Economic Justice, Labor and Community Practice

Facing economic upheaval and growing inequality, people in local communities are fighting for economic justice. Coalitions from labor, grassroots community organizations, the faith community, immigrant communities and other progressive forces are emerging across the U.S. and Canada and winning better jobs, benefits from local development and better working conditions. A multi-disciplinary group of scholars and activists provide background and analysis of these struggles and offer insights into successful community practice.

From the vantage points of community organizing, labor studies, political science, urban studies, social policy and active practitioners, this volume presents both background on the problem of economic and social inequality and portrays cases of how community practice is being redefined, how unions are pursuing their goals via labor-community coalitions, and the issues confronted as these new and vital alliances form. Community practitioners from social work, urban planning, active union members and leaders, labor educators, and those in the partnerships they have formed will find useful insights from these analyses.

This book was published as a special issue of the *Journal of Community Practice*.

Louise Simmons is Associate Professor of Social Work and Director of the Urban Semester Program at the University of Connecticut School of Social Work.

Scott Harding is Assistant Professor of Social Work at the University of Connecticut School of Social Work.

Economic Justice, Labor and Community Practice

Edited by Louise Simmons and Scott Harding

Routledge
Taylor & Francis Group

LONDON AND NEW YORK

First published 2010 by Routledge
2 Park Square, Milton Park, Abingdon, Oxon, OX14 4RN

Simultaneously published in the USA and Canada
by Routledge
270 Madison Avenue, New York, NY 10016

Routledge is an imprint of the Taylor & Francis Group, an informa business

Typeset in Garamond by Value Chain, India
Printed and bound in Great Britain by TJI Digital, Padstow, Cornwall

British Library Cataloguing in Publication Data
A catalogue record for this book is available from the British Library

ISBN10: 0-415-55975-8
ISBN13: 978-0-415-55975-1

Contents

On the Front Lines, in the Classrooms

INTRODUCTION

Economic Justice, Labor and Community Practice

The current economic and financial upheaval gripping the United States is widely seen as the worst crisis since the Great Depression of the 1930s. Unemployment has topped 10% in some states, mortgage foreclosures continue to rise, spending cuts are affecting sectors from education to health, and demand for public and private social services is surging. These conditions have challenged fundamental "free market" beliefs that have become economic orthodoxy, led to an unprecedented emergency investment in the banking and insurance industry, and spurred a short-term expansion of social safety net programs. For some observers, the turmoil appears to have no end and threatens the promise of the "American Dream."

While the current crisis is seen as a recent phenomenon, most working and poor people across the country have been facing a hostile economic and social environment for decades. Globalization and the implementation of "neo-liberal" policies have increased income inequality, devastated the social welfare state, undermined local communities, and facilitated an all-out assault on organized labor. As a result, double-digit unemployment, public disinvestment, and declining economic opportunity have been the norm in many parts of the country and for certain groups for some time.

Local communities are where global economic trends take actual form. In recent years some cities have successfully reinvented themselves to maintain or grow an economic base that supports changing demographics. However, the fate of many urban areas has not been as fortunate, never fully recovering from de-industrialization that began in the 1970s. The growth of low-wage work, particularly in the service sector, has accompanied the decline of unions and the loss of heavy industry. However, as service sector unions point out, there is nothing intrinsically better about manufacturing versus service sector employment. It is the fact that the former were highly unionized and provided reasonable wages, benefits, and protections that earned them the label of "good jobs." Thus, unionizing the growing low-wage service sector workforce is now an imperative for both the viability of the labor movement and the economic and social health of urban areas in which low-paid service sector workers live.

1

Within this context progressive forces face immense challenges. In recent years, labor and community activists have begun to build and refine organizing strategies to circumvent the weak enforcement of worker rights, especially the fundamental right to organize a union and create opportunities for economic mobility. The labor movement is developing new techniques to broaden its base and incorporate community organizing that have proven successful. Such efforts include living wage campaigns, community benefits agreements, and the building of progressive regional power (Dean & Reynolds, 2008). These collaborations have involved faith communities and community organizations, including social work activists in the community practice arena.

Communities across the United States are also witnessing a resurgence of movements for economic justice that are achieving a number of results of interest to both scholars and practitioners of social change. Partnerships encompassing grassroots neighborhood organizations, unions, the faith community, and other activists are redefining the terms of local economic development and public policy so that the benefits of these public projects accrue to local residents. Of note, the boundary between labor and community organizing is blurring, particularly in relation to low-wage workers who are also urban residents in localities where local organizing initiatives exist. This suggests an important paradigm shift.

The election of Barack Obama, a former community organizer, has also created optimism that new opportunities to build on these successes may emerge. His campaign crossed traditional boundaries and provided opportunities for new alliances and the use of community organizing tactics to achieve political goals. The hope is that the Obama administration will integrate—and motivate—the labor movement and community organizations to pursue policies that reverse widespread economic inequality, particularly by invigorating the role of the public sector.

What these new and revitalized economic justice movements are accomplishing in the realm of community practice is spurring activists to rethink and retool their work. The necessity of coalition building, overcoming historic divisions, building new relationships among disparate organizations, and achieving meaningful, concrete results are key challenges to surmount. Struggles to realize rights for immigrant workers and low-wage workers, more generally, have achieved some victories, even the in context of restrictive immigration policy, declining wages, and other exploitative practices against vulnerable workers.

The strands of these alliances have several origins. First there is the U.S. labor movement which has been attempting to reinvent itself in the last 15 years. Facing serious decline in union density for more than 30 years, unions have, of necessity, incorporated community organizing into their own repertoire and are reshaping urban politics, local economic development projects, and public policy (Dean & Reynolds, 2008; Reynolds, 2004;

Simmons & Harding, in press). Human service workers are also acting through their unions to improve services and working conditions. Community organizers are likewise concluding that in order to realize their goals, they must also partner with unions and others to reap any benefits from local development. Faith-based activists and other community-based advocates in the arenas of job training, social supports for low-income people, immigrant rights, and other areas are often coming to similar conclusions about how to attain their goals. Social activists, union members, and urban advocates all need to understand this changing political landscape as they mobilize for economic justice. We hope that this collection will help to facilitate greater understanding of these factors and the process of coalition building among these groups.

This book includes contributions by scholars from multiple disciplines, all involved in different aspects of *community practice* to advance economic justice. Our conception of this method includes community organizing and other forms of macro social work. These forms include policy practice, or the strand of urban planning that defines itself as advocacy or progressive planning, and the work of other organizations whose focus is on issues such as smart growth, immigrant rights, housing, homelessness, hunger, and other aspects of community life.

The convergence of interests in these issues from across varying fields highlights the salience of these organizing activities. Thus for organizing, community-labor partnerships are relevant because they represent a new form of strategy that transcends prior boundaries of community organizing. As organized labor has increasingly embraced community strategies, it has also become a key element of the rubric of community practice. Certain organizations such as immigrant worker centers blend community organizing, labor organizing, rights advocacy, and service provision (Fine, 2006). While often viewed as two sides of the urban trenches mapped out by Katznelson (1981), the boundaries between work and community are blurring as these two forms of urban politics and urban social movements coalesce.

Engaged scholars have an important role to play in helping community and labor movements achieve their goals. Careful, well-crafted investigations, from perspectives that are rigorous and at the same time sympathetic, offer practitioners insights to build effective practice approaches. The book foregrounds contributions from multiple disciplines with this objective. Several authors come from the vantage point of social work, particularly the realms of community organizing and policy, as well as social welfare history; others are involved in labor studies and labor education; some have ties to public affairs, urban studies, and political science. Importantly, other author teams include activists who are practicing on the front lines of the developments they analyze. The contributions included here all raise contextual issues or suggest forms of struggle and collaboration we believe are crucial in the study of economic justice movements.

CONTRIBUTIONS TO THIS BOOK

Our collection begins with several chapters that provide context and history for examining economic justice, labor, and community practice in a section we entitle "Economic Realities, History and Framing." In "Inequality and Its Discontents," Jill Littrell, Fred Brooks, Jan Ivery, and Mary Ohmer detail how the income and security of the individual, middle-class worker in the United States has declined and the gap between the rich and the poor has widened. They discuss why this is bad for democracy, the economy, and the aggregate health of the United States, and offer suggestions to address this inequality. Income inequality—the gap between the very wealthy and the poor—has widened to its highest point in 90 years. Inequality in the United States is also higher than in seven other industrialized countries: Australia, Denmark, France, Germany, Japan, Sweden, and the United Kingdom. The authors review the social programs, policies, and social movements around economic justice since the Depression of the 1930s and suggest what has to be done in today's crisis to restore economic security for the majority of Americans. They argue that there is a pivotal role for social movements and mobilization in order to insure that new policies and programs meet the mushrooming needs of this crisis.

Cynthia Rocha, in "Promoting Economic Justice in a Global Context: International Comparisons of Policies That Support Economic Justice," compares economic justice in terms of income inequality and child poverty rates within a number of industrialized countries including the United States. She examines labor market training, social service expenditures, unionization, and national tax rates to understand how social and fiscal policies promote or impede economic justice. Rocha also explores the implications for labor and community practitioners, including social work, as they devise new strategies to promote economic justice. Public attitudes toward social investment and strategies to ensure social inclusion emerge as fundamental to the equitable distribution of resources. Given the poor showing of the United States in her study—ranking last in income equality and next to last in child poverty—these findings highlight key barriers to social equality. Rocha suggests that a renewed focus on community and a strengthened labor movement, combined with a new administration, offers the promise of a fundamental shift in the role of the state in promoting economic justice.

The third chapter by Michael Reisch, "Social Workers, Unions, and Low Wage Workers: A Historical Perspective," explores the historical relationship between social work and labor, particularly the methods by which social workers have supported low-wage workers' efforts to improve their economic conditions and organize into unions. The relationship has varied over the past century as social work's professional identity and mission have evolved over time, and as political and economic climates shifted within the United States. Reisch argues that social work should become more involved with economic justice struggles, both in the practice arena, as well as in social work education and research. This is particularly important in light of the issues associated with globalization, such as immigration, and a more diverse constituency for social work.

Loretta Pyles, in "Where's the 'Freedom' in Free Trade? Framing Practices and Global Economic Justice," examines a critical but relatively neglected aspect of organizing and social movement work: the use of framing as a key tool to promote global economic justice issues. She uses three cases to highlight how popular education, consciousness raising, and democratic organizational structures inform the work of economic justice organizations: The Highlander Center, United Students Against Sweatshops, and the American Friends Service Committee's Economic Justice Project. The narratives used by these groups help define the meaning of their work. Despite the disparate nature of these organizations, Pyles finds key similarities in their use of framing. All three emphasize economic "globalization" and the power of transnational corporations as key sources of inequality and disempowerment—and as appropriate targets for change. As economic justice principles assume a more central place within social movements, understanding the centrality of the framing practices in this work will become essential. Thus understanding the issue frames employed by activists can help uncover the impact of these efforts. While working with different constituencies, these groups share an emphasis on the intersectionality of oppression, thus making important connections in their work among race, class, and gender. Pyles also notes that process goals assume an important place in the work of these organizations, underscoring the importance of organizational sustainability as integral to empowerment-based practice.

Our next group of contributions falls under the rubric of "Labor-Community Partnerships for Economic Justice." These selections discuss recent strategies in community practice that involve local movements striving for equity policies such as living wages, community-benefits agreements, and other aspects of the accountable development movement.

Virginia Parks and Dorian Warren, in "The Politics and Practice of Economic Justice: Community Benefits Agreements as Tactic of the New Accountable Development Movement," provide background and analysis of how community forces can reap benefits for local populations in the context of urban development. Over the past decade, community benefit agreements (CBAs)—arrangements or contracts between developers and local labor-community coalitions over specific development terms—have come to the fore as vehicles for leveraging improvements for workers and residents in areas where large development projects are taking place. The campaigns for CBAs are redefining urban politics as coalitions press local policy makers to endorse and enforce the agreements. Particularly in development that involves creation of service sector jobs, guarantees for living wages, decent benefits, and the right to unionize help turn potentially low-wage jobs into decent jobs for the local residents who end up in these positions. Local hiring provisions, environmental quality provisions, and housing provisions are often components of the CBAs. "Growth with equity" is the new paradigm for projects across the country. However, as Parks and Warren emphasize, the equity aspect comes about as a result of the organizing power of the CBA coalitions and their capacity to disrupt development if benefits do not accrue to local residents.

Next, David Dobbie in "Evolving Strategies of Labor-Community Coalition-Building" compares the trajectory of labor-community coalitions in Milwaukee, Chicago, and Pittsburgh over the past decade and analyzes the struggles involved in building and maintaining successful, enduring partnerships. Economic justice movements require careful attention to relationshipbuilding. Intentional strategies to accomplish this involve developing a shared vision and establishing "bridging institutions," or intermediaries that can help to link networks of activists and/or also offer technical assistance. Dobbie suggests that these coalitions need both short term and long term goals and strategies so that occasional losses or setbacks along the way do not derail progress in the broader movements for economic justice. He proposes that a "culture of solidarity" be nurtured to enable mutual understanding of labor and community forces.

In "Organizing Community and Labor Coalitions for Community Benefits Agreements in African American Communities: Ensuring Successful Partnerships," Bonnie Young Laing also analyzes two struggles for community benefits agreements in Los Angeles and Pittsburgh. Her focus is on what constitutes successful organizing that is inclusive of African American communities. She compares the various organizing models in the labor movement, the African American community, and those that have emerged in labor-community partnerships. In order for coalitions to work, careful attention must be paid so as not to replicate oppressive practices that African Americans and other people of color have experienced in cross-cultural organizations and alliances. The Los Angeles example, in which a successful multicultural coalition was built, is contrasted with the Pittsburgh experience in which tensions between African American community organizations and other coalition members made for a more contentious environment. Laing presents several methods by which to build stronger and more equitable partnerships.

A focus on consciousness-raising informs the Detroit-based labor and community collaboration analyzed by Roland Zullo and Gregory Pratt, in "Critical Pedagogy as a Tool for Labor-Community Coalition Building." In an effort to identify the conditions that can create a sustainable alliance between union members and local community activists, the authors designed a pilot project emphasizing critical pedagogy. Based in part on the work of Brazilian educator Paulo Freire, the authors offer important insights into the process of coalition building within a framework emphasizing member education and empowerment. Zullo and Pratt worked to identify union and community activists with shared interests who then cotaught their peers about a specific issue and developed a joint strategy for change. The use of such methods has the potential to uncover innovative principles and tactics that could make a valuable contribution to labor-community organizing. While this chapter offers a preliminary assessment of their work, the authors suggest that their efforts have already reduced existing tensions among some of participating organizations. Ultimately, Zullo and Pratt seek to create a template for use in other communities seeking to build and/or strengthen ties between organized labor and local activists.

The third set of contributions is presented in the section "On the Front Lines, in the Classrooms." These chapters provide frontline examples of different types of economic justice movements including work for immigrant rights, a strike by unionized social workers, a job training program, a classroom project on living wages, and the challenging process of building the capacity for economic justice movements in South Florida. We are also pleased that two of these contributions share experiences from Canada so that readers are afforded some examples from a country with many similarities to the United States, but with a different policy framework for dealing with similar economic and social problems.

In "'Social Justice Infrastructure' Organizations as New Actors From the Community: The Case of South Florida," Bruce Nissen traces the recent history of economic and social justice organizational development in the greater Miami area. In Miami, a variety of community organizations, worker centers, faith based coalitions, and unions have worked together in several specific campaigns over the last dozen years, but a more lasting coalition (as described in several of the previous chapters) has not been achieved. However, Nissen raises the concept of networks as a viable alternative vision of how economic and social justice movements can be sustained. A network need not be permanent in organizational form, but still can be the basis of building relationships for less permanent collaborations. He is optimistic that multiple "fronts" of organizing, in which mutual support is garnered through the South Florida network of organizations and activists, may be able to accomplish some of the goals of social justice movements.

A successful grassroots advocacy campaign involving social work students and faculty aimed at increasing the minimum wage in Nevada forms the basis of Susan Kerr Chandler's chapter, "Working Hard, Living Poor: Social Work and the Movement for Livable Wages." She describes a range of activities including the creation of a living wage study, media work, legislative lobbying and testimony, and the creation of a social policy curriculum that created multiple opportunities for political engagement. Chandler locates this effort within the history of professional practice with and advocacy on behalf of low-income groups. Like other scholars, she suggests that over time social work practitioners and educators have gradually lost sight of this mission. She argues that pedagogy offers an obvious entry for the next generation of social workers to engage in collective action to improve the lives of the working poor. By directly confronting the issue of social work's responsibility to promote economic justice, this multiyear class project enabled scores of students to work directly with a statewide coalition to improve the lives of working people. As such, this contribution offers important insights for those teaching social policy courses as well as social work activists as to how the academy and professional organizations can collaborate on critical social policy initiatives.

The struggles of immigrant workers in Canada and the issue campaigns of the Immigrant Workers' Centre in Montreal are analyzed by Jill Hanley and Eric Shragge in "Organizing for Immigrant Rights: Policy Barriers and Community Campaigns." Immigrant workers in Canada, much like in the United States, face a host of barriers, often endure a precarious legal status, and also often work in low-wage and unsafe jobs. The Immigrant Workers' Centre represents a hybrid type of organization that incorporates some elements of community organizing and some elements of labor organizing. Its activities have included campaigns to repeal the three month waiting period for immigrants in obtaining free public health insurance, the inclusion of domestic workers in health and safety policies that provide compensation for workplace injuries, and compensation for workers who were laid off from textile sector jobs and were ineligible for Canadian "collective layoff benefits." These are illustrative of the problems and exclusions from public programs faced by immigrants in Canada, and workers' centers provide the type of response that addresses their needs, protects their status, and incorporates culturally relevant practice.

Job-training programs are an area of social programs that potentially create economic opportunity. Yet without careful planning, recruitment, and placement, they often don't meet their goals, particularly for people of color who train for employment in the construction industry. In "Outcomes of Two Construction Trades Pre-Apprenticeship Programs: A Comparison" by Helena Worthen and Rev. Anthony Haynes, the outcomes of two training programs are compared. In the first, a high level of support was provided to participants and a close organizational relationship to the United Brotherhood of Carpenters (UBC) existed, while the second program lacked these qualities. If new job programs are created as a result of initiatives of the Obama administration, this comparison is instructive. Effective job training programs ought to be designed to open up access to good jobs for those who face employment barriers and this includes substantial support for participants and viable linkages to entities that control access to the work such as union apprenticeship programs.

Tara LaRose relates the story of job actions and a six-week long strike in 2000 by child welfare workers in Toronto in "One Small Revolution: Unionization, Community Practice, and Workload in Child Welfare." In a retrospective study, members of the Canadian Union of Public Employees (CUPE) Local 2190 shared their experiences of gaining a new contract with stronger provisions to insure the quality of services and better working conditions, including caps on caseloads and language on workloads. Under province policies that preceded the strike, social workers endured a shift to a new method of practice under the Ontario Risk Assessment Model (ORAM). ORAM featured a series of standardized practice tools and service eligibility criteria. The emphasis of this system was on efficiency, however, workers felt that their professional autonomy and the quality of their services were undermined, and they experienced a great deal of workplace stress under ORAM. Ultimately, through the strike, CUPE Local 2190 achieved not only greater control over their work environment, but a sense of personal and professional empowerment that has been sustained in the ensuing years.

OUR THANKS

Our thanks go out to the many people who made this book possible. We particularly want to acknowledge Alice Johnson Butterfield, Tracy Soska and Benson Chisanga, members of the editorial team with us for the *Journal of Community Practice,* who encouraged us to undertake the special issue of the journal on which this book is based. We are, of course, grateful to all of the contributors for their outstanding chapters. Likewise, we had the benefit of expert reviewers in providing meaningful comments and suggestions. Ana Santiago, Managing Editor of the *Journal of Community Practice,* was immensely helpful, as have been several individuals at Taylor and Francis. Finally, this book recounts the struggles of individuals and communities across communities in North America, with ties to many parts of the world. Ultimately we are thankful to them for their tenacity and courage in the pursuit of economic justice.

Scott Harding
Louise Simmons

REFERENCES

Dean, A., & Reynolds, D. (2008). Labor's new regional strategy: The rebirth of central labor councils. *New Labor Forum, 17*(1), 45–55.

Fine, J. (2006). *Worker centers: Organizing communities at the edge of the dream.* Cornell, NY: ILR Press.

Katznelson, I. (1981). *City trenches: Urban politics and the patterning of class in the United States.* New York: Pantheon Books.

Reynolds, D. (Ed.). (2004). *Partnering for change: Unions and community groups build coalitions for economic justice.* Armonk, NY: M.E. Sharpe.

Simmons, L., & Harding, S. (in press). Community-labor coalitions for progressive change. *Journal of Workplace Behavioral Health.*

ECONOMIC REALITIES, HISTORY, AND FRAMING

Inequality and Its Discontents

JILL LITTRELL, FRED BROOKS,
JAN M. IVERY, and MARY L. OHMER
School of Social Work, Georgia State University, Atlanta, Georgia, USA

In the last two decades, the income and security of the individual middle class worker has declined, and the gap between the rich and the poor has widened. In contrast to the last twenty years and the "gilded age" that preceded it, from the time of the first New Deal through the 1970s, the middle class prospered. Wealth and income were more equitably shared in America. This article examines policies that strengthened the middle class during the New Deal, during World War II, and after World War II. These policies strengthened the bargaining power of labor. This article offers suggestions for reviving the middle class now with particular focus on empowering labor.

THE THREATENED MIDDLE CLASS

Inequality in Income and Wealth: The United States Over Time

During the last two decades, inequality has been increasing; the income/wealth gap between the rich and the poor has been steadily augmenting (Kawachi & Kennedy, 2002; Krugman, 2007; Piketty & Saez, 2003; Reich, 2007). Today's income distribution statistics mirror the statistics of the "gilded age" (1877–1900) made infamous by the robber barons (Krugman, 2007, p. 16). The share of total income (excluding capital gains) for the highest ten percent of the U.S. population was 44.3% in 2005, similar to the 1920 statistic of 43.6%. Moreover, the highest 1% of Americans earned approximately the same percentage of the nation's total income in 2005 as in 1920, with both figures at roughly 17%. Piketty and Saez (2003, 2006), illustrate graphically (see Figure 1) how the level of the nation's total income captured by the very rich has fluctuated over the century, peaking in the gilded age and at the present time.

Today's income equality contrasts sharply to income distribution during the 1950s and 1960s. Beginning in 1973, "the affluent sections of society" began pulling away sharply from the poor and middle class (Kawachi & Kennedy, 2002, p. 22; Wolff, 1998). Data collected by the U.S. Census Bureau appears in Table 1 (Jones & Weinberg, 2000). Table 1 illustrates that while the share of aggregate income held by the lowest fifth actually grew slightly from 4.0 to 4.3% between 1967 and 1980, after 1980, the percentage of the pie captured by the poorest quintile declined. In contrast, while the wealthiest fifth of households captured 43.8% of all earned income in 1967, their share of the pie had risen to 50.4% by 2005. What happened to the middle quintile? The middle quintile (i.e., those earning an average of $46,301 in 2005) also lost ground, declining to 14.6% of aggregate income in 2005, from 17.3% of aggregate income in 1967. It should be noted that disparities in income distribution have grown even as American workers have become more productive (Kawachi & Kennedy, 2002; Krugman, 2007; Sawhill & Morton, 2007).

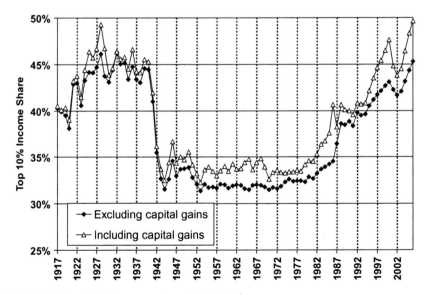

FIGURE 1 The top decile income share, 1917–2006.

Note. Income is defined as market income (and excludes government transfers). From Piketty and Saez (2003), series updated to 2006; http://elsa.berkeley.edu/~saez/TabFig 2006prel.xls.

TABLE 1 Distribution (In Percentages) of All Earned Income Across Various Quintiles: 1967 to 2005

Income quintiles	1967	1970	1975	1980	1985	1990	1995	2000	2005
Lowest quintile	4.0	4.1	4.4	4.3	4.0	3.9	3.7	3.6	3.4
Second quintile	10.8	10.8	10.5	10.3	9.7	9.6	9.1	8.9	8.6
Middle quintile	17.3	17.4	17.1	16.9	16.3	15.9	15.2	14.8	14.6
Fourth quintile	24.2	24.5	24.8	24.9	24.6	24.0	23.3	23.0	23.0
Highest quintile	43.8	43.3	43.2	43.7	45.3	46.6	48.7	49.8	50.4

Note. 2005 average income: $10,655 for lowest quintile, $27,357 for second, $46,301 for middle, $72,825 for fourth, and $159,583 for highest. From U.S. Census Bureau (2005). *Current Population Survey, 1968 to 2006 Annual Social and Economic Supplements.*

We have been talking about how aggregate income is distributed among tiers of income earners in the society. We can also examine how adjusted dollar earnings have fluctuated over time. In contrast to the dismal times during the Great Depression, median household income in 2005 dollars roughly doubled from $22K to $44K during the period from 1947 to 1973 (Krugman, 2007, p. 54). By the mid 1950s, almost half of all families fell comfortably within the middle range, earning between $4,000 and $7,500 after taxes in 1953 dollars (Krugman, 2007, pp. 36–37). While family incomes have held steady in adjusted dollars over the last several decades, it should be noted that most households now have two income earners in contrast to the 1950s, when many women did not work (Palley, 1998, p 63). Moreover, the incomes of even college graduates have declined by 5% from 2000 to 2004 (Krugman, 2006). Coupled with the decline in earnings over time, employee benefits have eroded over the last several decades, and job insecurity has risen (Hacker, 2006; Kawachi & Kennedy, 2002; Krugman, 2006; Uchitelle, 2007).

While income refers to "the flow of dollars over a year," wealth is "the net dollar value of the stock of assets minus debts held by a household at one point in time" (Kawachi & Kennedy, 2002, p. 24). Wealth has become even more concentrated in fewer hands than income (Kawachi & Kennedy, 2002; Reich, 2007). Beginning in the 1970s, according to Reich (2007, p. 114) "the nation's richest one percent—comprising roughly one and a half million families in 2004—has more than doubled their share of total national wealth." On current estimates, the wealthiest one percent of American society owns 48% of the nation's financial assets, and 39% of the nation's total assets, including real estate (Wolff, 1998).

Comparing the U.S. to Other Industrialized Countries

The Gini index measures intra-national inequality using a scale from 0.00 to 1.00, with 0 indicating uneven distribution across families and 1.00 signifying

TABLE 2 Measures of Income Inequality: The U.S. Compared to Selected Industrial Countries

Country	Gini index 2004	Decile ratio 2000
United States	0.47	5.7
United Kingdom	0.36	4.6
Australia	0.35	4.2
France	0.33	3.4
Germany	0.28	3.4
Sweden	0.25	3.0
Japan	0.25	4.2
Denmark	0.25	2.8

Note. Source for Gini Index: United Nations Human Development Report, 2004; Source for Decile Ratio: Brandolini & Smeeding, 2007, p. 30.

even distribution among families (Ohmer & DeMasi, 2008). Practically, an index of between .40 and .49 is interpreted as serious inequality. While the Gini Index for the United States was 0.34 in 1967, it rose to 0.47 in 2004, the highest among a number of selected industrial nations (U.S. Census Bureau, 2005). The Decile Ratio is another way to assess distribution of aggregate earnings in a country. The Decile Ratio uses the income of a person in the top 10% of the population as the numerator and the income of a person in the bottom 10% as the denominator, with both figures having been indexed to the median income level in the country (Kawachi & Kennedy, 2002, p. 25). As seen in Table 2, the United States exhibits the highest level of inequitable income distribution on this indicator as well. The United States is an extreme case compared to other industrialized nations with an index of 5.7, compared to the lowest index of 2.8 in Denmark (Brandolini & Smeeding, 2007).

The proverbial "American dream" signifies the opportunity to move from a lower economic status to a higher one given personal initiative. How is the American dream faring today contrasted with the rest of the world? Examining the correlation between parents' and children's income as an indicator of relative mobility, data show that a number of countries, including Denmark, Norway, Finland, Canada, Sweden, Germany, and France have more relative mobility than does the United States (Corak, 2006). In addition, when measuring mobility using the "transition rate out of poverty between one year and the next, economic mobility was lower in the United States (13.8%) than in France (27.5), Germany (25.6), Ireland (25.2), the Netherlands (44.4), and Sweden (36.8) in the mid 1980s" (Kawachi & Kennedy, 2002, p. 166).

When America Catches Cold, African Americans Catch the Flu

The economic downturn since the beginning of 2008 has been particularly hard on African Americans. In November of 2008, unemployment for African

Americans was at 11.2% versus 6.7% for the nation. Unemployment for autoworkers rose by 13.9% versus 4.4% for other manufacturing jobs during the last year. African Americans workers are over-represented in the auto-industry compared to white Americans (Chapman, 2008).

Policies and Protest Movements that Expanded the Middle Class in the United States

The period after World War II through 1972 expanded the size of the middle class and narrowed the gap between the rich and the poor. Goldin and Margo (1992) report that wage inequality began to decrease with the passage of the first New Deal legislation in 1933, but the "Great Compression" continued throughout the 1940s. Was the "invisible hand of the market"—to borrow Adams Smith's metaphor—the cause of the emergence of the healthy middle class? Many economists have argued that post World War II legislation and governmental policies played a major role in the emergence of the middle class (Krugman, 2007; Levy & Temlin, 2007; Murolo & Chitty, 2001; Piven, 2006). This legislation bolstered the bargaining position of labor, increased marginal tax rates on the wealthy, and placed advanced education and home ownership within the reach of a board spectrum of Americans. Some of the governmental policies that built the middle class will be considered in the next sections.

UNIONS BEFORE THE DEPRESSION

From 1890 to 1920, organization of labor occurred primarily in cities and among mine workers. Union membership peaked at 5 million members (almost 20% of the industrial labor force) in 1920 after the mobilization of WWI. Union organizing drives before the depression were often met with fierce, violent resistance. Private security firms (e.g., the Pinkertons) or sometimes government troops (e.g., the Pullman Strike of 1894) crushed organizing drives and strikes (Murollo & Chitty, 2001; Piven, 2006). Court decisions almost always backed employers in labor-management disputes in the 1920s and early 1930s. Unemployment during the depression created a labor surplus, weakening the bargaining position of workers. By 1933, union membership had declined to less than 10% of the non-agricultural labor force (Krugman, 2007).

THE FIRST NEW DEAL

With the advent of the Great Depression, unemployment rose to unprecedented levels. Social unrest also reached unprecedented levels in the form of unemployed protests at relief centers, hunger marches, rent riots, and

eviction resistance actions (Piven & Cloward, 1971). In response, the first
New Deal was passed in 1933. The centerpiece of the first New Deal was
the National Industrial Recovery Act (NIRA) which, according to Murolo and
Chitty (2001), was intended as only token support to unions. The real objective of NIRA was to revive the industrial sector by diminishing excessive
competition between companies. In collaboration with the business community NIRA formulated new codes of conduct that regulated production
quotas, product standards, prices and labor conditions. Section 7A of NIRA
gave workers "the right or organize and bargain collectively . . . free from
the interference, restraint or coercion of employers" (Murolo & Chitty, 2001,
p. 193). Although businesses never intended to comply with Section 7A, and
the federal government initially did nothing to enforce business compliance,
labor unions used the language in Section 7A to launch major organizing
drives in the last half of 1933. Hundreds of thousands of new members
joined unions. The United Mine Workers adapted the phrasing of Section
7A to proclaim on recruitment flyers and hand bills that "the President
wants you to join a union" (Murolo & Chitty, 2001, p. 195), and quickly
signed-up 300,000 new members shortly after the NIRA passed. By the end
of 1933, over 750,000 new union members had been recruited across industries; this represented unprecedented union growth in the midst of the
depression (Murolo & Chitty, 2001). Thus, the first New Deal had unintended consequences that bolstered the bargaining position of the unions.

Union membership continued growing into 1934 and so did labor
unrest in the form of strikes. The 1933–34 organizing drives resulted in
3,500 strikes, with another 2,000 strikes in 1935. Several strikes were large,
multi-state uprisings capturing national attention. In September 1934, over
400,000 textile mill workers from Alabama to Maine walked off the job. This
was the largest strike in United States history. The primary worker demand
was for the federal government to force the textile mills to comply with
NIRA regulations, prohibiting obstructions to the formation of unions. On
September 21, 1934, U.S. President Roosevelt agreed to appoint new officials
to enforce NIRA and asked for workers to end the strike. The strike ended,
but companies continued to ignore NIRA. In many southern mills, companies
refused to re-hire returning workers. The strike's defeat constituted labor's
biggest loss in 1934 (Murolo & Chitty, 2001). In contrast to the unsuccessful
textile strike, other large strikes of 1934, including the Auto-Lite workers in
Toledo, stevedores in San Francisco, and truckers in Minneapolis, won
many of their demands (Murolo & Chitty, 2001).

What was accomplished by the first New Deal? Goldin and Margo
(1992) argue the minimum wages in NIRA were "probably" the cause of inequality beginning to decline after 1933. However, Piven (2006) places more
emphasis on strikes, protests, and widespread labor unrest as instrumental
factors in reducing inequality. NIRA was declared unconstitutional by the
U.S. Supreme Court in May of 1935, ending the first New Deal.

THE SECOND NEW DEAL

In 1935, with the Depression still very deep (14% unemployment), the Roosevelt administration decided to align itself more closely with labor. New strategies were needed. The "Second New Deal" legislation included the National Labor Relations Act (NLRA), the creation of the National Labor Relations Board (NLRB) to enforce the NLRA, and the creation of the Works Progress Administration (WPA).

Compared to NIRA, the NLRA went much further in support of workers' rights to organize. The NLRA specifically prohibited employer tactics previously used to defeat organizing drives. (These tactics included "using threats, coercion, or restraint against an organizing drive; . . . discriminating against union members in hiring, firing, or job assignments; . . . and refusing to bargain with a union voted in by the workers," Murolo & Chitty, 2001, p. 201). Moreover, those enforcing NLRA regulations were mandated to be "impartial government members" who were not partisan to labor or business (Levy & Temlin, 2007, p. 25).

Whether the Second New Deal was instrumental in ending the Great Depression is an open question. What is not in dispute is that the Great Depression ended following the next huge government employment program: World War II.

WORLD WAR II

With a labor shortage created by enormous numbers going into the military and diversion of goods from the consumer markets to the needs of the military, huge inflationary pressures were anticipated. In 1942, shortly after Pearl Harbor, Roosevelt revived the National War Labor Board (NWLB) that had been in place during WWI. This agency arbitrated labor management disputes to prevent war-time strikes and work stoppages. During WWII, the NWLB supported workers' rights to organize, bargain collectively, and earn living wages (Krugman, 2007). Union membership almost doubled during WWII. Roosevelt's NWLB established wage controls in many industries to ward off the inflationary pressures of war time labor shortages. These wage controls raised the wages of lower-paid workers and compressed wage differentials between high-paid and low-paid workers, both within and between industries (Goldin & Margo, 1992; Krugman, 2007).

THE POST-WAR PERIOD

All of the activity from New Deal legislation, robust union organizing, militant labor strikes and protests, WWII wage controls, and increased taxation on the richest Americans reduced inequality and expanded the middle class. The zeitgeist had changed. In 1950, we witnessed a new paradigm between business and labor called the "Treaty of Detroit". The "Treaty of Detroit" was the label given by *Fortune* magazine in 1950 to the landmark labor contract between the United Auto Workers (UAW) union and General Motors (GM), which had been notoriously anti-union for decades. This precedent-setting contract included automatic cost-of-living adjustments to wages, pay increases tied to productivity gains, a pension plan, and an agreement by GM to pay half the cost of comprehensive health care. Some concessions went to management: management got more control over production and investment policies (Levy & Temlin, 2007). Between 1948 and 1950, similar concessions were again made to workers, and in 1949, GM posted record profits. The new arrangement between labor and GM turned out to be a win-win for labor and GM's bottom line. The empirical evidence suggested that record profits and generous wage and benefit packages could coexist. After a bitter strike at Chrysler, the GM-UAW contract was quickly replicated among the "Big Three" automakers and became a precedent in union management contracts across many industries (Levy & Temlin, 2007; Moberg 2007).

REFLECTION ON THE EBB AND FLOW OF UNIONS

Organized labor and membership in labor unions grew dramatically from the 1930s to the 50s, peaking in 1957 at 17.7 million (Troy, 1965), or 35% of the labor force. According to the Economic Policy Institute (Mishel & Walters, 2003), unionized workers earn 20% more than their non-unionized counterparts. The differential between union versus non-union wages is even more pronounced for minorities and women (Sklar, Mykyta, & Wefald, 2001). Not only does membership in unions directly increase compensation for members, but high levels of union membership indirectly affect compensation in open-shop companies who find that to attract and keep good employees, they have to raise wages and benefits to compete with unionized firms (Krugman, 2007). In addition to increasing wages, because unions represent large voting blocks, they are instrumental in organizing support for auxiliary issues such as affordable housing, better education, better unemployment benefits, civil rights, and so on (Shulman, 2007). As union membership declined after 1950 to its present level of 11% (Krugman, 2007, p. 18), so did the size and security of the middle class.

Other Factors that Contributed to a Growing Middle Class in the 20th Century

FHA AND VA HOUSING LOANS

While a militant labor movement was probably the strongest change-agent in creating a middle class (especially among blue collar workers), other policies and social movements helped expand the middle class. Home ownership is widely considered a hallmark of being middle class. In the 1930s, only 40% of families in the United States owned their own home. The Federal Housing Act, passed during the first New Deal in 1934, provided Federal Housing Authority (FHA) insurance to encourage the private sector to provide mortgages to families who otherwise would not qualify for a traditional mortgage. Between 1940 and 1980, the percentage of American families owning their own home almost doubled (Chevan, 1989). Moreover, the G.I. Bill of 1944 included similar mortgage insurance for veterans. Between 1944 and 1952, 2.4 million homes were purchase with the help of Veteran's Administration Insurance (U.S Department of Veteran's Affairs, 2008). The FHA and VA programs insured about one-third of all homes purchased during the 1950s (Sklar et al., 2001, p. 149).

G.I. BILL AND EDUCATION BENEFITS

While labor unions were responsible for expanding the middle class to include blue collar workers, policies that made higher education more attainable and affordable also contributed to a larger, more affluent middle class. In 1944, President Roosevelt signed legislation which allocated federal funding for the educational expenses of 7.8 million World War II veterans. Few federal policies are considered more successful than the Servicemen's Readjustment Act of 1944, known as the G.I. Bill. Not only did the G.I. Bill enable many veterans to move into the middle class, but the benefits of the G.I. Bill continue to accrue (as evidenced by high SAT scores) to the descendants of those who received G.I. Bill funding (Tillery, 2008). As America emerged as an industrial, high-tech economy, the G.I. Bill produced the skilled workforce required to operate in the high-tech economy. The increase in worker productivity witnessed in the post World War II period (Krugman, 2007) is in large measure attributable to having a well trained workforce (Dickens, Sawhill, & Tebbs, 2006).

It is difficult to assess the degree to which fear of organized demands from returning veterans contributed to the passage of the G.I. Bill. By the end of World War II, populist attitudes and concern about the modal person had probably grown as a result of experiencing the Great Depression and the rise in unions. However, in 1944, many politicians in Washington remembered the 1932 tent city (on the banks of the Anacostia River) erected by 20,000 World War I veterans and their families, protesting the government's lack of payment of $100 war bonuses promised to be paid 12 years after the war. The veterans and their families were dispersed by U.S. infantry, cavalry, and tanks, led by Generals Eisenhower and McArthur (Murolo & Chitty, 2001; Piven & Cloward, 1971). The Department of Veterans Affairs' own website (see http://www.gibill.va.gov/GI Bill Info/history.htm) says the urgency of the 1944 G.I. Bill "stemmed from a desire to avoid the missteps following WWI when discharged veterans got little more than a $60 allowance and a train ride home" (para. 5). The VA website offers empirical support for Piven's (2006) hypothesis that progressive legislation in the USA is directly or indirectly related to protest and disruption. Congress' desire in 1944 to avoid the debacle of 1932 had much to do with the prompt passage and signing of the G.I. Bill.

RACISM IN G.I. BILL AND HOUSING POLICIES

The benefits which accrued to white Americans as a result of the G.I. Bill and FHA and VA housing loans left out African Americans (Jackson, 1985; Tillery, 2008). FHA and VA loans went overwhelmingly to white applicants. While African Americans were eligible for FHA and VA loans, most banks were unwilling to underwrite mortgages in either black or integrated neighborhoods. The process was called "redlining", and though it was discriminatory, it was legal for many years (Jackson, 1985, pp. 208–214). Since most middle-class wealth is related to equity in homes (Wolff, 1998), it also contributed to racial disparities in wealth that persist to this day.

EMERGENCE OF THE AFRICAN AMERICAN MIDDLE CLASS

The migration of African Americans from southern farms to northern cities between 1910 and 1970 changed the demographics and social structure of U.S. society (Lemann, 1991). Despite the discriminatory practices toward minorities in the wider society, small numbers of African American-owned businesses catering to southern migrants emerged in cities such as Chicago and New York's Harlem before World War II (Jackson & Stewart, 2003). Howard University graduated African American Scholars. Eminent individuals such as Percy Julian and Zora Neal Hurston made significant contributions to chemistry and art. A. Phillip Randolff organized the Brotherhood of Sleeping Car Porters into an effective union in 1925. Despite these glimmers of African American middle class, most African Americans remained poor until the emergence of a middle class following the passage of Civil Rights legislation between 1959 and 1978 (Collins, 1983). The African American poverty rate declined from 55.1% in 1959 to 30.6% in 1991. As the poverty rate declined, the proportion of middle-and upper-class African Americans increased. Families with incomes greater than $35,000 grew from 5.9% of African American households to 14.8% of African American households between 1967 and 1991 (Katz-Fishman & Scott, 1994, p. 575). Without government legislation and enforcement of the legislation, it is unlikely that middle class expansion would have occurred during this time period, although some scholars argue that other factors contributed to this expansion as well (Donohue & Heckman, 1991). We now consider seminal institutions and developments established by Civil Rights Legislation.

The Equal Opportunity Employment Commission (EEOC). The Equal Opportunity Employment Commission (EEOC) was established to monitor enforcement of Title IV of the Civil Rights Act of 1964 that prohibited discrimination in wages, hiring, and promotion. Private firms with 100 or more employees reported on the number of minority workers they employed. Initially, the EEOC was limited in scope to the processing of complaints and investigating cases under litigation. In an effort to expand the EEOC's role, Congress granted the commission power to initiate civil suits in 1972 (Collins, 1983; Donohue & Heckman, 1991). Following this expansion in responsibility, companies that reported under EEOC requirements opened jobs to African Americans at a faster rate compared to firms not required to report (Brimmer, 1976).

Office of Federal Contract Compliance (OFCC) and Affirmative Action. The Office of Federal Contract Compliance (OFCC) was established through Executive Order 11246 in 1962. Federal contractors were required to develop "affirmative action plans" to increase the number of persons of color (and later women) who were employed by federal contractors. Sanctions for contractors that did not comply included loss of eligibility to receive federal contracts, fines paid to the government, and compensation in back-pay to aggrieved individuals (Donohue & Heckman, 1991). The Office of Minority Business Enterprise was created to increase federal contracts with minority-owned businesses. The Interagency Council of Minority Business Enterprise was created to coordinate these procurements.

The war on poverty. During the War on Poverty in the 1960s, the number of federally-funded social welfare organizations increased and became sources of employment for African Americans. Community Action Programs specifically sought to employ indigenous persons to administer federally-funded programs. The expanding social service bureaucracy led to a disproportionate increase of African Americans working in federal, state, and local government. Between 1960 and 1970, the proportion of African American managers in the public sector increased 67%, compared to a 15% increase for white managers. Wages in the public sector were higher than those in the private sector (Collins, 1983; Lemann, 1989).

Reflection. The expansion of the African American middle class correlated with a change in legislation and government policy, just as had the development of the white middle class following particular governmental initiatives of the New Deal. But, could these governmental initiatives have occurred without a rallying cry from the people? Disruptive protests and acts of civil disobedience by hundreds of thousands of civil rights activists led to significant civil rights legislation passed between 1963 and 1967. Similarly, disruptive protests in the 1930s led to the governmental initiatives that precipitated the emergence of the middle class in white America following the Great Depression. For the development of both the white middle class and the African American middle class, more than spontaneous market forces were required to reduce inequality and move people from poverty to the middle class. Cloward and Piven (2000) aver that governments only respond with policies that reduce inequality when they are forced to by powerful, disruptive social movements. The sequence of historical events supports their conclusion.

WHERE TO NOW?

Thus far, we have established that the size and security of the middle class has been jeopardized since the 1970s. We have enumerated those policies that effectively created a middle class in the United States following the Great Depression. Drawing on the lessons of the past, we now focus on government initiatives that can return this nation to its former status as nation in which most of the people are members of a secure middle class.

With the collapse of the world's financial sector in the fall of 2008, a global recession/depression threatens the world. Ironically, America may be once again witnessing the hard times of depression (which led to social unrest and eventually policies to bolster the middle class during the 1930s). Certainly, everyone is concerned about the collapse of consumer demand (Chossudovsy, 2008). The imperative of getting money into the hands of those who will spend it, in other words, the middle class, may infuse additional vigor into the cause of strengthening and widening the middle class.

Galbraith (2008a; 2008b) argues that monetary policy alone (i.e., lowering interest rates by the Federal Reserve and saving the banks) will not be sufficient to avert a looming depression. The government must inject currency into the economy, spending money to employ people. Given the imperative of a government stimulus package, opportunities for strengthening the position of labor and reinvigorating a middle class have fortuitously arisen. Questions remain regarding where to direct the employment of individuals and how to ensure that employment will result in sufficient consumer demand to keep the capitalist machinery working. We argue that fiscal policy should be directed to improving the American educational system, to rebuilding infrastructure, and to developing alternative sources of energy. Since government will be funding job creation, we can learn from the government's role in invigorating the position of organized labor during the New Deal. Government funding for new jobs should be contingent on mandatory living wages and strengthened bargaining position of unions.

Globalism

We have considered the governmental policies that strengthened the middle class following World War II. However, the world has changed since the 1950s. In the 1990s, India, China, and the former Soviet block joined the global economy, doubling the world labor pool from 1.46 billion workers to 2.93 billion workers (Freeman, 2007). Trade agreements such as North American Fair Trade Agreement (NAFTA) have facilitated the free movement of labor in the form of immigration as well as the exchange of products. During the 1950s, when the middle class was strong, American industry had little competition. American industry could grant concessions to labor and pass costs along to consumers. Businesses did not have to compete on price (Reich, 2007). With competition on pricing at cut-throat levels attributable to the global economy, businesses have moved production to nations with lower wages in order to lower prices. However, with reports that China is currently being abandoned for cheaper workers in Cambodia (Bradsher, 2008), businesses seem to be running out of laborers who work cheaply. In terms of American policy, the goal should be to turn the world into markets (and not just for sales of American cigarettes). To advance the cause of creating markets in Asia, South America, India, and Africa, trade agreements should be tied to living wages for workers in their respective countries.

Fortunately, the labor movement has also "gone global". On November 15, 2008, when global leaders (G-20 leaders) met in Washington, three international labor organizations (the International Trade Union Confederation, the Trade Union Advisory Council to the Organization of Economic Corporation and Development, and the Global Union Federations) called for a Bretton Woods system that would reduce economic inequality and reign in unbridled capitalism (Meyerson, 2008a).

Economists have applauded free trade: trade allows individual countries to specialize in those sectors in which they have a competitive advantage with the overall effect of local economies of scale achieving greater productivity (Krugman & Obstfeld, 2006). Initially, the assumption was that America's highly skilled labor pool would position America to enjoy a competitive advantage in the high technology sector of production (Freeman, 2007). However, by 2005, both Korea and European Union had a greater proportion of their citizens in universities. By 2010, China will graduate more science and engineering PhDs than the United States. Presently, China has a burgeoning niche in nanotechnology. Moreover, if work can be sent via the Internet to a person offshore—which includes about 10% of employment in the United States—then tasks can be delegated to a lower wage worker in India or China (Freeman, 2007). For America to remain competitive in high-technology sectors, money must be spent on education. If America educates its labor force and makes trade agreements that strengthen worker rights globally, America can compete even with a well-paid workforce.

Where to Create Jobs

A strong case can be made for funneling funding into education. Better educated individuals are more productive. A highly educated work force is a big incentive to businesses pondering over where to locate production (Thurow, 2003, p. 36). America needs to provide low-cost education to all citizens. The G.I. Bill did a great deal to create more productive workers. Jim Webb (2008) has argued for a G.I. Bill for returning Iraq veterans. Although a G.I. Bill would be a start, it cannot have the same effect as it did after World War II, because World War II involved such a large percentage of the population as soldiers. Thus, a G.I. Bill for everyone is required. Moreover, individuals who are displaced because of the global economy should be retrained in a needed skill (Thurow, 2003). Young children should be in daycare, not only as a support to families, but also because Head Start programs expand the capacity of children to learn once they get in grade school and will later contribute to economic growth (Dickens, Sawhill, & Tebbs, 2006). American needs to invest in a highly-skilled work force, and this investment will require hiring more educators. Part of a stimulus package should be spent on education.

Fiscal policy intervention should be coupled with employing Americans in jobs that will improve the productivity in the long run—that is, building roads, bridges, and other infrastructure. Government spending on infrastructure has gone from four percent of government spending in 1960 to two percent in 1998 (Palley, 1998). By investing in improvements in infrastructure, America could employ those truly disadvantaged minorities who have been left out of the larger economy (Wilson, 1996). Moreover, the productivity of labor (i.e., the capacity to produce more at a lower cost) would improve. Decreasing the number of unemployed should increase the bargaining position of labor and increase wages (Palley, 1998).

Oil prices have currently declined, probably as result of decreased demand occasioned by the current global recession. The temporary decline in the price of oil does not imply that the imperative of developing alternative sources of energy has abated. For national security, America must lessen its dependence of foreign oil. For purposes of saving the planet, global dependence of fossil fuels must be stopped. Finally, many argue that the world supply of oil is running out–period (Cohen, 2007). Research and development of alternative sources of energy need to occur. Better uses of extant energy sources (e.g., electric cars, more efficient heating systems, better insulation, mass transit systems) need to be developed. Madrick (2007) argues that costs of research and development on new technology won't be borne by private investment because "returns to such investments are typically diffused throughout the society". Government has to assume responsibility. Massive investment must occur. These investments can be expected to increase employment as well as creating a new niche for America in the global economy.

Strengthening Unions

Thus far, we have argued for policies that will employ more people and will increase the productivity of those who are employed. Economists have argued that wage levels are coupled to the productivity of workers. However, during the current past two decades the productivity of the American worker has increased without a commensurate increase in wages (Dew-Becket & Gordon, 2005; Krugman, 2007; Levy & Temlin, 2007; Sawhill & Morton, 2007). We have learned that more than "the invisible hand of the market" is required. Looking to the lessons of how the middle class was expanded following World War II suggests that policies are needed to strengthen the bargaining position of labor.

Hilda Solis, Obama's Secretary of Labor, has a record of strong commitment to unions (Meyerson, 2008b). This is encouraging. In addition to the Secretary of Labor, the new administration needs to appoint members of the NLRB who are willing to adjudicate labor-management disputes fairly without bias towards management. With the exception of Clinton administration appointees, the NLRB has been demonstratively pro-management for most of the past 30 years. History suggests unions were only able to reach a critical mass when labor laws were enforced by an unbiased NLRB. The NLRB needs to be strengthened. Another opportunity for strengthening labor is through the enforcement of the NLRA. The Justice Department should enforce the NLRA, which makes it illegal for employers to prevent employees from organizing. Employers in violation of labor laws need to pay stiff fines and punitive damages. Aggrieved employees should receive back pay and those who file legitimate claims should be reinstated while their cases are adjudicated (Sklar et al., 2001, p. 152).

In addition to enforcing extant laws, organized labor is advocating the passage of the Employee Free Choice Act (EFCA). A key provision of EFCA would provide an alternative mechanism for workers' authorization of unions to represent them: employees would need only to sign cards endorsing union right to bargain for them. This practice would replace the previous extended bureaucratic election process that often was accompanied by fierce anti-union campaigns initiated by management. Organizers refer to the new system as "card-check recognition". With "card-check recognition," union organizers hope to replicate the enormously successful organizing drives of the past 20 years by Las Vegas UNITE/HERE Local 226, a.k.a. 'The Culinary' union. Thanks to the "Culinary," hospitality workers in Las Vegas enjoy the highest pay scales and most generous benefits for culinary workers in the United States: waiters and waitresses make $10.50 an hour before tips (Greenhouse, 2004).

Unions, as well as other social movement organizations such as the Association of Community Organizations for Reform Now (ACORN), strive to influence the passing of living wage legislation. The efforts of social movement organizations have met with success, as evidenced by the 150 cities that have passed living wage ordinances. We need a "real living wage" minimum wage law at the national level. If government funding expands the creation of new jobs, minimum wage legislation would set a floor for the wages offered for these new jobs (Shulman, 2007). It will be critically important to monitor the precise terms of stimulus packages to ensure that protections for labor are included.

Roles for the Practitioners

The 2008 presidential election was witness to the vital role of practitioners and volunteer activists in changing U.S. policy. Project Vote, ACORN, Rock-the-Vote, along with hundreds of unions, churches, and civic organizations registered 9 million new voters. Obama won the election by 10 million votes, and his margin of victory in some states—for example, in North Carolina—was less than the number of newly registered voters. Obviously, activism and organization made a difference in the recent election. Social workers need to continue to partner with community organizations to ensure the votes will be there in coming elections.

The reader has undoubtedly recognized that many of our recommendations for fiscal policy have been endorsed by President Obama. In order to implement these policies, legislation must be passed through a Senate where filibuster is still possible. Enormous pressure from grassroots organizations and unions will be required. It will be important to remain ever vigilant to the wording of new legislation and the wording of regulations in the Federal Register to ensure that clever ways to circumvent good intentions are not found. Will we need to "take to the streets" in order to achieve our objectives? Piven (2008) argues that the protests of labor and workers were needed to change the zeitgeist paving the road for the reforms of the New Deal. Politicians are by nature compromisers. Only the voice of the people can shift the center or starting point from which politicians can negotiate components of legislation. For inequality to decline, the unemployed, the uninsured, those losing their homes through foreclosure, and the majority of workers whose wages have stagnated over the past 30 years need to unify in demanding change. Social work practitioners should join with community organizations to make that happen.

A Role for Social Workers in Jobs Created by the Stimulus Package

With unprecedented numbers of Americans losing their jobs as a result of the current recession coming atop of job losses attributable to globalization, a new practitioner role seems likely to emerge. Matching displaced workers with jobs created by government stimulus packages seems to be a more efficient mechanism than allowing people to find their own way through the employment maze, haphazardly matching skills with vacancies. The practitioner tasked with matching persons to jobs could also ensure that new workers are apprised of their right to join the union. Tactics formerly used by employers to discourage unionizing (see Sklar et al., 2001, p. 152) can be circumvented.

CONCLUDING REFLECTIONS

The present economic crisis offers opportunities for creating a better America with a stronger middle class. Strengthening union membership and mandating a "living wage" minimum wage are vital components to seizing the opportunities for creating more equitable America. Social work practitioners must continue to organize politically to ensure that the promised stimulus packages really will result in a stronger middle class.

REFERENCES

Brandolini, A., & Smeeding, T. A. (2007). *Inequality patterns in Western-type democracies: Cross-country differences and time changes.* Centre for Household, Income, Labor & Demographic Economics. Retrieved June 20, 2008, from http://www.maxwell.syr.edu/moynihan/Programs/euc/May6-7_Conference_Papers/BrandoliniSmeeding.pdf

Brimmer, (1976). The economic position of black Americans. In *A special report to the National Commission for Manpower Policy* (Special Report No. 9). Washington, DC: Commission for Manpower.

Bradsher, K. (2008, June 18). Investors seek Asian options to costly China. *New York Times.* Retrieved December 25, 2008, from http://www.nytimes.com/2008/06/18/business/worldbusiness/18invest.html?_r=1&sq=china%20and%20labor&st

Chapman, M. M. (2008, December 30). Black workers in auto plants losing ground: Middle-class dreams suffer with Detroit. *New York Times*, pp. A1, B4.

Chevan, A. (1989). Growth of homeownership 1940–1980. *Demography, 26*(2), 249–266.

Chossudovsky, M. (2008). *The Great Depression of the 21st century: Collapse of the real economy.* Centre for Research on Globalization. Retrieved December 25, 2008, from http://www.globalresearch.ca/index.php?context=va&aid=10977.

Cloward, R., & Piven, F. F. (2000). Disruptive dissensus: People and power in the industrial age. In J. Rothman (Ed.), *Reflections in community organization* (pp. 165–193). Itasca, IL: F.E. Peacock.

Cohen, D. (2007). *The perfect storm.* Association for the Study of Peak Oil and Gas USA. Retrieved June 20, 2008, from http://www.aspo-usa.com/archives/index.php?option=com_content&task=view&id=243&Itemid=91.

Collins, S. M. (1983). The making of the middle class. *Social Problems, 30*, 369–382.

Corak, M. (2006). Do poor children become poor adults? Lessons from a cross country comparison of generational earnings mobility. In J. Creedy & G. Kalb (Eds.), *Research on income inequality, Vol 13. Dynamics of inequality and poverty* (pp. 143–188). The Netherlands: Elvesier.

Dew-Becket, I., & Gordon, R. (2006). Where did the productivity growth go? Inflation dynamics and the distribution of income. In G.L. Perry & W. C. Brainard (Eds.), *Brookings papers on economic activities 2: 2005* (pp. 67–127). Washington, DC: Brookings Institution.

Donohue, J. J., & Heckman, J. (1991). Continuous versus episodic change: The impact of civil rights policy on the economic status of blacks. *Journal of Economic Literature, 26,* 1603–1643.

Freeman, R. B. (2007). The great doubling: The challenge of the new global labor market. In J. Edwards, M. M. Crain & A. L. Kalleberg (Eds.), *Ending poverty in America: How to restore the American dream* (pp. 55–65). New York: New Press.

Galbraith, J. K. (2008a). *The predator state.* New York: Free Press.

Galbraith, J. K. (2008b, September 29). How much will it cost and will it come soon enough? *American Prospect.* Retrieved December 3, 2008, from http://www.prospect.org/cs/articles?article=how_much_will_it_cost_and_will_it_come_soon_enough

Goldin, C., & Margo, R. (1992). The great compression: The wage structure in the United States at mid-century. *Quarterly Journal of Economics, 107,* 1–34.

Greenhouse, S. (2004, June 3). Local 226, 'the Culinary' makes Las Vegas the land of the living wage. *New York Times,* p. A22.

Hacker, J. S. (2006). *The great American risk shift: Why American jobs, families, health care, and retirement aren't secure—and how you can fight back.* New York, NY: Oxford University Press.

Jackson, K. (1985). *Crabgrass frontier: The suburbanization of the United States.* Oxford: Oxford University Press.

Jackson, P. B., & Stewart, Q. T. (2003). A research agenda for the Black middle class: Work stress, survival strategies, and mental health. *Journal of Health and Social Behavior, 44,* 442–455.

Jones, A. F., Jr., & Weinberg, D. H. (2000). The changing shape of the nation's income distribution: 1947 to 1998. *Current population reports.* Washington, DC: U.S. Census Bureau. Retrieved July 20, 2007, from http://www.theatlantic.com/politics/poverty/lemunf2.htm

Katz-Fishman, W., & Scott, J. (1994). Diversity and equality: Race and class in America. *Sociological Forum, 9,* 569–581.

Kawachi, I., & Kennedy, B. P. (2002). *The health of nations: Why inequality is harmful to your health.* New York: New Press.

Krugman, P. (2007). *Conscience of a liberal.* New York: W.W. Norton.

Krugman, P. R., & Obstfeld, M. (2006). *International economics: Theory and policy* (7th ed.). Boston, MA: Addison Wesley.

Lemann, N. (1989). The unfinished war [Electronic version]. *The Atlantic.* Retrieved on June 26, 2008, from http://www.theatlantic.com/politics/poverty/lemuf2.htm

Lemann, N. (1991). *The promised land: The great Black migration and how it changed America.* New York: Vintage Press.

Levy, F., & Temlin, P. (2007, June). *Inequality and institutions in the 20th Century America* (Document No. 07-17). Cambridge, MA: Industrial Performance Center, MIT Department of Economic Working Papers. Retrieved April 22, 2009, from http://web.mit.edu/ipc/publications/pdf/07-002.pdf

Madrick, J. (2007). Breaking the stranglehold on growth: Why policies promoting demand offer a better way for the U.S. economy. *Economic Policy Institute* (EPI Briefing Paper No. 192, pp. 1–22). Retrieved December 21, 2007, from http://www.sharedprosperity.org/bp192/bp192.pdf

Meyerson, H. (2008a, January/February). A global New Deal. *American Prospect*, *20*, 10–12.

Meyerson, H. (2008b, December 18). Hilda Solis is great. *American Prospect*. Retrieved December 25, 2008, from http://www.prospect.org/csnc/blogs/tapped_archives?month=12&year=2008&base_name=Hilda_solis_is_great

Mishel, L., & Walters, M. (2003). How unions help all workers. *Economic Policy Institute* (EPI Briefing Paper No. 143). Retrieved December 3, 2008, from http://www.epi.org/page/-/old/briefingpapers/143/bp143.pdf

Moberg, D. (2007, November 13). Treaty of Detroit is repealed. *In These Times*. Retrieved April 22, 2009, from http://www.inthesetimes.com/article/3408/

Murolo, P., & Chitty, A. B. (2001). *From the folks who brought you the weekend: A short illustrated history of labor in the United States*. New York: New Press.

Ohmer, M., & DeMasi, K. (2008). *Consensus organizing: A community development workbook*. Thousand Oaks, CA: Sage.

Palley, T. I. (1998). *Plenty of nothing: The downsizing of the American dream and the case for structural Keynesianism*. Princeton, NJ: Princeton University Press.

Piketty, T., & Saez, E. (2003). Income inequality in the United States, 1913–1998. *Quarterly Journal of Economics, CXVII*, 1–39.

Piven, F. F. (2008, November 13). Obama needs a protest movement [Electronic version]. *The Nation*. Retrieved December 25, 2008, from http://www.thenation.com/doc/20081201/piven.

Piven, F. F. (2006). *Challenging authority: How ordinary people change America*. Lanham, MD: Rowan & Littlefield.

Piven, F. F., & Cloward, R. (1971). *Regulating the poor: The functions of public welfare*. New York: Vintage.

Reich, R. B. (2007). *Supercapitalism*. New York: Barzoi.

Sawhill, I., & Morton, J. E. (2007). *Economic mobility: Is the American dream alive and well?* Washington, DC: Pew Charitable Trusts.

Sawhill, I., Tebbs, J., & Dickens, W. (2006). *The effects of investing in early education on economic growth*. Washington, DC: Brookings Institution. Retrieved on June 14, 2008, from http://www.brookings.edu/papers/2006/04education_dickens02.aspx

Shulman, B. (2007). Making work pay. In J. Edwards, M., M. Crain & A. L. Kalleberg (Eds.), *Ending poverty in America: How to restore the American dream* (pp. 114–124). New York: New Press.

Sklar, H., Mykyta, L., & Wefald, S. (2001). *Raise the floor: Wages and polices that work for all of us*. New York: Ms. Foundation for Women.

Thurow, L. C. (2003). *Fortune favors the bold*. New York: Harpers.

Tillery, A. B. (2008, June 23). *The long shadow of the GI Bill: Intergenerational effects of U.S. social policy on the racial gap*. Paper presented at the Woodrow Wilson Center, Washington, DC.

Troy, L. (1965). Trade union membership, 1897–1962. *Review of Economics and Statistics, 47*(1), 93–113.

Uchitelle, L. (2007). *The disposable American: Layoffs and their consequences*. New York: UCS Labor Books.

U.S. Census Bureau. (2005). *Current population survey, 1996, 2004, and 2005 annual social and economic supplements.* Washington, DC: U.S. Government Printing Office. Retrieved April 22, 2009, from http://www.gibill.va.gov/ GI_Bill_Info/history.htm

U.S. Department of Veteran's Affairs. (2008). *GI-Bill history.* Retrieved June 2, 2008, from http://www.gibill.va.gov/GI_Bill_Info/history.htm

United Nations. (2004). *United Nations human development report.* New York: United Nations Development Programme. Retrieved February 24, 2007, from http://www.undp.org/annualreports/2004/english/

Webb, J. (2008). *Leading veteran's groups advocate comprehensive "21st Century G. I. Bill".* Retrieved April 21, 2009, from http://webb.senate.gov/email/ 022608.html

Wilson, W. J. (1996). *When work disappears: The world of the new urban poor.* New York: Vintage.

Wolff, E. N. (1998). Recent trends in size distribution of household wealth. *Journal of Economic Perspectives, Summer, 12*(3), 131–150.

Promoting Economic Justice in a Global Context: International Comparisons of Policies That Support Economic Justice

CYNTHIA ROCHA

College of Social Work, University of Tennessee, Knoxville, Tennessee, USA

This study compares economic justice, measured by income inequality and child poverty rates, across industrialized countries. Labor market training, social service expenditures, unions and taxes were significantly related to economic justice. The United States had the highest income inequality and the second-highest child poverty rate of the countries studied.

PROMOTING ECONOMIC JUSTICE IN A GLOBAL CONTEXT: INTERNATIONAL COMPARISONS OF POLICIES THAT SUPPORT ECONOMIC JUSTICE

Economic justice is an increasingly important issue in the United States and abroad for governments, community practitioners, and numerous others concerned with growing global interdependence. Because unequal access to economic resources within many countries participating in the global market economy continues to grow, it is important to discern what policies are essential in promoting economic justice. Yet there is little agreement about what constitutes economic justice and, more importantly, how to attain it. At the heart of this disagreement is whether the global marketplace can meet social needs without creating policies that will restrain economic growth, or whether government intervention is needed to restrain unfettered capitalism that may increase a country's global competitive edge, but at a cost to economic justice for its citizens. This article analyzes which policies may help or hinder a country's advancement toward a more equitable distribution of resources and thus promote greater economic justice. Comparing countries' attainment of economic justice helps to pinpoint what types of policies have the most impact on issues of equality.

This article first defines economic justice and discusses the theoretical underpinnings of conflicting views on how to attain it in an international market economy. Next the literature on potential policies related to economic justice is reviewed. Based on the various theories and research findings from a national and international perspective, indicators related to social welfare, the economy, labor, and fiscal policies are analyzed from an international data set to ascertain which policies are indeed related to conditions of economic justice. The focus of this study is on industrialized nations, specifically the United States and OECD countries, and therefore, does not address economic inequality in developing nations. Specific countries that have attained the highest and lowest degrees of economic justice are reviewed in light of the policies found to be highly correlated with economic justice indicators. Finally, given the findings, the article examines the implications for social workers, organized labor, and other community practitioners in how best to promote economic justice.

Defining Economic Justice

While the concept of economic justice is mentioned frequently in the literature, there are a multitude of theories and definitions of economic justice. Although social scientists may not agree on what defines economic justice, Hahnel (2005) asserts that most "believe they know injustice when they see it" (p. 19). Hahnel also maintains that the question that social scientists grapple with is what constitutes equitable distributions of resources. Distributions of benefits vary and may be accorded to people based on their human capital, their efforts, or their needs. Thus, economic justice is controversial because, depending on how it is defined, the policies needed to achieve it will determine how scarce resources will be divided among people (Kapstein, 2006).

Measuring economic justice is also problematic. Lundy and van Wormer (2007) provide a more precise definition of economic justice as simply equitable standards of living, where people have an opportunity to work for an income that provides adequately for their families. This definition is more measurable if we can agree on what "adequately" means. The Social Work Dictionary (2003) offers more specificity and defines economic justice as a principle "where governments and other social institutions adhere to policies ensuring that all people receive adequate incomes above an agreed upon poverty threshold" (p. 137). Therefore, if all people receive an "adequate income," it would speak to equality of income, or how income is distributed. Poverty threshold, although defined differently across countries, would place emphasis on an agreed upon floor that people cannot fall below. Therefore, both income equality and poverty levels allow us to define the degree to which a nation achieves economic justice. Because both terms are measurable, they will be used to operationalize economic justice in this study.

Theoretical Arguments Regarding Economic Justice and the Global Economy

It is important to look at the theoretical arguments on how to best reach economic justice in a society because these underpin much of current behavior of governments competing in the global economy. There are two main theoretical arguments regarding economic wellbeing. The first is the notion that in a globalized economy, capitalism must embrace a decentralized decision making model toward development relying on the private sector of the economy to provide for basic economic common goods (O'Connor, 2002). O'Connor purports that the decentralized capitalist global economy "creates new and better jobs, greater demand for society's output, a rising GNP and an improved quality of life" (p. 100). These are essentially neo-classical supply-side economic and neoliberal political theories that purport that privatization, deregulation and reductions in social programs will increase economic efficiency in the market, resulting in a higher standard of living for its citizens (Babe, 2000). This is also known as an individual (or laissez-faire) approach to development and assumes a country's economic status will drive their social welfare outcomes, rather than the other way around (Midgley, 1995). By the 1980s, many western nations began adopting neoliberal policies, believing social and human development would occur naturally as a result of economic growth.

On the other hand, there are industrialized countries that have taken a position that the best course of political action is to ensure some basic pro-tections for workers, requiring regulation of the capitalist market place, "rejecting the idea that the economy is a self-regulating system" (Midgley, 1995, p. 144). Under more traditional welfare models, regulations of the market place are needed "to ensure the fruits of development are distributed equitably" (Waldhorn, 2002, p. 5). This is a Keynesian economic approach, which suggests that economic intervention is necessary to foster economic growth. This theoretical approach is widely cited as the inspiration for the modern welfare state in the United States.

Although the United States eventually adopted the more neoclassical neoliberal models of deregulation and decentralization of social welfare, most European welfare states adopted a more regulated approach to their economies, choosing to leave the welfare state relatively unscathed. They believe that, rather than the economy determining economic justice, policies that support justice can contribute to economic efficiency. Hemerijck (2002) explains that the European social model presumes that "social policy is an essential factor in promoting economic adjustment, that there is no contra-diction between economic competitiveness and social cohesion" (p. 174).

These are two seemingly contradictory arguments. The first is that an effi-cient unregulated economy leads to economic well-being. The other is the notion that economic efficiency and social well-being are interdependent, and that social welfare policies may in fact lead to economic efficiency. As Caputo (2007) emphasizes, the theoretical task at this point is to identify the compo-nents of the state that can foster conditions of justice and to find the links between economics and social benefits. Thus, the conceptual framework in this study will address to what degree economic efficiency (defined as per cap-ital gross domestic product, or GDP); social welfare policies (including social welfare expenditures, taxes, and investments in education and training); and organized collective bargaining are related to greater economic justice.

Literature on Income Inequality and Poverty

Whether economic efficiency leads to economic justice or whether government regulations are necessary to ensure justice will be discussed throughout the literature review as we look at the state of economic justice in the industrialized world, as well as what the literature indicates the predictors of justice might be. Many industrialized countries are currently grappling with the pressures of globalization and its impact on income inequality and poverty (United Nations, 2005; Waldhorn, 2002; Weller, Scott & Hersh, 2001).

In the United States, disparities in both income and child poverty rates have continued to grow since 1969 despite public income transfers (Ozawa & Kim, 2000). From where are these growing inequalities emerging? The Economic Policy Institute estimates that between 1973 and 2006 U.S. trade lowered wages of workers with less than a college degree by 4%, while college-educated workers' incomes increased by 3% (Bivens, 2008). The trade disparities that impact low wage labor are largely caused by increases in industries for less-skilled workers that pay lower wages. But industrial shifts account for only part of the increased economic inequalities. In the United States, where income inequality is at an all time high, the minimum wage has not kept up with inflation, social welfare has taken major cuts, CEOs of corporations have made multi-million dollar salaries while 40 hour-a-week workers may still live under the poverty level, and union membership is at an all time low (Abramovitz, 2001; DeCarlo, 2006; Mishel et al., 2007).

The United States is not the only industrialized country that has experi-enced increases in income inequality over the last several years, however. Jaumotte, Lall and Papageorgion (2008) found that the benefits of growth rates associated with globalization have not been equally shared. Income inequality has risen in many countries despite "improvements in technology, liberal market-oriented reforms and . . . unprecedented levels of integration of the world economy" (p. 3).

Yet, the commitment to economic justice has continued in those countries where "equality is a broadly accepted societal norm" (Armingion, 2004, p. 235). For example, Armingion studied 14 industrialized countries targeted by the Organisation for Economic Cooperation and Development (OECD) for recommendations to cope with domestic economic problems that might deter them from more efficiently competing in the global economy. The OECD is a highly influential policy research organization whose member countries are from the richest most industrialized nations in the world. However, Armingion found that when reductions in social welfare do not reflect a country's cultural norms of equity, the neo liberal OECD recommendations often go unheeded. For example, Denmark, Sweden, and Norway ignored OECD recommendations that would have retrenched policies believed to reduce inequalities. In France, OECD proposals to introduce competition into health care policy to increase efficiency were resisted; and in Finland, recommendations to increase the age of retirement, deregulate labor relations, and privatize vocational training were not followed. This suggests if the recommendations to retrench social policies in order to become more efficient in the international economy are correct, then these are the same countries that should be suffering economically from decreased ability to compete internationally; thus decreasing employment, reducing income equality and increasing poverty. This study will test these assumptions using the OECD data base.

Literature Review on Potential Predictors of Economic Justice

Although the OECD and other neoliberal and neoclassical theoreticians suggest that a strong economy will lead to greater economic stability and thus greater economic justice, other researchers disagree, suggesting that governments must invest in social welfare policies to attain greater income equality and decreased poverty levels (Abramovitz, 2001; Mishel, Bernstein & Allegretto, 2007). There is also evidence that collective bargaining has helped decrease wage inequality for workers, and thus predicts greater economic justice (Mellor, Barnes-Farrell, & Stanton, 1999; Traxler, Brandl, Glassner & Ludvig, 2008). To understand these arguments further, the potential predictors of economic justice are reviewed.

Social Welfare and Fiscal Policies

Ozawa and Kim (2000) suggest the increase in income inequality for children in the United States is due in part to the ineffectiveness of social welfare policies to counter this inequality. Although U.S. social welfare is commonly regarded as serving only poor people, in reality most social welfare programs serve the middle and upper classes (Abramovitz, 2001). The actual percentage of redistributive effort from U.S. social welfare programs is quite small. Abramovitz suggests the same holds true for fiscal policies, where the U.S. tax system provides middle and upper income people with considerably more benefits than are available to poor families.

In an international analysis comparing the importance of government expenditures on social welfare versus relying on market forces (measured by per capita GDP) to increase nations' well-being, Rocha (2007) found that an infrastructure that supports both government spending on social welfare as well as relying on the market were important in decreasing infant mortality and increasing life expectancy.

Economic Indicators

As discussed earlier, proponents of laissez-faire economics suggest that social development will occur naturally as a result of economic growth, and that a rising Gross Domestic Product (GDP) will increase overall quality of life (O'Connor, 2002). GDP measures the market value of all goods and services produced within a country. Thus per capita GDP is often used to measure wealth, or living standards, of a country by assuming the total value of goods sold in a nation is distributed evenly across the population. GDP has become the most important economic statistic in western culture, using it as a measure of social progress (Robbins, 2005). Does economic expansion alone, in the face of social welfare retrenchment, decrease inequality?

Research results have been mixed. Korukond and Bathala (2004), for example, found that developing countries that increased their economic output (GDP) also had increased unemployment at the same time. They go on to say that cut throat competition strains the ability of nations to provide for human welfare and that central government must monitor and regulate capitalist enterprises in order to obtain the most efficient allocation of resources. Furthermore, in a longitudinal review of U.S. Census data from 1967 through 2000, Rocha and McCarter (2003/4) found that the U.S economic expansions of the late 1990s continued to benefit the upper 20% of wage earners.

Education and Human Capital

There is general agreement in the literature that human capital investments in education and training increase individuals' access to better jobs and increased wages (Mishel, Bernstein & Allegretto, 2007; O'Connor, 2002; Rocha & McCarter, 2003/4). As Mishel and associates suggest, it is "common to point out that the wages of 'more educated' workers have grown faster than the wages of less-educated workers since 1979, with the real wages of less-educated workers falling sharply . . . in the 1995–2000 period" (p. 149).

The cost of acquiring post-secondary education has soared in recent years, while Pell grants have declined in the percent of coverage of educational costs. In 1975–76, Pell grants covered 84% of tuition costs compared to 39% in 2002 (King and Bannon, 2002). Half of all college students drop out without completing their degree. Dynarski (2008) found that students who received subsidies in addition to Pell grants and loans were more likely to complete college than other students. For students who do finish their degree, 39% of student borrowers graduate with unmanageable amounts of debt (defined as more than 8% of their income; King & Bannon, 2002). For low-income and minority students, the amount is even higher. Thus, it is important to look not only at the amount of education achieved, but how much the central government is investing in education and training and how that is related to economic justice.

Unions and Collective Bargaining

The growth of globalization has created new challenges for unions world-wide, particularly in industrialized countries, where unions had a strong-hold on industry before the deindustrialization period of the 1980s and 1990s. Union membership in the U.S. fell from 43% in 1978 to 12.1% in 2007 (Bureau of Labor Statistics, 2008). U.S. workers who are unionized still have wages and benefits that exceed nonunion workers. Overall in 2007, union members had median weekly earnings of $863, while those who were not represented by unions had median weekly earnings of $663 (BLS, 2008). But the union wage advantage for low wage earners and women was even greater. In 2007 unionization raised women's wages by 11.2%, and women were almost 20% more likely to have health insurance than their non-union counterparts (CEPR, 2008). Low wage earners benefited even more, increasing their wages by 20.6%.

Unions have always been "premised on the limited ability of capital to exit or threaten to exit from economic relations" (Piven & Cloward, 1998, p. 14). Now with the interdependence of trade, corporations have greater opportunities to relocate to other countries, decreasing the bargaining power of unions in many industries. However, for those who have been able to remain unionized, their collective power has won them substantial benefits over nonunion workers.

While unions have had challenges across all industrialized countries, those in other countries have not all declined to the extent that U.S. unions have. In the Scandinavian countries, for example, there is a long history of negotiation and collective bargaining. For example, Elvander (2002) reports that in Denmark collective bargaining units have always been considered social partners and are included in the decision making over legislation that affects the labor market. Although in each Scandinavian country collective bargaining is very different, they all are part of negotiations or mediation in the decisions regarding labor policy. The European Union has not integrated their unions into government decision-making to the extent the Scandinavian countries have, and in fact has had declines in union density over the last several years.

RESEARCH QUESTIONS

Given the definitions of economic justice, both nationally and internationally, the focus in this article is on two facets of economic justice: (a) adequate incomes, and (b) providing people with resources above a poverty threshold. Using 2000 data from the Organization for Economic Cooperation and Development 30 member nations (OECD, 2005) the research questions are:

1. Which OECD member nations have obtained greater economic justice?
2. What are the social, fiscal, labor, and economic conditions present in countries that have greater economic equity? and
3. Which countries have the highest and lowest levels of economic justice, and how do these findings compare with policies and other indicators found significantly associated with economic justice?

METHODOLOGY

Sample and Design

The sample consists of the thirty member nations of the OECD for the year 2000 (OECD, 2005). The members of the OECD are largely the most industrialized countries, producing two-thirds of the world's goods and services (Rocha, 2007). Member countries in the OECD have a market economy and a pluralistic democracy. The original core group of North American and European nations (Austria, Belgium, Canada, Denmark, France, Germany, Greece, Iceland, Ireland, Italy, Luxembourg, the Netherlands, Norway, Portugal, Spain, Sweden, Switzerland, Turkey, The United States and the United Kingdom) has expanded to include Australia, the Czech Republic, Finland, Hungary, Japan, Korea, Mexico, New Zealand, Poland and the Slovak Republic (Rocha, 2007, pp. 7–8).

The design of the study is descriptive and cross-sectional. Because of the small sample size, more sophisticated analyses are not possible. However, much can be gleaned from a descriptive study regarding the relationships among industrialized countries and their commitment to economic justice.

MEASUREMENT AND ANALYSIS

The measures in this study are highly reliable across nations. All variables have been collected and measured consistently by the OECD, overcoming much of the past difficulties in attempting to compare across nations. The two variables used to assess economic justice are income inequality and child poverty rates. The independent variables are training, education, public social expenditures, per capita GDP, taxation, and union membership. The variables are operationalized as follows:

Income inequality: Incidence of low pay as a percent of workers earning less than two-thirds of the median income.
Childhood poverty: Percent of children living in poverty.
Training: Public expenditures as a percent of GDP on training and education.
Education: All levels of education combined.
Public Social Expenditures: Public social expenditures as a percent of GDP.
Per Capita GDP: Gross Domestic Product divided across a nation's population.
Taxation: Total tax wedge for married couples, including employer's social security contributions (average rate in %). Tax Wedge, as defined by the OECD (2004) is the difference between what employers pay out in wages and social security charges and what employees bring home after taxes and social security deductions.
Union Membership: Percent of workforce membership in unions.

Analyses are restricted to descriptive statistics and correlations between dependent and independent variables. The five countries exhibiting the highest scores in economic justice will also be compared with the bottom five countries. These countries will then be compared with the independent variables found significantly correlated with economic justice.

RESULTS

The first research question asked which OECD member nations have obtained greater economic justice. Table 1 examines the countries with the highest and lowest economic justice scores as measured by income inequality and child poverty rates. The top and bottom five countries are shown for each dependent variable. As Table 1 indicates, the top countries (Sweden, Denmark, Finland, Italy, and Belgium) ranged from a low of 5.3–7.3% in income inequality (the incidence of low pay as a percent of workers earning less than two-thirds of the median income) while the bottom five countries (United States, Korea, Hungary, Ireland, and Canada) ranged from 20.9–24.5% in income inequality. The top countries in the alleviation of children in poverty (Finland, Sweden, Denmark, Belgium, and Norway) had child poverty rates from 2.1–4.4% of poverty, while the bottom five countries (Mexico, United States, Turkey, Italy, and the United Kingdom) ranged from 18.6–26.2%.

TABLE 1 Countries With the Highest and Lowest Economic Justice Scores as Measured by Income Inequality and Child Poverty Rates

Highest economic justice top five countries	Lowest income inequality (% of median income)	Top five countries	Lowest child poverty (% of children)
Sweden	5.3%	Finland	2.1%
Denmark	5.6%	Sweden	2.7%
Finland	5.9%	Denmark	3.4%
Italy	6.1%	Belgium	4.1%
Belgium	7.3%	Norway	4.4%
Lowest economic justice bottom five countries	Highest income inequality	Bottom five countries	Highest child poverty
United States	24.5%	Mexico	26.2%
Korea	23.8%	United States	23.2%
Hungary	22.0%	Turkey	19.7%
Ireland	21.1%	Italy	18.8%
Canada	20.9%	United Kingdom	18.6%

Note. From OECD (2005). The OECD Statistics Portal. Organisation for Economic Cooperation and Development. Retrieved January 28, 2008, from http://www.oecd.org/statistics.

The second research question asked, what are the social, fiscal, labor and economic conditions present in countries that have greater economic equity? In bi-variate correlation analyses, greater percentage of GDP on labor market training, increased public social expenditures, higher taxes, and union membership were significantly related to decreased income inequality (see Table 2). Per capita GDP and level of education were not related to income inequality. Labor market training, education, public social expenditures, tax rate, and union membership were significantly related to child poverty. However, per capita GDP was not related to child poverty rates.

The final research question is which countries have the highest and lowest levels of economic justice, and how do these compare with policies and other indicators found significantly associated with economic justice?

TABLE 2 Correlations Between Indicators of Economic Justice and Social, Political, Labor, and Economic Variables

Variable	Income inequality	Child poverty rates
% GDP labor market training	$-.517^*$	$-.592^*$
Education	$-.422$	$-.629^{**}$
Public social expenditures	$-.698^{**}$	$-.793^{**}$
Per capita GDP	$-.177$	$-.421$
Taxes for married couples	$-.546^{**}$	$-.536^*$
Union membership	$-.756^{**}$	$-.702^{**}$

Note. $^*p < .05$, $^{**}p < .01$.

This allows us to take a closer look at the countries that had significant correlations between economic justice indicators and the policies and conditions related to economic justice that were found in Table 2.

Table 3 illustrates how the above differences in income inequality and child poverty rates across countries compare with variables found significant in the correlation analysis. For the countries found in the top five for either income equality or lower child poverty rates, individual scores on labor market training, education, social expenditures, tax wedge, and union membership are given. Likewise, individual scores are given for the countries scoring in the bottom on income inequality and child poverty rates. Also shown are the ranges and averages of these scores so the reader can easily see the differences.

The greatest variation among countries was in the percentage of GDP devoted to training, the percent of social expenditures spent, and union membership. Countries high in economic justice spent on average almost two

TABLE 3 Indicators Associated With Countries Who Have the Highest and Lowest Economic Justice

High economic justice countries	Labor market training as % GDP	Education (total years)	Social expenditures (% of GDP)	Tax wedge married (incl. social security)	Union membership %
Belgium	.24	18.7	24.0	41.3	55.6
Denmark	.85	17.8	30	31.0	74.4
Finland	.30	18.7	29	40.3	76.2
Italy*	.05	15.8	27	37.4	34.9
Norway	.06	17.9	25	26.2	54.3
Sweden	.31	20.2	33	44.3	79.1
Range	.05–.85%	15–20	24–33%	26–44%	34–79%
Average	.301%	18.18	28%	36.75%	62.41%

Low economic justice countries	Labor market training	Education	Social welfare expenditure	Tax wedge	Union membership
Canada	.17	16.5	17	23.0	28.1
Hungary	.07	16.4	.	35.3	.
Ireland	.	15.9	18	19.9	37.8
Italy*	.05	15.8	27	37.4	34.9
Korea	.09	16.0	5	14.6	11.4
Mexico	.03	12.6	8	22.0	.
Turkey	.	10.1	10	31.1	.
United Kingdom	.05	18.9	22	23.8	31.2
United States	.04	16.7	16	24.5	12.8
Range	.03–.17%	10–18	8–27%	14–37%	11–37%
Average	.071%	15.43	15.37%	25.7%	26.03%

Note. Only variables with significant correlations with one or more dependent variables reported.

From OECD (2005). The OECD Statistics Portal. Organisation for Economic Cooperation and Development. Retrieved January 28, 2008, from http://www.oecd.org/statistics.

*Italy is a special case since it was in the top five countries for income equality but the bottom five countries for childhood poverty.

times the percent of their GDP on public social expenditures, were 2.39 times more likely to be in a union, and spent four times the percent of GDP on labor market training. Although taxes were only 1.4 times higher on average in high economic justice countries, this variable is difficult to interpret, since it is unknown what different countries employers' share of social security taxes are.

DISCUSSION

The most interesting finding in this study was the insignificance of per capita GDP in its relationship to economic justice. So much emphasis is put on GDP as a predictor of well-being and development in the economic literature, yet it was not related to either income inequality or child poverty rates. It was also interesting that education was significantly related to decreases in child poverty but not income inequality. Early in the article, it was noted that while human capital theory suggests that education is important in increasing income, how one achieves that education is an unknown. Is it personal income or government assistance? Thus, the percentage of GDP that the governments spend on education and training was included in the analysis to try to tease this out a bit. While this is in no way definitive, it does pose the question: how is it that personal education does not correlate with decreased income inequality, but government investments in education and training does? More research needs to be done to ascertain if greater government assistance in education and training give low-income people a head start in decreasing income inequality.

It is clear that government social expenditures, greater taxes, and increased union membership decrease income inequality and child poverty rates. These variables are to some degree related. Taxes pay for social expenditures, for example. However, it is also true that each country decides, based on their value system, how taxes should be spent. Concomitantly, increased union membership leads to greater power in collective bargaining and a greater voice in income distribution and other social welfare issues regarding the health of the labor force. Thus, each of these variables are important in their relationship to economic justice, but taken together may provide a more comprehensive picture in achieving greater economic justice.

Finally, the neoliberal argument that a strong economy alone will lead to greater economic justice does not have support in these findings. Higher GDP was not related to economic justice overall; it was how the governments chose to distribute the GDP that was associated with economic justice. Indeed, if the neoliberal argument were the case, Scandinavian countries should have been lower in economic justice because they provide more social welfare than any of the other countries; instead, they were in the top five of each of the indicators for economic justice. Having said this, the results should be viewed with caution, since the sample size is small and the design is cross-sectional. More research is needed in this area; particularly with larger data sets and with longitudinal analyses.

LIMITATIONS

Some limitations in this study are evident. First, there is the curious case of Italy, which rather ironically made it to both the top and bottom five countries in terms of economic justice; bottom five in child poverty rates, but top five in income equality. By including Italy in both high and low economic justice countries in Table 3 it may have obfuscated some of the results. A second limitation is the tax variable. There is no way to know for all countries, how much employers pay for their part of social security taxes. Even though the OECD probably reported this reliably, the importance of how taxes affect families is still relatively unknown, since we do not know how much of the tax burden is given to families versus to their employer. Also, as mentioned above, larger sample sizes would increase the power of the results.

Nevertheless, the outcomes of this study assist us in understanding which policies and social conditions are associated with greater economic justice, provide evidence to support policies that are related to greater income equality and reduced poverty rates, and offer guidance for action campaigns that target specific policy changes at the national level that will increase economic justice.

Implications for Social Work, Social Movements, and Community-Based Efforts to Address Inequality

Mizrahi (2004) suggests it is time for community practitioners and advocates to become better organized strategically and create new opportunities to address economic justice. According to the literature, because the state plays such a vital role in ensuring economic justice for its citizens, it seems logical that social work's focus should be on changing policy (as advocates) and educating the public (as community practitioners) on what policies could create a better infrastructure to protect workers. Educating the public on what other industrialized countries do to increase economic justice may supplement our understanding of more effective strategies to take in the United States.

The historical development of social work practice focusing on social and economic justice has been influenced by external social movements, including economic issues associated with worker and trade union movements, civil rights, women's rights, gay liberation, and the grey power movement, just to name a few. These movements, often external to our profession, have influenced social work practice in a number of ways. First, they challenged the profession's assumption that "we know best" (Thompson, 2002, p. 717). Second, they pushed social work to recognize clients as stakeholders and partners, potentially increasing client participation in their own service provision. Thus, as global challenges to social and economic justice have increased, our code of ethics and our accrediting body for social work education have put social justice for poor and oppressed populations at the forefront of our professional goals, ethics, and standards (Council on Social Work Education, 2008; National Association of Social Workers, 1999).

In professional social work practice in the United States, there has always been and continues to be a fundamental tension between being agents of social control or a force for justice and change. But this tension exists in other industrialized nations as well. In Britain, for example, social work is seen as "supportive of state initiatives . . . but can also run counter to these and be a thorn in the side of the formal power structure . . . Clearly, there are constraints upon social work [in Britain], given its roots in the statutory framework" (Thompson, 2002, p. 719).

Also in Canada over the last 20 years, social welfare benefits have eroded as the United States and Canada continue integrating their economies under trade agreements such as NAFTA (Lundy & van Wormer, 2007). As the Canadian and U.S. economies become more integrated "social workers have often found themselves torn between the values instilled in them in schools of social work and the realities of trying to help clients against an increasingly lean and mean social system" (Lundy et al., p. 733). Thus it is quite clear that social work, although a potential political force for change to increase economic justice, has been caught between the government and reform efforts in many western countries.

There is, however, a strong, albeit small, cadre of social workers in the political and community practice arena. There are also national associations, such as the National Association of Social Workers (NASW), The International Federation of Social Workers (IFSW), and the Association for Community Organization and Social Administration (ACOSA) that have infrastructures in place that can be used to mobilize social workers both here and abroad. As we learn more about what policies and strategies relate to global economic justice, there are social workers with the skills to assume those political and community roles. Furthermore, the political arena in the U.S. administration has recently changed, bringing a platform of reform with the sweeping victory in the 2008 elections, a more community-oriented President, and more moderate representatives in the majority in Congress. This not only assists the small group of social workers already in policy and community practice roles, but may ultimately release some of the old tensions direct practitioners have felt between government-funded work and reform.

Implications for Labor Movements and Community Based Efforts to Address Inequality

In the United States, there has been a decline in collective bargaining over the last twenty years or so. There are current attempts underway to strengthen and revitalize unions that involve (a) including community organizations as partners in union organizing, and (b) coordinating collective bargaining transnationally. Lopez (2004) suggests the way to revitalize labor in the United States is to forge labor-community coalitions, transitioning unions from what he terms business unions to social movement unions. There is some evidence that by incorporating a wide range of community groups, and moving unions toward a social justice stance, it would attract more than just the workers in one sector, but would gain the interest of the community at large. In this way, community organizations would be included in a bottom up approach to union organizing.

The second idea to strengthen collective bargaining that has been developed and tested to a limited degree in Europe has been termed *transnational organizing* or *cross-border bargaining*. Traxler et al., (2008) provides the first analysis of transnational bargaining and concludes that cross-border pattern bargaining, comprising a large country and neighboring smaller ones, are likely to work together effectively in collective bargaining if they are in similar industries. Generally, the larger of the countries would bear the main burden of coordinating the effort. This idea may be particularly well-suited for countries with specific trade agreements. For example, NAFTA includes Canada, the United States, and Mexico. If developed internationally, it would also address the issue that Piven and Cloward (1998) discussed regarding the flight of capital across borders. As Waldhorn (2002) states: "the movement for free trade is irreversible . . . the best course of political action now is to insure future agreements include important protection for workers" (p. 3).

Efforts at cross border bargaining have not had a great deal of success in the United States (c.f. Bacon, 1998; Watts, 2003), although most are still in their infancy. Part of the problem is that the low level of union representation in the United States and the anti-union tactics of U.S. employers have decreased bargaining power of both U.S. unions and other organizing attempts in neighboring countries (AFL-CIO, 2008). For example, some U.S. unions that supported their Mexican counterparts have had their own plants shut down, allegedly in retaliation (Brooks & Fox, 2004). There have been some organizing success stories, most of them in the border regions with Maquiladoras. Beyond the border, however, U.S. and Mexican labor unions have held many discussions that have led to proclamations of worker rights, but relatively few actual partnerships. So far, most cross-border unions and social networks between the United States and Mexico have not resulted in sustained movements. The idea to strengthen unions through transnational organizing between the United States and smaller neighboring countries that Traxler (2008) found effective in Europe, has not evolved similarly in the United States and requires much more research to understand under what circumstances these relationships succeed.

CONCLUSION: WHY HAVE OTHER OECD COUNTRIES ADDRESSED ECONOMIC JUSTICE BETTER THAN THE U.S.?

It is disappointing to see the United States at the bottom of income equality, and second to the last in child poverty among countries included in this study. Why have we done so poorly in taking care of our workers and our children? There are several related answers to this, much of it evident in the results from this study. It is clear that the United States must invest more in the social welfare infrastructure of the country. First, much of the reluctance in investing in social welfare has to do with a value system that focuses on individual change and a laissez-faire economy. Popular education may be an important avenue for community practitioners to pursue for changing knowledge and attitudes. The more the public knows what protections other countries have for their workers, the more they will demand the same. Second, the literature indicates that workers must believe that unions can make a difference and understand that this must be an international effort. From the data in this study it is clear that several other countries have more organized collective bargaining and that this variable is significantly related to increased economic justice. Linking union activity to community activities may provide promise in strengthening collective bargaining. Rather than looking at individual explanations for our failures, we must begin to focus on community solutions. Rather than look at what individual workers can get from collective bargaining, people must see what their community can gain in terms of overall well-being. Ultimately this represents a shift from individual to community thinking.

Finally, economic justice in the global economy requires national level leadership. The state must have an infrastructure in place to support and protect workers, their families, and communities. Values, again, can be seen in the lack of government leadership focusing on the community. It requires education and a shift in our value system to understand why thinking in terms of community works. It requires that social workers be trained in popular education techniques, policy practice, and community practice in order to empower ourselves and others to make the changes necessary to increase economic justice in the United States. As the new President takes office, there is hope that a shift toward community thinking may occur.

REFERENCES

Abramovitz, M. (2001). Everyone is still on welfare: The role of redistribution in social policy. *Social Work*, 46(4), 297–308.

AFL-CIO (2008). *Global focus on collective bargaining coverage: U.S. Congress meets the world labor movement*. Retrieved January 23, 2009, from http://www.cwa-union. org/news/cwa-news/u-s-congress-meets-the-world-labor-movement.html

Armingeon, K. (2004). OECD and national welfare state development. In K. Armingeon & M. Beyeler (Eds.), *The OECD and European welfare states* (pp. 226–241). Bedmin, Cornwall, UK: MPG Books.

Babe, R. E. (2000). *Canadian communication thought: Ten foundational writers.* Toronto, CA: University of Toronto Press.

Bacon, D. (1998, December 2,). A blow for cross-border organizing. *San Francisco Guardian*, p. 27. Retrieved January 23, 2009, from http://www.hartford-hwp.com/archives/40/040.html

Barker, Robert L. (Ed.). (2003). *The social work dictionary* (5th ed.). Washington, DC: NASW Press.

Bivens, L. J. (2008). Trade, jobs, and wages: Are the public's worries about globalization justified? (Issue Brief No. 244). *Economic Policy Institute*, Retrieved December 8, 2008 from http://www.epi.org/content.cfm/ib244

Brooks, D., & Fox, J. (2004). NAFTA: *Ten years of cross-border dialogue.* IRC America Program Special Report. Retrieved Januuary 29, 2009, from http://americas.irc-online.org/reports/2004/0403nafta.html

Bureau of Labor Statistics (2008). *Union members in 2007.* Washington, DC: U.S. Department of Labor. Retrieved December 15, 2008, from http://www.bls.gov/news.release/pdf/union2.pdf

Caputo, R. K. (2007). Social theory and its relation to social problems: An essay about theory and research with social justice in mind. *Journal of Sociology and Social Welfare, 34*(1), 43–61.

Council on Social Work Education. (2008). *2008 education policy and accreditations standards.* Retrieved August 21, 2008, from http://www.cswe.org/cswe/accreditation/

DeCarlo, S. (2006, April 20). Special report: What the boss makes. *Forbes Magazine.* Retrieved October 22, 2008, from http://www.forbes.com/2006/04/20/ceo-pay-options-cz_sw_0420ceopay_print.html

Dynarski, S. (2008). Building the stock of college educated labor. *Journal of Human Resources, XLIII*(3), 576–610.

Elvander, N. (2002). The labour market regimes in the Nordic countries: A comparative analysis. *Scandinavian Political Studies, 25*(2), 117–137.

Jenson, J. (2004). Changing the paradigm: Family responsibility or investing in children. *Canadian Journal of Sociology, 29*(2), 169–193.

Hahnel, R. (2005). *Economic justice and democracy: From competition to cooperation.* New York: Routledge.

Hemerijck, A. (2002). The self transformation of the European social model(s). In G. Esping-Andersen (Ed.), *Why we need a new European welfare state* (pp. 173–215). Oxford, UK: Oxford University Press.

Jaumotte, F., Lall, S., & Papageorgion, C. (2008). Rising income inequality: Technology or trade and financial globalization? (IMF Working Paper, wp/08/185). International Monetary Fund. Retrieved December 18, 2008 from http://www.imf.org/external/pubs/ft/wp/2008/wp08185.pdf

Kapstein, E. B. (2006). *Economic justice in an unfair world: Toward a level playing field.* Princeton, NJ: Princeton University Press.

King, T., & Bannon, E. (2006). The burden of borrowing. *A report on the rising state of student loan debt: State PIRBs.* Washington, DC: State PIRG Higher Education Project.

Korukonda, A. R., & Bathala, C. R. (2004). Ethics, equity, and social justice in the new economic order: Using financial information for keeping social score. *Journal of Business Ethics, 54*, 1–15.

Lopez, S. H. (2004). *Reorganizing the rust belt: An inside study of the American labor movement.* Berkeley: University of California.

Lundy, C., & van Wormer, K (2007). Social and economic justice, human rights and peace. *International Social Work, 50*(6), 727–739.

Midgley, J. (1995). *Social development.* Thousand Oaks, CA: Sage.

Mizrahi, T. (2004). Are movements for social and economic justice growing? Reports on protest and social action in the U.S. and Israel. *Journal of Community Practice, 12*(1/2), 155–160.

Mishel, L., Bernstein, J., & Allegretto, S. (2007). *The state of working America: 2006/2007.* Ithaca, NY: ILR Press.

National Association of Social Workers. (1999). *Code of ethics of the National Association of Social Workers.* Retrieved August 21, 2008, from http://www.socialworkers. org/pubs/Code/code.asp

O'Connor, D. E. (2002) *Demystifying the global economy.* Westport, CT: Greenwood.

Organization for Economic Cooperation and Development (2004). *OECD study shows tax wedges continue to fall.* Retrieved January 23, 2009, from http://www. oecd.org/document/51/0,3343,en_2649_201185_30486387_1_1_1_1,00.html

Organization for Economic Cooperation and Development (2005). *The OECD statistics portal.* Retrieved January 28, 2008, from http://www.oecd.org/statistics/

Ozawa, M. N., & Kim, R. Y. (2000). The increasing income inequality among children. *Journal of Poverty, 4*(3), 1–18.

Piven, F. F., & Cloward, R. (1998). Eras of power. *Monthly Review,* 49(8), 11–23.

Robbins, R. H. (2005). *Global problems and the culture of capitalism* (3rd ed.). New York: Pearson.

Rocha, C. (2007). The relationship of government social expenditures and market driven economic indicators to measures of well-being: An international comparison. *Social Development Issues, 29*(2), 1–14.

Rocha, C., & McCarter, A. (2003/04). Strengthening economic justice content in social work education. *Arete, 27*(2), 1–16.

Schmitt, J. A. (2008a). *The union wage advantage for low skilled workers.* Washington, DC: Center for Economic and Policy Research. Retrieved December 14, 2008, from http://www.cepr.net/index.pnp.publications/reports/the-union-wage-advantage-for-low-skilled-workers/

Schmitt, J. A. (2008b). *Unions and upward mobility for women workers.* Washington, DC: Center for Economic and Policy Research. Retrieved December 14, 2008, from http://www.cepr.net/index.pnp.publications/reports/union-and-upward-mobility-for-women-workers/

Thompson, N. (2002). Social movements, social justice and social work. *British Journal of Social Work, 32*, 711–722.

Traxler, F., Brandl, B., Glassner, V., & Ludvig, A. (2008). Can cross-border bargaining coordination work: Analytical reflections and evidence from the metal industry in Germany and Austria. *European Journal of Industrial Relations, 14*(2), 217–237.

United Nations (2007). *Report on the world social situation.* United Nations Department on Economic and Social Affairs. Retrieved December 16, 2008, from http://www.un.org/esa/socdev/rwss/index.html

U.S. Census Bureau (2006). *1968 to 2006 annual social and economic supplements.* Current Population Survey Series (p. 60–204). Retrieved on December 18, 2008 from http://www.census.gov/hhes/www/income/histinc/ineqtoc.html

Waldhorn, S. (2002). On the wrong track. *Social Policy, 32*(4), 3–5.

Watts, J. (2003). *Mexico-U.S. migration and labor unions: Obstacles to building cross-border solidarity.* Retrieved December 21, 2008, from http://www.ccis-ucsd.org/publications/wrkg79.pdf

Weller, C. E., Scott, R. E., & Hersh, A. S. (2001). *The unremarkable record of liberalized trade* (Economic Policy Institute Briefing Paper No. 113). Retrieved December 14, 2008, from http://www.epi.org/content.cfm/briefingpapers_sept01inequality

Social Workers, Unions, and Low Wage Workers: A Historical Perspective

MICHAEL REISCH

School of Social Work, University of Maryland, Baltimore, Maryland, USA

Using primary and secondary sources, this article explores the relationship between social workers' and low-wage workers' efforts to improve their economic conditions, especially through unions. It examines ways in which the profession's mission has been interpreted and suggests some implications for social workers' roles in contemporary economic justice struggles.

Work has a greater effect than any other technique of living in the direction of binding the individual more closely to reality.

– Sigmund Freud, *Civilization and Its Discontents* (1930)

Good work is not just the maintenance of connections . . . but the enactment of connections. It is living, and a way of living.

– Wendell Berry, *Work and the Life of the Spirit* (1998)

INTRODUCTION: THE RELATIONSHIP BETWEEN SOCIAL WORK AND LOW WAGE WORKERS

Efforts to organize and provide income support for low-wage workers, inside and outside unions, have been among the central activities of social workers in the U.S. since the 1890s. Yet, their dedication to these goals has been neither ideologically nor politically consistent. The diverse and occasionally contradictory roles social workers have played in assisting low-wage workers in their struggles for economic justice reflect several interrelated factors: the changing class composition of the profession; the relationship between social workers and communities of color and immigrants; the role of the social work profession in the broader political-economy; and the evolution of social workers' attitudes toward social work unions and professionalism (Fisher, 1994; Karger, 1988; Reisch & Andrews, 2001). Using primary and secondary sources, this article explores the interplay of these factors in four periods: the Progressive Era and its aftermath; the New Deal/Fair Deal/McCarthy period; the War on Poverty; and the Reagan and Post-Reagan years. These time frames provide a clear demarcation of the development of U.S. social policy and social work which reflect the evolution of the profession's approach to issues involving low wage workers and its attitudes toward unions. In the conclusion, the article discusses the implications of this history for future endeavors in this arena.

THE PROGRESSIVE ERA: IMMIGRATION, TRADE UNIONS, AND THE ORIGINS OF SOCIAL WORK

Between the end of the Civil War and the start of World War I, the United States underwent a period of economic expansion unprecedented in the nation's history. The nation's Gross National Product (GNP) increased about 250%, although its benefits were distributed unevenly (Axinn & Stern, 2008). In addition, rapid industrialization and urbanization expanded and intensified the poverty experienced by American workers and their families, and produced major increases in virtually every negative social indicator—from street crime to epidemic disease, from alcoholism to child abuse (Patterson, 2001). Between 1890 and 1912 "the wage earner's share of the net product in manufacturing had actually declined" and nearly 80% of the nation's male breadwinners earned below the annual income established for "minimum decency" by the Commission on Industrial Relations (Axinn & Stern, 2008, p. 130). The Commission concluded that one-half to two-thirds of working-class families lived in poverty and another third lived in "abject poverty" (p. 131). A well-publicized study of poverty by Robert Hunter (1904), a settlement house worker, drew similar conclusions.

Both public and private aid programs lacked adequate or coordinated responses to the problems of increased poverty among industrial workers and higher levels of unemployment, particularly during the twelve depressions which occurred in this "boom and bust" period. Conditions were particularly harsh for new immigrants from Europe, Asia, and Mexico, newly emancipated African Americans, and working and lower class women. Existing poor laws discriminated against all of these groups and were particularly harsh toward women and persons of color in terms of their eligibility requirements and level of benefits. Their punitive nature "disrupted family life and released poor women for work in the poorhouse or the bottom rungs of the labor market" (Abramovitz, 1985, p. 130).

Although they often expressed mainstream prejudices about gender, race, ethnicity, and religion, many Progressive Era social workers, particularly those in the settlement house movement, possessed greater trust in the working class than their movement allies. Some, like Florence Kelley and Ellen Gates Starr, regarded union organizing as a means to achieve socialism or an expanded social wage. Others, like Jane Addams, supported unions as part of her efforts to promote social democracy and diminish the level of class conflict in U.S. society. Based on diverse motives both religious and secular, settlement workers fought for labor legislation, provided ongoing support for union organizing efforts, especially among women, and through their own initiatives, created groups like the Women's Trade Union League (Carson, 1990; Chambers, 1967). In sum, participants in the settlement movement regarded the creation and strengthening of labor unions as critical to the improvement of the lives of low income workers and their families.

Leaders of the Charities Organization Societies (COS) and the child-saving movements that dominated organized social welfare in the late 19th and early 20th centuries, however, distrusted and feared low-wage workers, particularly those from immigrant backgrounds. Not unlike anti-immigration advocates today, they argued that the influx of millions of low-wage workers would have disastrous effects on the U.S. economy. They also believed that the introduction of diverse religions and cultures would lead to the decline of American civilization (Reisch, 2008). These concerns led them to make common cause with conservative, anti-union business interests, whose support they cultivated to advance the professionalization of social work (Richmond, 1906).

The arguments of these social welfare leaders against the creation of state-funded policies that would benefit low-wage workers, such as those developed in Great Britain, France, and Germany, therefore, reflected a combination of class prejudice, anti-immigrant sentiment, fear of the social dangers produced by masses of beggars and tramps, and consternation that an organized working class, inspired by socialist, social democratic, or anarchist ideas, would fundamentally alter the nation's political status quo, particularly in major cities. Mainstream social welfare leaders also resisted efforts to rethink the causes of poverty—for example, to replace individualistic or moralistic explanations with environmental ones—and to substitute government-sponsored programs for either older, more aristocratic systems of charity or the emerging "scientific" model of charities organization developed by the COS. Even in the aftermath of the severe depression of 1893, they proposed solutions to unemployment and poverty which would require mandatory work programs and cooperation between municipal officials and voluntary organizations, such as those developed in Boston (Reisch & Andrews, 2001).

In addition to proposing tighter restrictions on immigration, their strategy included the establishment of city and county employment bureaus with well-organized systems of investigation; adequate graded work tests; and the creation of trade schools and prison-like institutions (such as farm colonies and workshops) which would house able-bodied individuals who refused to work. It emphasized worker discipline, compulsion, the denial of workers' demands for a "living wage," suppression of trade unions, state control of the conditions of work, and the maintenance of long-standing distinctions between the "worthy" and "unworthy" poor (Katz, 1996). An 1894 statement by John Graham Brooks exemplified these ideas: "It seems clear that for such work [government-funded jobs in time of depression] the "living wage" cannot be paid but something below even the market wage for kindred tasks . . . It goes without saying that if the "right to work" be granted, the conditions of that right cannot be set by those who demand the work" (Brooks, p. 21). This focus on the social control of low-wage workers was also reflected in the methods of scientific charity introduced by the COS (Margolin, 1997).

A few COS leaders like Mary Richmond, however, regarded the social divisions in U.S. society as impediments both to social reform and the expansion of scientific charity. Her ideas regarding low-wage workers and unions reflected a curious blend of compassion, social control, and Progressivism. For example, in the same December 1906 presentation in which she proposed denying aid and shelter to "tramps" and the strict enforcement of municipal anti-begging ordinances, she also called for the abolition of child labor and the provision of relief as a supplement to wages or during periods of temporary unemployment. Yet, in contrast to Addams and other settlement house workers, Richmond consistently sought individual and personal solutions to the prevailing "social question" rather than structural ones. In remarks that forecast the future direction of the social work profession, she stated "those who write and lecture with such enthusiasm about socialism, individualism and anarchism would all be benefited by a good stiff dose of case work" (Richmond, 1906, pp. 4–5).

Although many settlement house workers were also wary of the economic and political consequences of trade unionism, they believed in its potential to promote peaceful industrial progress and the democratization of U.S. society. Unlike socialists like Kelley, Starr, or Lillian Wald (the founder and director of the Henry Street Settlement in New York), Addams viewed the mission of unions in terms of Christian altruism and the fulfillment of the fraternal spirit, rather than as a means to achieve social justice. Although she frequently acknowledged the socioeconomic conditions that motivated workers to unionize, Addams held unions equally accountable for the emergence of seemingly irreconcilable class conflict. She hoped that as the labor movement "matured" it would evolve away from class warfare and toward greater cooperation with capitalists to democratize industrial affairs (Knight,

2005). She argued that the settlement movement had an obligation to influence unions in a direction similar to that followed by those in Great Britain—that is, away from radical action and toward an evolutionary approach to resolving the problems of industrialization (Addams, 1895).[1] While the craft unions of the American Federation of Labor (AFL) followed this course, more militant unions, such as those organized by the Industrial Workers of the World (IWW), resisted. Ironically, both union leaders and their supporters in the settlement movement were persecuted in the "Red Scare" that followed World War I.

THE 1920s AND THE NEW DEAL: SOCIAL RESEARCH, SOCIAL POLICY, AND THE WELFARE STATE

Despite their efforts to cultivate the support of political and economic elites such as President Woodrow Wilson and industrialist Henry Ford, social workers were not immune from the effects of the repressive climate of the post-World War I period. Hundreds of labor organizers and left-wing political activists, such as Emma Goldman—a long-time friend and ally of Lillian Wald—were arrested and deported. Radical and pacifist social workers, such as Addams, Kelley, and Wald, were investigated by state legislators and the courts, and viciously attacked by newspapers, politicians, and right-wing groups, often with government assistance. Even moderate reformers like Julia Lathrop, Director of the Children's Bureau, and their causes, such as the Sheppard-Towner Maternal and Infant Care Program, were labeled subversive.

As a result, between 1918 and the early 1930s, the social work profession largely retreated from its modest efforts on behalf of low-wage workers and trade unions (Reisch & Andrews, 2001). Most settlement houses abandoned their policy advocacy and community organizing in favor of the creation of recreational and social service programs, and casework became the dominant form of social work practice. Even here, the earlier emphasis on reaching individuals by way of their social environment (Richmond, 1917) was replaced by an increased focus on individual behavior and theories of personality. Conditions such as alcoholism, truancy, and family conflict were now viewed through this lens rather than as a consequence of structural forces (Richmond, 1920; Taft, 1922).

This trend was reflected most pointedly in the near total absence of presentations on the plight of working Americans at the National Conference of Social Work in the early 1920s, despite the sharp rise in joblessness during these years. Throughout much of the decade, there was also scant mention of the issues of poverty and unemployment in the Conference *Proceedings*. As Frank Bruno (1957) recounted, "It was as if the public [and the social work profession] really believed that the rapidly increasing national income was filtering down to the lower income groups and that those who had the desire to work, could find means of establishing or improving their standard of living" (p. 298).

The most important exceptions to this retreat were the studies produced by social work researchers, such as Mary van Kleeck and Helen Hall, to document the effects of industrial conditions and unemployment (Andrews, 1997). Their work built upon earlier investigative activities of the Consumers' League established by Josephine Shaw Lowell, the National Child Labor Committee, Paul Kellogg's *Survey* magazine, and the American Association for Labor Legislation, which had advocated for unemployment insurance and public works projects for decades (Chambers, 1971). As Director of Industrial Studies at the Russell Sage Foundation, van Kleeck had initiated such research prior to World War I with a particular emphasis on factory conditions affecting women and girls and studies of specific industries such as coal mining, longshore work, and steel (Selekman & van Kleeck, 1924). Although van Kleeck described this research as fact-finding and analysis rather than advocacy, the studies she and others directed had several positive effects in the policy arena. These included the elimination of the 12-hour day in the steel industry, the reduction of industrial accidents, and greater public attention to the problem of unemployment (Klein, 1923; van Kleeck, 1932). In addition, by the mid-1920s, social workers like Kelley and Arthur Kellogg helped organize the National Unemployment League which focused on the social, familial, and economic problems created by unemployment (Morrissey, 1996).

In the late 1920s, social workers became increasingly concerned about joblessness as economic conditions worsened in certain industrial sectors such as mining. In response, the National Federation of Settlements (NFS) commissioned a 1928 study of unemployment and appointed Helen Hall to direct the project. (Van Kleeck also served on the project's executive committee.) The study, based on the personal narratives of over 300 families suffering from the effects of job loss, conclusively "demonstrated that unemployment was a structural problem of the economic system, requiring built-in protection for workers even in good times" (Morrissey, 1996, p. 5). Unlike previous research, however, which reached largely an academic or professional audience, the NFS deliberately tried to influence public opinion in the direction of policy change. As a result of the study, the government began to gather data on unemployment through the Federal Bureau of Labor Statistics for the first time.

The publications produced by the study (Calkins, 1930, 1931) also revealed for the first time the emotional, physical, and psychological impact of joblessness. The timing of these publications could not have been better, as the Depression deepened and unemployment soon reached crisis proportions. In van Kleeck's view (1932) the publication of this research exemplified the most suitable role social workers could play regarding the issue of unemployment, that is "giv[ing] testimony . . . on the relation of wages to the cost of living and [their impact on] actual standards of living" (p. 12). In so doing, social workers could:

> speak for those who are the least strong economically in the community . . . and speak for the community as a whole and not for any one group, except where the interest of one group must be protected against another group for the sake of the common welfare, . . . for instance, when children are exploited in industry or when selfish competitive interests depress conditions below the level of a desirable standard of living. . . . (p. 16)

Well ahead of her time, van Kleeck proposed institutionalizing this role through the formation of permanent university-community partnerships in which workers and community members would be involved in all aspects of the research. She also proposed greater recognition within the profession and its educational programs of the potential contributions of social research and the importance of adequate government recordkeeping. Many of her ideas were implemented during the New Deal and Fair Deal.

Even before the NFS studies were published, "the first realistic statement of what the lack of work was doing to the country was made in [a] 1931 [paper at the National Conference of Social Work] by Jacob Billikopf, of the Philadelphia Federation of Jewish Charities" (Bruno, 1957, p. 301). Citing the well-known economist and future U.S. Senator Paul Douglas, he called for a national social insurance program to replace the "dole of public or private charity" (p. 301). At the same conference, other speakers, including Harry Lurie of the Bureau of Jewish Social Research, argued that the problem of unemployment was a public obligation which could only be solved through government-funded intervention, financed by taxation. These ideas became the basis for the labor, welfare, and industrial policies of the New Deal, designed and implemented by influential social workers such as Harry Hopkins (Director of the Federal Emergency Relief Administration and the Works Progress Administration) and Frances Perkins (a former settlement house worker and Roosevelt's Secretary of Labor). Their role was both abetted and complicated, however, by the changing dynamics of the social work field during this tumultuous decade.

By the time of Franklin Roosevelt's inauguration in March, 1933, the demographic composition of the social work profession had significantly changed from what it was at the height of the Progressive era (Walkowitz, 1999). Social workers of the "second generation" were no longer predominantly from elite backgrounds. They were often the children of the populations which the COS and settlement houses served (Carson, 1990).

This demographic shift was reflected in social workers' attitudes about immigrants, low-wage workers, and unions, including the unionization of social workers themselves. For example, social workers' support for the newly emerging Congress of Industrial Organizations (CIO) was accompanied by the creation of social work unions in public and private agencies and by a radically different view of professionalism. These views were reflected in the growth of the Rank and File Movement, which by the mid-1930s had more members than the mainstream American Association of Social Workers (Wenocur & Reisch, 1989). Many social workers now openly acknowledged the similarity between their interests and those of their clients, particularly those who belonged to unions. For nearly two decades, this recognition fostered alliances on issues like unemployment, workers' rights, corporate abuses, and the need for the United States to develop an industrial policy and expand its nascent welfare state.

At the 1934 National Conference of Social Work, Mary van Kleeck expressed this widely held sentiment clearly:

> [Social workers and] labor groups . . . have [both] sought to maintain the standard of living of the workers; to ask that the return in the pay envelope bears some proportion to the productivity of labor; to ask that there be leisure, growing also out of the increased productivity of labor. (1935, p. 295)

Even mainstream organizations, such as the American Association of Social Workers (AASW), which often criticized the more radical members of the profession, took a leadership role in advocating for federally-funded relief programs for the unemployed. Spokespersons for the settlement movement, however, like Hall and Kellogg, wanted the Roosevelt Administration to go beyond relief measures and address issues like social insurance, long-term income security, and the rights of labor to organize and bargain collectively (Chambers, 1971; Morrissey, 1996). At the same time, more radical social workers, particularly those in the Rank and File Movement, criticized the tepid reforms of the New Deal and proposed more sweeping structural changes which addressed the fundamental problems of a market-oriented economy (Reisch & Andrews, 2001). Social workers also cooperated with organized labor during the New Deal in three other ways: involving union representatives on public and non-profit boards; organizing social work unions in the public and private sectors; and endorsing the labor movement's agenda in the formal statements of professional social work organizations (Karger, 1988). At the neighborhood level, social workers, often affiliated with left-wing political parties, engaged in community organizing to resist evictions and advocated for more rapid and more equitable distribution of public relief funds and public sector employment (Reisch & Andrews, 2001). Their efforts, however, were dwarfed by the activities of organizers such as Saul Alinsky in Chicago, CIO-sponsored unions in Pittsburgh and Detroit, and Communist Party members in New York.

The position of organized social welfare in the legislative arena and in relation to the burgeoning labor movement was strengthened by the growing emphasis among social workers of the importance of collective bargaining on their own behalf. By the mid-1930s, both the American Association of Social Workers (AASW) and its more radical counterpart, the Rank and File Movement, had endorsed the use of collective bargaining. The AASW even acknowledged the right of social workers to strike when the conditions were "exceptional" and clients' interests were protected (Social Service Employees Division, 1938). Social work leaders such as van Kleeck, Bertha Capen Reynolds, Paul Kellogg (editor of *The Survey*), Wayne McMillen, Stanley Isaacs, and Philip Klein all endorsed this principle.

During World War II, many social workers saw a clear connection between their professional responsibilities and the goals of organized labor (King, 1944; Otto, 1945). They collaborated on the creation of social services in defense industries, such as child care (Stotzfus, 2003), and the development of worker education programs in unions. Inspired by the global battle against fascism and for freedom and democracy, the aim of programs such as those sponsored by the International Ladies Garment Workers Union (ILGWU) was to "analyze the clashes of ideas involved in [the current] revolutionary struggle and . . . critically evaluate economic and social values from a national and international point of view . . . [and] make available to the masses information that will clarify for them the possible consequences of a victory of our enemies" (Cohn, 1943, p. 6). Educational content included a reinterpretation of American civilization, analysis of recent social legislation, and material on leadership development and policy advocacy. Particularly striking for its day was the integration of materials on the role of women and African Americans, and an international perspective which emphasized potential post-war developments in Asia and Latin America.

During these years, both reform-minded social workers and their union allies expressed a persistent fear that a major depression would follow the cessation of hostilities, as it did after the previous world war. To prevent this, they urged the government to pass Roosevelt's Second Bill of Rights, drafted in 1944, which included the right to work, fair and adequate wages, provision of life's basic necessities, including education and health care, and protection of civil rights and civil liberties (Gross, 1988, 1989; Grosswald, 1998). They also opposed the militarization of the U.S. economy occurring under the guise of the Cold War and challenged openly anti-labor legislation such as the Taft-Hartley Act (Marcus, 1948). In May 15, 1947, leaders of a wide range of social service organizations, churches, professional schools, and left-leaning social work unions wrote a telegram to President Truman and other officials which stated:

We wish to register . . . our objections to the Taft and Hartley bills. To weaken in any way the full and free right of labor to organize and bargain collectively is to undermine the structure of American democracy. The[se] bills . . . will wipe out the gains of labor made under the Roosevelt Administration . . . [which] were hailed not only by labor but by all decent Americans as carrying forward the American way of life.

As social workers and religious leaders, we know from experience the direct relationship between the gains and losses of labor and the common welfare. We are deeply concerned with the implications of a depression now threatening our nation. In our opinion, that depression will be hastened and deepened by the proposed legislation which will limit labor's ability to protect the economic interests of working people. (United Office and Professional Workers of America, 1947)

During the late 1940s and early 1950s, social workers regarded these interests as closely linked to the protection of labor's right to organize and strike, the reorientation of the nation's priorities away from militarism and war, and the "promotion of an adequate welfare program [which would] . . . advance standards of service" (Social Service Employees' Union [SSEU], 1948, p. 3). Social work unions like SSEU and the United Office and Professional Workers of America (UOPWA) fought for decent salaries for social workers and other low paid white collar workers, better working conditions, coverage of all workers by the Social Security Act, improved services to the community, and the protection of members' civil liberties (Livingston, 1951). Without using the term, they also sought the empowerment of workers and community members through ". . . broaden[ing] the base of control of the agencies; . . . encourag[ing] them to work jointly with labor and other groups in obtaining health and welfare legislation; [and] . . . stop[ping] waste and duplication of services through adequate planning and coordination on local and national levels" (SSEU, 1948, p. 14). Social workers actively debated issues such as "should social workers organize?" (King, 1946) and the place of union affiliation in the voluntary non-profit social service sector (Conference on Union Affiliation of Employees of Voluntary Health & Welfare Agencies, 1947a, 1947b).

Some non-profit social service organizations which were active during this period, like the Young Women's Christian Association (YWCA), had a long history of cooperating with unions and supporting the rights of working people. As far back as its 1910 convention, the YWCA adopted a recommendation calling for a "minimum living wage" for working women and the regulation of working hours. In 1919, at its First National Industrial Conference, it called for the eight-hour day, the prohibition of night work for women, gender equality in employment and wages, the prohibition of child labor, and the right of workers to organize and bargain collectively (Bishop, 1946, p. 58). The following year, in addition to affirming these recommendations, the

YWCA convention adopted a platform which included the "abatement and prevention of poverty . . . protection of the worker from dangerous machinery, occupational disease and mortality, . . . the protection of workers from the hardships of enforced unemployment, [and] suitable provision for the old age of the workers and those incapacitated by injury" (Bishop, 1946, p. 59). In addition to ongoing legislative advocacy, the YWCA cooperated with labor unions through the creation of various service, recreation, and educational programs; collaborative fundraising; loaning or renting facilities; and joint sponsorship of special projects. It often linked the expansion of labor rights with recognition of the rights of women and persons of color.

Within a few years, however, the repressive climate of McCarthyism decimated left-leaning unions, including social work unions in the public and private sectors, and resulted in mainstream social service organizations blacklisting and marginalizing social workers and clients who supported social justice causes. In some states, suspected communists or "Reds" who were unemployed were even declared ineligible for public relief payments (Lush, 1950). As a result, activism among social workers declined and was replaced by an inward-looking drive for enhanced professional status (Wenocur & Reisch, 1989).

As organized labor purged its left-leaning members and radical unions, the overall power of unions declined. At the same time, the demographic composition of low-wage workers began to change and social workers refocused their attention away from the alleviation of structural inequalities toward the enhancement of individual or family life. The political environment shifted so rapidly that by 1951 the profession had to be persuaded that its middle class interests were compatible with those of organized labor (Wolfson, 1951). By the mid-1950s, the "retreat" of social work from an emphasis on services to low-income people became an issue of pressing concern to the minority of advocates and activists within the profession (Specht & Courtenay, 1994).

THE WAR ON POVERTY: WELFARE, WORK, AND THE RETREAT FROM UNIVERSALISM

The "rediscovery" of poverty by the social work profession during the 1960s was not accompanied by significant increases in unionizing efforts among social workers or a diminution of the field's professionalizing impulse. In fact, for the past several decades, social workers, particularly in the public sector and in health care institutions, have tried—largely without success—to reconcile their professional aspirations with union membership, and their ethical imperative to pursue social justice goals with their desire to maintain scientific detachment and professional objectivity (Alexander, 1980; Alexander, Lichtenberg, & Brunn, 1980; Reeser & Epstein, 1990). As a result, residents of low-income communities, many of whom belong to unions, have often criticized social workers for their patronizing attitudes toward clients and constituents.

The failure to reestablish ongoing alliances with low-wage workers and unions has significantly weakened social workers' ability to respond to the neo-liberal policy agenda which emerged during the past quarter century to rationalize the structural transformations accompanying economic globalization. Class, racial, and cultural gaps between social workers and low-wage workers have compounded the difficulties of coalition-building directed at economic justice issues. Although the field of community organizing within social work expanded somewhat during the 1960s and early 1970s, this expansion was short-lived (Reisch & Wenocur, 1986). One notable exception has been the participation of social workers in the organizing efforts of Local 1199 of the Hospital and Health Care Employees Union, now known as 1199SEIU.

Founded in June, 1932, by a small group of clerks and pharmacists in New York, 1199 joined the AFL-CIO in 1936 and the CIO in 1937. From the outset, it demonstrated a strong commitment to civil rights; by winning a 1936 fight to allow African Americans to work as pharmacists in Harlem drug stores and providing financial help to the Montgomery bus boycott in 1954, it earned the label "my favorite union" from Martin Luther King, Jr. In 1964, hospital social workers in some of New York's voluntary hospitals joined the union and, in 1969, 1199 expanded its organizing efforts on a national scale (Local 1199, 1978). Since the 1970s, its "Bread and Roses" project has successfully integrated cultural activities with popular education and advocacy on behalf of low wage workers and their families. Today, the union has grown to include health care workers in New York, New Jersey, Maryland, Massachusetts, and Washington, DC. There are also other branches of 1199 in Connecticut and Philadelphia.

Although social workers paid increased attention to issues of poverty and welfare during the 1960s, they analyzed these issues in different ways from how they had been viewed in the past. Instead of focusing on improving wages and working conditions, expanding unionization, and reducing structurally-based class inequalities, the profession emphasized the development of programs in the areas of job training, education, and social services designed to overcome the "culture of poverty" that appeared to entrap many of its clients (Cohen, 1964; Mandell, 1966). Particularly after the passage of Medicare in 1965, organized social welfare drifted away from the universal focus which had dominated its policy agenda since the New Deal, despite warnings from influential spokespersons of the risks involved (Garfinkel, 1978; Lekachman, 1981).

This drift occurred in two ways. First, growing concerns about poverty soon blended in the public's mind with concerns about the plight of welfare recipients (Dinerman, 1977; Donovan, Jaffe, & Pirie, 1987). This shifted attention away from the needs of low wage workers who were caught in the "notch" just above the official poverty line (the so-called "working poor") and exacerbated schisms between social workers and white working class communities, who began to rediscover their ethnicity in the late 1960s and early 1970s. It also encouraged the tendency of political elites and the media to equate social work with welfare (i.e., AFDC) and to conflate the needs and demographic composition of the welfare poor and the working poor. This unintentionally reinforced the racial backlash against civil rights, anti-poverty legislation, and activism on behalf of welfare rights that erupted in the late 1960s and early 1970s and ultimately undermined support for both labor and social welfare policies (Edsall & Edsall, 1991). The explicitly anti-union and anti-welfare policies of the Reagan Administration, with their not-so-subtle racial overtones, further weakened and discredited the role of unions as instruments of social change and social justice.

Secondly, problems like poverty and unemployment were increasingly viewed by social workers through much narrower conceptual lenses. At first, this change corrected long-standing omissions of the unique needs of low income African Americans and women (Ozawa, 1976; Rosenman, 1976, 1979). Later, however, the focus became even specialized, emphasizing more specific groups such as African American youth (Moss, 1982), African American men (Gary & Leashore, 1982), single parents (Jones & Wattenberg, 1991), new immigrants (Day, 1989), and older women (Ozawa, 1995). Another important development during this period was renewed attention to the relationship between economic issues like unemployment and the expansion of social work practice in such areas as mental health, substance abuse treatment, family services, and child welfare (Biegel, Cunningham, Yamatani, & Martz, 1989; Beckett, 1988; Donovan, Jaffe, & Pirie, 1987; Hagen & Davis, 1992; Sherraden, 1985).

The linkage between economic issues and health or mental health concerns was also reflected in the growth of employee assistance programs (EAPs) in both public and private sector organizations. Most of these EAPs were established under corporate rather than union auspices, however, and few of them reflected a structural analysis of the needs of low-wage and unemployed workers or union members. In fact, they underscored the growing distinctions between the professional status goals of social workers and the needs and aspirations of workers. These trends have persisted during the past three decades.

THE REAGAN AND POST-REAGAN ERAS

Although in recent years social workers have substantially retreated from their previous advocacy on behalf of working class individuals and families and the proportion of social workers involved in community organizing has significantly decreased (Reisch, 2006), concerns about unemployment and low-wage employment have appeared periodically in the social work literature (Cloward, 1993; Danziger, 1997; Piven & Cloward, 1993; Sherraden, 1985; Wagner, 1990). A few social workers have also spoken out in other venues such as religious social justice-oriented publications (Amidei, 1987) and statements by advocacy coalitions like the Women's Economic Agenda Project (1988). The Radical Alliance of Social Service Workers (1981) consistently addressed the relationship between social work and organized labor in its limited circulation newsletter, although its concerns represented a minority perspective among social workers.

In addition, the official pronouncements of the profession continued to reflect strong support for low income wage earners and their families. For example, in a 2003 policy statement, the National Association of Social Workers (NASW) "reaffirm[ed] its support for the right of workers to organize, to engage in collective bargaining to improve their working conditions and to strike to draw attention to their grievances." It also "oppose[d] any abrogation of these rights by administrative regulation, legislation, or judicial action, . . . as well as "the use of medical screenings to deny workers access to health benefits, the imposition of mandatory drug testing in the workplace, and the use of electronic or computer surveillance of employees to monitor job performance" (NASW, 2003, p. 44). The organization's publication, *Social Work Speaks*, makes no mention, however, of social workers as workers or potential union members and the legislative priorities of NASW have rarely focused on legislation to strengthen the role of unions.

At the level of national policy, in language strikingly similar to that used during the post-World War II period (Marcus, 1948), NASW's 2000 Delegate Assembly stated unequivocally, "private profit must be reexamined as the sole criterion for motivating economic activity. The U.S. government must ensure that basic necessities are available to all people at a level that promotes human dignity, whether or not the production and distribution of those necessities are profitable" (2003, p. 97). NASW also endorsed the creation of "a comprehensive international industrial policy" and the goal of a more equitable redistribution of available resources and wealth. Yet, these broad statements were not accompanied by specific policy proposals as they had been in the past.

In the 1990s and early 2000s, however, NASW made some specific policy recommendations to improve the economic conditions of low wage workers, whose plight had seriously deteriorated during the past quarter century as a consequence of globalization, deindustrialization, the decline of labor unions, and the retrenchment of public social welfare with deleterious effects on their ability to provide decent housing for their families, obtain access to health care, and cover the cost of basic expenses (Bernstein, 2007; National Association of Social Workers, 1994, 2000, 2003; Piketty & Saez, 2003; Sherman, 2007; Urban Institute, 2008). These recommendations included the indexing of the minimum wage to the cost of living, the provision of a living wage to workers by for-profit and nonprofit organizations, the expansion of the Earned Income Tax Credit (EITC), and a revision of the formula used to calculate the unemployment rate. Other, less well-defined policy goals included "a more comprehensive, progressive, fair, and equitable tax system," the end of all forms of wage and workplace discrimination, the reduction of wage gaps between workers, managers and owners, the provision of family friendly benefits, and protection of workers and communities "from the impact of corporate downsizing, plant closures, outsourcing, conversion of full-time employees to part-time status, and excessive use of overtime through tougher legislation" (NASW, 2003, pp. 98–99).

These largely rhetorical policy statements contrasted sharply with more concrete institutional actions during the past decade. In the mid-1990s, despite its long-time advocacy on behalf of low wage workers, NASW did not use its much-touted leverage with the Clinton Administration to oppose or alter its punitive welfare reform legislation. During this period there was also a consistent and precipitous decline in attention to labor and working class issues in social work journals and the curricula of schools of social work (Council on Social Work Education, 2007). These developments weakened the ability of organized social welfare to advocate for policy changes on behalf of unions and low-wage workers in the wake of economic globalization and the recent worldwide economic crisis. The absence of a well-coordinated response from social workers to the increased economic risk confronting low wage workers, even prior to the current crisis, contradicted the profession's ethical imperative to pursue social justice.

CONCLUSION

Social workers' relationship to issues affecting low-wage workers and unions has evolved through several distinct phases during the past century. During the Progressive Era, a combination of religious and secular values and a certain "noblesse oblige" inspired sympathetic social workers, largely within the settlement house movement, to regard solutions to the needs of low wage workers and their families as important steps toward either structural change or societal reconciliation. Reform-minded and radical social workers viewed the development of unions as a necessary means to achieve these broader social goals. Their concerns, however, were tempered by persistent ambivalence toward union members, particularly immigrants, who comprised a large majority of the low-wage workforce, often based on religious and ethnic prejudice. During the post-World War I era, they were also influenced in opposing directions by the political-economic pressures of professionalization and the changing demographics of the social work field.

From the New Deal until the early 1950s, social workers and organized labor forged an alliance based on common interests, organizational bonds, strategic necessity, and shared class consciousness. Many social workers regarded themselves as workers with problems and needs comparable to those of their clients and coalition partners. This led to support not only for expanded government intervention in the social welfare field in the form of universal social policies, but also for state-sponsored protections for workers and organized labor. The repressive climate of the post-World War II McCarthy period largely destroyed this alliance and shifted the focus of organized social welfare away from unionism and policy advocacy and toward professional status enhancement.

Consequently, since the 1950s, as the professional aspirations of social workers increased and became entrenched, the objective and subjective gaps between them and low income workers and their families expanded. Social workers no longer consider themselves part of the working class, and while they may occasionally still be regarded as a "semi-profession," they have largely rejected unionization as a means of enhancing their occupational status or improving their working conditions. To a considerable extent, they have also turned away from prior support of the labor movement as a means to achieve more equitable social policies. These trends have been most clearly reflected in the decline of social work unions, the paucity of discussion in the social work literature about issues of class, and the distinctions frequently made by scholars and practitioners between the welfare poor and the working poor. To paraphrase an earlier observation by Cloward and Epstein (1965), it has produced a disengagement from the (working) poor, often bemoaned but seldom acted upon by the field. As a result, organized social welfare now lacks the alliances it once had to play a leadership role in the current economic crisis around such "natural" social work issues as unemployment and underemployment, housing foreclosures, the environment, occupational safety and health, and the lack of health care coverage which many low income working families experience.

Throughout these different phases, several key themes emerge. First, the active involvement of social workers in policy advocacy around issues affecting low-wage workers, such as unemployment and unemployment benefits, a living wage, and safe working conditions appears to correlate closely with the congruence or lack of congruence between their perceived class interests and those of other workers (Glickman, 1997). In the past, social workers have forged effective coalitions with labor unions and organizations of the unemployed which produced important public policy changes. In recent decades, the ideological and political bases for these alliances have diminished considerably despite the profession's rhetorical adherence to social justice.

Second, advocacy among social workers on behalf of the needs of low-wage workers and unions has been closely tied to support for universal

social policies and services. Both unions and organized social welfare recognized that for political reasons the needs of their clients and constituents
could best be addressed through the institutionalization of such policies into
the U.S. social welfare system. This mutual awareness was strongest
between the 1930s and 1960s, producing such landmark legislation as the
Social Security Act, the Fair Labor Standards Act, and Medicare.

For the past forty years, however, social workers have focused their
policy advocacy increasingly on selective policies, such as Medicaid, the
McKinney Act, and Affirmative Action, which have been largely targeted
toward welfare recipients and other disadvantaged populations. This trend
has both reflected and been exacerbated by the recent emphasis within the
profession, particularly in schools of social work, on issues of identity and
the embrace of post-modern perspectives. While the inclusion of previously
ignored or marginalized groups within social work discourse has corrected
long-standing problems of omission or commission, it has also diminished
public support for expanding the nation's social welfare system and heightened racial and class divisions among potential coalition partners. It remains
to be seen whether such partnerships can be reestablished under a more
sympathetic Presidential Administration.

Third, the response of social workers to the needs of low-wage workers
and their unions has been linked to their attitudes about immigrants and
immigration. From the Progressive Era until the early 1930s, sympathy for
the plight of immigrants was often tempered by cultural prejudice and
benign condescension. For the most part, social workers acted *on behalf of*
rather than *in alliance with* low-wage immigrant workers. This relationship
changed considerably during the New Deal as a result of several factors: the
new demographics of the social work field, which now consisted of many
children of immigrants; the influence of socialist ideas among social workers
(which fostered the notion of class solidarity across ethnic and religious
lines); the decrease in immigration rates and the gradual assimilation of the
existing immigrant population; and the depth of the nation's socio-economic
crisis. After World War II, the linkage between immigration and low-wage
employment disappeared to a considerable extent. For several decades, the
needs of immigrants were defined in terms of their assimilation into the
American cultural mainstream.

When issues regarding immigration re-emerged in the public arena
during the 1980s, the immigrant population was vastly different (comprised
largely of Latin Americans and Asians). Their problems were now closely
associated with issues affecting individuals and communities of color rather
than with those of low-wage workers in general (Reisch, 2008). At present,
the approach of many social workers to immigrants is similar to that of their
Progressive Era ancestors, although it lacks both their condescending tone
and their emphasis on structural analysis and broad social goals. Social
workers today are largely at a loss as to how best to meet the needs of

immigrant workers. They lack the knowledge, skills, organizational forms and, above all, the inter-organizational relationships to be effective allies.

The implications of this assessment of social work's past is that the social workers of the 21st century will need to address several issues *concurrently* to play an effective part in future social justice struggles. These include recognizing the role of unions in protecting the rights and well-being of low wage workers in the United States and other nations, defending the place of universal social policies in the U.S. social welfare system, creating and sustaining multicultural inter-organizational alliances, reexamining the structure and goals of social service organizations, reassessing the role of social work research, and rethinking the content of social work education. Addressing these issues is particularly critical during the present economic crisis as the effects of globalization and the three-decade long retrenchment of progressive government policies have exacerbated long-standing socio-economic inequalities (Bernstein, 2007; Macarov, 2003; Sherman, 2007; Smith, McHugh, Stettner, & Segal, 2003).

Finally, in the future social workers must articulate a more comprehensive vision of social welfare which avoids the pitfalls of appearing to promote the needs of some elements of the population at the expense of others. Analyses of the impact of Hurricane Katrina on low-income women and people of color on the Gulf Coast conducted by the Institute for Women's Policy Research provide a good example of how this might be done (Gault, Hartmann, Jones-DeWeever, Werschkul, & Williams, 2005). Social workers will also need to grapple with the complex policy implications of an increasingly multicultural society around issues like Affirmative Action and the socio-economic effects of immigration (Schmidt, 2008). In addition, the profession must adapt its perspectives and its advocacy to the realities of the new global economy (Ghosh, 2008). Lastly, social workers will need to redefine the meaning of professionalism in a manner which bridges the current gap between the profession's rhetoric and reality. While the reemergence of social work unions appears to be an unlikely outcome of this process, a reexamination of social workers' relationship with unions and low wage workers—in the United States and abroad—is essential if the profession is to reestablish itself as a viable force for social justice and social change in the decades ahead.

NOTE

1. Ironically, the approach which Addams proposed complemented efforts by industrialists like Henry Ford to preempt radical trade union or ethnically-based organizing through the establishment of corporate-sponsored educational and social services. Through the company's sociological department, Ford's brand of welfare capitalism focused on the assimilation of the diverse immigrant communities which comprised his workforce into "American" values and habits. It enforced these goals by restricting its well-publicized $5/day wage to those workers who met certain standards of behavior (Schwarz, 1971).

REFERENCES

Abramovitz, M. (1985, March). The family ethic: The female pauper and public aid, pre-1900. *Social Service Review*, 37(1), 121–135.

Addams, J. (1895). The settlement as a factor in the labor movement. In J. Addams (Ed.), *Hull House maps and papers* (pp. 183–204). New York: T.Y. Crowell.

Alexander, L. B. (1980). Professionalization and unionization: Compatible after all? *Social Work*, 26(6), 476–482.

Alexander, L. B., Lichtenberg, P., & Brunn, D. (1980). Social workers in unions: A survey. *Social Work*, 25(3), 216–223.

Amidei, N. (1987, June). American Sullivan principles. *Seeds*, 13–15.

Andrews, J. L. (1997). Helen Hall and the settlement house movement's response to unemployment: Reaching out to the community. *Journal of Community Practice*, 4(2), 65–75.

Axinn, J., & Stern, M. J. (2008). *Social welfare: A history of the American response to need* (8th ed.). Boston, MA: Allyn & Bacon.

Beckett, J. O. (1988). Plant closings: How older workers are affected. *Social Work*, 33(1), 29–33.

Beckett, J. O. (1976). Working wives: A racial comparison. *Social Work*, 21(6), 463–471.

Bernstein, J. (2007, December 13). Updated CBO data reveal unprecedented increase in inequality (Issue Brief No. 239). Washington, DC: Economic Policy Institute. Retrieved July 20, 2008, from http://www.epi.org/publications/entry/ib239

Biegel, D. E., Cunningham, J., Yamatani, H., & Martz, P. (1989). Self-reliance and blue collar unemployment in a steel town. *Social Work*, 34(3), 389–406.

Bishop. D. H. (1946). *What about the YWCA and labor?* New York: YWCA.

Brooks, J. G. (1894). The future problem of charity and the unemployed. *Annals of the American Academy of Political and Social Science*, 5, 1–27.

Bruno, F. J. (1957). *Trends in social work, 1874–1956: A history based on the proceedings of the National Conference of Social Work*. New York: Columbia University Press.

Calkins, C. (1931). *Case studies of unemployment*. Philadelphia: University of Pennsylvania.

Calkins, C. (1930). *Some folks won't work*. Rahway, NJ: Quinn and Goden.

Carson, M. (1990). *Settlement folk: Social thought and the American settlement movement, 1885–1930*. Chicago, IL: University of Chicago Press.

Chambers, C. (1981). *Paul U. Kellogg and the Survey: Voices for social welfare and social justice*. Minneapolis: University of Minnesota Press.

Chambers, C. (1967). *Seedtime of reform: American social service and social action, 1918–1933*. Ann Arbor: University of Michigan Press.

Chambers, D. E. (1975). Reform of workmen's compensation. *Social Work*, 20(4), 259–265.

Cloward, R. A. (1993). The reordered class structure. *BCR Reports*, 5(2), 1, 7.

Cloward, R. A., & Epstein, I. (1965, May). *Private social welfare's disengagement from the poor: The case of family adjustment agencies*. Paper presented at the Social Work Day Conference, School of Social Work, State University of New York at Buffalo.

Cohen, J. (1964). Social work and the culture of poverty. *Social Work*, 9(1), 3–11.

Cohn, F. M. (1943). *Workers' education in war and peace.* New York: Workers' Education Bureau of America.

Conference on Union Affiliation of Employees of Voluntary Health and Welfare Agencies. (1947a, June). *Report of the Conference on Union Affiliation of Employees of Voluntary Health and Welfare Agencies.* Unpublished manuscript, Archives of the University of Pennsylvania School of Social Work, Philadelphia.

Conference on Union Affiliation of Employees of Voluntary Health and Welfare Agencies. (1947b, June). *Report on Discussion.* Unpublished manuscript, Archives of the University of Pennsylvania School of Social Work, Philadelphia.

Council on Social Work Education. (2007). *Statistics on social work education in the United States.* Alexandria, VA: Author.

Danziger, S. (1997, March). *America unequal: The economy, the labor market and family incomes.* Paper presented at the Annual Program Meeting of the Council on Social Work Education, Washington, DC.

Day, P. J. (1989). The new poor in America: Isolationism in an international political-economy. *Social Work, 34*(3), 227–233.

Dinerman, M. (1977). Catch 23: Women, work and welfare. *Social Work, 22*(6), 472–477.

Donovan, R., Jaffe, N., & Pirie, V. M. (1987). Unemployment among low income women: An exploratory study. *Social Work, 32*(4), 301–305.

Edsall, T. B., & Edsall, M. D. (1991). *Chain reaction: The impact of race, rights, and taxes on American politics.* New York: Norton.

Fisher, R. (1994). *Let the people decide: A history of neighborhood organizing in America* (Rev. ed.). New York: Twayne.

Garfinkel, I. (1978). Welfare reform. *Proceedings of the National Conference on Social Welfare,* (pp. 80–95). New York: Columbia University Press.

Gary, L. E., & Leashore, B. (1982). High-risk status of Black men. *Social Work, 27*(1), 54–58.

Gault, B., Hartmann, H., Jones-DeWeever, A., Werschkul, M., & Williams, E. (2005, October). *The women of New Orleans and the Gulf Coast: Multiple disadvantages and key assets for recovery, Part I: Poverty, race, gender and class* (IWPR Briefing Paper #D464). Washington, DC: Institute for Women's Policy Research.

Ghosh, J. (2008, October 24). Global inequity must end. *The Guardian,* Retrieved on October 26, 2008, from http://www.guardian.co.uk/commentisfree/2008/oct/24/economics-development

Glickman, L. B. (1997). *A living wage: American workers and the making of consumer society.* Ithaca: Cornell University Press.

Gross, B. (1988, May, August, September, October, December; 1989, February). The rise and fall of full employment, Parts I-VI, VIII-X. *Labor Center Reporter,* Nos. 239, 241, 244, 245, 247, 248, 253, 256, 257, Berkeley, CA: Institute of Industrial Relations.

Grosswald, B. (1998). *Full employment policy in the United States: A policy analysis.* Unpublished manuscript, University of California School of Social Welfare, Berkeley.

Hagen, J. L., & Davis, L. V. (1992). Working with women: Building a policy and practice agenda. *Social Work, 37*(6), 495–503.

Hunter, R. (1904). *Poverty.* New York: Grossett & Dunlap.

Jones, L. E., & Wattenberg, E. (1991). Working, still poor: A loan program's role in the crisis of low-income single parents. *Social Work, 36*(2), 146–153.

Karger, H. J. (1988). *Social workers and labor unions.* Westport, CT: Greenwood.

Katz, M. B. (1996). *In the shadow of the poorhouse: A social history of welfare in America* (Rev. ed.). New York: Basic Books.

King, C. (1944, May). *Common goals of social work and labor.* Paper presented at the National Conference of Social Work, Russell Sage Foundation Library, Cleveland, Ohio.

King, C. (1946, January). Should social workers organize? A round table—with apologies to "Harvey." *Woman's Press,* 1–3.

Klein, P. (1923). *The burden of unemployment.* New York: Russell Sage.

Knight, L. W. (2005). *Citizen: Jane Addams and the struggle for democracy,* Chicago, IL: University of Chicago Press.

Lekachman, R. (1981). President Reagan and the human services. *Proceedings of the National Conference on Social Welfare* (pp. 36–45). New York: Columbia University Press.

Livingston, D. (1951, January). *Report to the General Council of the United Professional and Office Workers of America.* Unpublished manuscript, Archives of the University of Pennsylvania School of Social Work, Philadelphia.

Local 1199. (1978). *History of the national union of hospital and health care employees.* New York: Union of Hospital and Health Care Employees, Local 1199. (Available at Ruth Smalley Archive, School of Social Work, University of Pennsylvania, Philadelphia).

Lush, G. H. (1950, May 24). Reds ineligible for state relief, Chidsey rules. *Philadelphia Inquirer,* pp. 1, 3.

Macarov, D. (2003). *What the market does to people: Privatization, globalization, and poverty.* London: Zed Books.

Mandell, B. (1966). The crime of poverty. *Social Work, 11*(1), 11–15.

Marcus, G. (1948, June). *A social work platform in 1948.* Address delivered at a meeting of the Social Welfare Division, National Council of Arts, Sciences, and Professions, New York.

Margolin, L. (1997). *Under the cover of kindness: The invention of social work.* Charlottesville, VA: University of Virginia Press.

Morrissey, M. H. (1996, February). *A public face for private troubles: Helen Hall and the unemployment study of 1928.* Paper presented at the 42nd Annual Program Meeting of the Council on Social Work Education, Washington, DC.

National Association of Social Workers (1994, 2000, 2003). *Social work speaks* (3rd, 5th, and 6th eds.) Washington, DC: Author.

Otto, M. M. (1945, October). Organized labor's participation in social work: A selected bibliography. *Bulletin of the Russell Sage Foundation Library, 163,* 2–7.

Ozawa, M. N. (1995). The economic status of vulnerable older women. *Social Work, 40*(3), 323–331.

Ozawa, M. N. (1976). Women and work. *Social Work, 21*(6), 455–462.

Pannekoek, A. (1941–1942). *Workers Councils,* Greenwich, CT: Fawcett.

Patterson, J. (2001). *America's struggle against poverty in the 20th century.* Cambridge, MA: Harvard University Press.

Picketty, T., & Saez, E. (2003). Income inequality in the United States, 1913–1998. *Quarterly Journal of Economics, 118*(1), 1–39.

Piven, F. F. & Cloward, R. A. (1993). Poor relief and theories of the welfare state. In *Regulating the poor: The functions of public welfare* (Rev. ed., pp. 407–456). New York: Vintage Books.

Radical Alliance of Social Service Workers. (1981). Editorial: The human services and organized labor. *The Social Service Alternate View, 6*(3), 1, 5.

Reeser, L. C., & Epstein, I. (1990). *Professionalization and activism in social work: The sixties, the eighties, and the future.* New York: Columbia University Press.

Reisch, M. (2006). Workforce study falls short. *Social Work, 51*(4), 291–293.

Reisch, M. (2008). From melting pot to multiculturalism: The impact of racial and ethnic diversity on social work and social justice in the U.S. *British Journal of Social Work, 38*(4), 788–804.

Reisch, M., & Andrews, J. L. (2001). *The road not taken: A history of radical social work in the United States.* Philadelphia, PA: Brunner-Routledge.

Reisch, M. & Wenocur, S. (1986). The future of community organization in social work: Social activism and the politics of profession building. *Social Service Review, 60*(1), 70–91.

Richmond, M. E. (1906, December). Industrial conditions and the charity worker. Unpublished manuscript, Mary Richmond Papers, Columbia University, New York.

Richmond, M. E. (1917). *Social diagnosis.* New York: Russell Sage Foundation.

Richmond, M. E. (1920). Some next steps in social treatment. *The Family, 1*(4), 6–10.

Rosenman, L. (1976). Inequities in income security. *Social Work, 21*(6), 472–477.

Rosenman, L. (1979). Unemployment of women: A social policy issue. *Social Work, 24*(1), 20–25.

Ross, J. A. (1982). Unemployment among Black youths: A policy dilemma. *Social Work, 27*(1), 47–53.

Schmidt, P. (2008, February 8). Bans on affirmative action help Asian Americans, not Whites, report says. *Chronicle of Higher Education, 54*(22), A20.

Schwarz, J. (1971). Henry Ford's melting pot. In O. Feinstein (Ed.), *Ethnic groups in the city* (pp. 191–198). Lexington, MA: Heath Lexington Books.

Selekman, B. M., & van Kleeck, M. (1924). *Employees' representation in coal mines, a study of the industrial representation plan of the Colorado Fuel and Iron Company.* New York: Russell Sage.

Sherman, A. (2007, December 14). *Income inequality hits records levels new CBO data show.* Washington, DC: Center on Budget and Policy Priorities. Retrieved from http://www.cbpp.org/reports/index.cfm?fa=expert&id=38&year=2007&numreturn=50

Sherraden, M. W. (1985). Chronic unemployment: A social work perspective. *Social Work, 30*(5), 403–408.

Smith, R., McHugh, R., Stettner, A., & Segal, N. (2003). *Between a rock and a hard place: Confronting the failure of state unemployment insurance systems to serve women and working families.* New York: National Employment Law Project.

Social Service Employees Division. (1938, July). *Collective bargaining in social work: Then and now.* New York: United Office and Professional Workers of America.

Social Service Employees' Union (1948, April). *Our Union.* New York: United Office and Professional Workers of America. (Available at Archives of the University of Pennsylvania School of Social Work, Philadelphia)

Specht, H., & Courtenay, M. (1994). *Unfaithful angels: How social work abandoned its mission.* New York: Free Press.

Stotzfus, E. (2003). *Citizen, mother, worker: Debating public responsibility for child care after the second world war.* Chapel Hill: University of North Carolina.

Taft, J. (1922). The social worker's opportunity. *The Family, 3*(6), 149–153.

United Office and Professional Workers of America. (1947, May 15). *Telegram to President H.S. Truman.* Unpublished manuscript, Archives of the University of Pennsylvania School of Social Work, Philadelphia.

Urban Institute. (2008, September 3). *Q & A: New income and poverty statistics and the social safety net.* Washington, DC: Author. Retrieved September 15, 2008, from http://www.urban.org/welfare/index.cfm

Van Kleeck, M. (1932). Social research and industry. *Proceedings of the Second International Conference of Social Work, Frankfurt Main, Germany* (4th section, 1–20). (Available at Archives of the University of Pennsylvania School of Social Work, Philadelphia)

Van Kleeck, M. (1935). The common goals of labor and social work. *Proceedings of the 1934 National Conference of Social Work.* Chicago, IL: University of Chicago.

Wagner, D. (1990, March). *Social work and labor: Partners in assisting dislocated workers.* Paper presented at the annual program meeting of the Council on Social Work Education, Reno, NV.

Walkowitz, D. (1999). *Working with class: Social workers and the politics of middle class identity.* Chapel Hill, NC: University of North Carolina.

Wenocur, S. & Reisch, M. (1989). *From charity to enterprise: The development of American social work in a market economy.* Urbana: University of Illinois.

Wolfson, T. (1951, June). *Can the middle class work with organized labor?* Paper presented at the meeting of the Ninth Annual Conference of the Philadelphia Labor Education Association, Haverford College. Unpublished manuscript, Archives of the University of the Pennsylvania School of Social Work, Philadelphia.

Women's Economic Agenda Project. (1987). *Women's economic agenda: A call to action by and for California women.* Oakland, CA: Author.

Where's the "Freedom" in Free Trade? Framing Practices and Global Economic Justice

LORETTA PYLES

School of Social Welfare, University at Albany,
State University of New York, Albany, New York, USA

This study analyzes the work of three progressive organizations—
the Highlander Center, American Friends Service Committee's
Praxis/Economic Justice Project, and United Students Against
Sweatshops. Drawing from social movement theory's framing
perspective, I explore key components of the frames and framing
practices of these organizations working on global economic justice
issues. Special attention is paid to the role that popular education
techniques, critical consciousness-raising, and democratic organi-
zational structures play in framing practices. These methods have
proven to be vital tools for both community practitioners working
on economic justice issues, particularly in the context of a global-
izing economy.

Social movement theorists have noted that social action necessarily requires a change in attitude or consciousness, a fundamental restructuring of beliefs that subsequently inform actions (Jasper, 1997). Such changes are known as framing practices, which critique status quo social relations, policies or practices and offer a vision for a new way forward (Noakes & Johnston, 2005). Like other social movement actors, labor and economic justice organizers have fashioned new frames that fundamentally question specific capitalist practices and present new ideas for labor grounded in economic justice.

Contemporary innovations in labor organizing have transpired in a context of transnational and global economic justice movements. These movements have flourished because of the abilities of groups of affected constituents to find common ground and reframe the meaning and impact of economic globalization on citizens. Such practices are founded on the ability of groups of affected individuals to proffer critical analyses of lived experiences in democratic settings.

This article is concerned with key elements of contemporary framing practices of global economic justice organizations. Specifically, through this study, I seek to answer several questions: (a) What are the frames of global economic justice activists, and how do these frames differ from mainstream frames about economic globalization? and (b) What internal organizational activities and practices facilitate reframing?

To answer these questions, I analyze three examples of global economic justice framing, including that of the popular education practices of the Highlander Center, the transnational organizing work of United Students Against Sweatshops (USAS), and the popular education work of the American Friends Service Committee's Praxis/Economic Justice Project. With a stated commitment to social and economic justice, including poverty alleviation, framing practices of such organizations within the growing global economic justice movement are relevant to community organizers and social workers.

LITERATURE REVIEW

This study is grounded in several key areas of social movement and community organizing studies. In the following sections I analyze framing perspectives in social movement literature and the research on global economic justice organizing. Finally, I discuss popular education techniques and practices of critical consciousness-raising.

FRAMING PERSPECTIVES

According to social movement theorists, frames are "ways of presenting issues that identify injustices, attribute blame, suggest solutions, and inspire collective action" (Staggenborg, 2005, p. 755). Such framing patterns serve to explain injustices and are necessary conditions for collective action (Noakes & Johnston, 2005). Breaking through status quo socially constructed narratives of unfettered capitalism in favor of new frames of progressive economic justice has always been an essential practice of social movements including the labor movement and other economic justice work. The frames employed by organizers are not always directly influenced by strategic cal-culations; rather, frames are constructed as an expression of organizational ideologies and practices, as well as cultural conditions, political conditions, emotions and existential meaning (Goodwin & Jasper, 2004; Reese & Newcombe, 2003).

Schneider (2005) has noted that one of the key determinants of the success of a social movement frame is the movement's understanding of political opportunity structures, i.e. openings in power structures that can allow for change. Bobo, Kendall and Max (2001) identify four types of power available to achieve reforms—political/legislative power; consumer power; legal/regulatory power, and strike/disruptive power. Thus, Southern African Americans and their allies in the 1950s and 1960s framed their campaign around civil rights because the courts represented the most accessible aspect of the political opportunity structure at that time.

Lakoff (2004) has studied conservative social movements in the United States and noted how its actors utilize alluring language to garner support for issues. For example, through the development of the Clean Air Act, conservatives took words like "healthy," "clean" and "safe" and used them strategically. Multinational corporations and other proponents of policies such as the North American Free Trade Agreement (NAFTA) invoke words, e.g. "free," that are attractive to mainstream U.S. citizens and employ them to frame a debate in a way that has a broad appeal.

The job of progressive labor and other economic justice organizers has often been to break through these mainstream frames of corporations and other actors, making new meanings transparent, and exposing the assumptions and impacts of social policies and practices. Thus, the practice of "breaking through" frames allows activists to re-frame issues that can ultimately "suggest solutions [and] inspire collective action" (Staggenborg, 2005, p. 755).

GLOBALIZATION

The intensive globalization of the last 30 years has been referred to as the most significant re-structuring of political and economic arrangements since the Industrial Revolution (Mander, 2001). The expansion of capitalist enterprises into new markets across the globe has resulted in a variety of complex outcomes depending on one's social standpoint. Structural adjustment programs and free trade agreements, which have sought to alleviate debts and "develop" the Global South, have exacerbated the poor conditions of the most marginalized workers (Polack, 2004). As transnational corporations have hired local labor across the globe, it more often than not occurs without attention to living wages or the quality of life of vulnerable citizens and families (Streeten, 2001).

Free trade policies and structural adjustment programs as implemented by the World Trade Organization, World Bank, and International Monetary Fund have continued to defy attempts to protect workers' wages and conditions worldwide. Studies have shown that the policies of governments ignited by these financial institutions have had deleterious consequences for the environment and the quality of life of workers and poor people throughout the world (Lechner & Boli, 2004). These policies have contributed to displacement from indigenous land, sub-standard working conditions, health problems, and a growing discrepancy between the rich and poor (Fort, Mercer & Gish, 2004).

Global Justice Movement

Global justice activists are not against globalization per se. Instead they advocate for a globalization that is citizen-directed not corporate-driven. Citizen-directed globalization, or "globalization from below" occurs when democratic practices are employed to determine community priorities (Lechner & Boli, 2004; Shiva, 2005). Human welfare is prioritized over corporate welfare.

Marx predicted that the inequities of capitalism would eventually minimize the differences among workers (nationality, race, culture, etc.), igniting the development of international labor organizing (Armbruster-Sandoval, 2005). Global justice activists have begun actualizing this prediction and sought to connect across national, cultural, ethnic, linguistic and religious barriers. These activists have found common ground in their plight and strengths as workers, displaced farmers, indigenous people, students and global citizens. Contemporary transnational labor organizing has included organizing in the *maquiladoras* in Latin America (Armbruster-Sandoval, 1999), anti-sweatshop organizing in Asia and the Americas (Armbruster-Sandoval, 2005; Featherstone, 2002) and the development of fair-trade organizations across the globe, to name a few. Organized events such as the World Social Forum in Porto Alegre, Brazil and the Seattle protest of the World Trade Organization (WTO) have proven to be vital lynchpins for fostering transnational alliances across a range of arenas impacted by economic globalization including labor, the environment, race, gender and health (Beausang, 2002; Katsiafacas, 2004).

The research on economic justice organizing with a global frame has focused on a variety of dimensions of this progressive organizing practice. Such studies have centered on: negotiating class, gender and racial complexities in transnational networks (Armbruster-Sandoval, 2005); the role of consciousness-raising and the empowerment of immigrant women organizers in the U.S. (Chandler & Jones, 2003); and the framing practices of global social movement actors (Finnegan, 2003; Micheletti & Stolle, 2007; Wapner, 2003). The frames employed by global economic justice actors are the focus of this study.

Global economic justice framing practices can be understood initially by considering the language of "free trade," "trade rights" and "open markets" in relation to the global economy. It is clear that this language attempts to give the impression that unregulated economic growth is congruent with the democratic ideals of freedom and rights. However, if one investigates the realities of free trade policies, one will find that they have resulted in the exact opposite for many people – low wages, unsafe working environments, lack of access to clean water, poor healthcare; indeed, a lack of freedom and rights (Klein, 2002; National Labor Committee, 2004; Polack, 2004). The "free" part appears to apply to corporations, i.e. the wealthy and powerful. Transnational labor organizers have questioned such Orwellian ideas of freedom noting that free trade masks the negative effects of a deregulated economy. Indeed, they question, where exactly is the "freedom" in free trade? Thus, it would appear that the ability to "break the frame" of top-down globalization discourse is an essential task of global economic justice activists and organizers.

Popular Education and Critical Consciousness-Raising

Popular education is an educational approach for political and social change that stresses pedagogical techniques that empower citizens to learn about the connections between individual experiences and social systems (Peters & Bell, 1989; Pyles, 2009). With roots in Latin American liberation movements and Danish folk schools, popular education strategies emphasize adult education that is geared toward illuminating the critical consciousness of marginalized people (Freire, 1970; Gadotti, 1994). Groups of individuals with the help of a trained facilitator have the opportunity to discuss and articulate their life experiences. These discussions are conducted through a critical lens that clarifies historical marginalization and pathways to empowerment.

Brazilian critical educator Paulo Freire differentiated between what he called *banking* education and *problematizing* education (Gadotti, 1994; Shor, 1993). Problematizing education is a critical dialogical reflection on knowledge that is usually taken-for-granted. To problematize something goes beyond mere critique and involves the use of dialectical questioning by a teacher encouraging students to "question answers rather than merely to answer questions" (Shor, 1993, p. 26). In Freire's work in Brazil, for example, when working with illiterate peasant farmers, he would show them pictures of a peasant working in the fields with an owner/boss overseeing their work. Asking them to describe what they saw, he sought to enhance their understanding of economic power relations encouraging them to articulate this in their own terms. Developing strategies for action is also a necessary component of such popular education techniques. These strategies are commensurate philosophically and practically with the innovations of the feminist movement, known as consciousness-raising (Ferree & Hess, 2000; Pyles, 2009).

Learning more about the framing practices of global justice actors can contribute to the scholarly dialogue on framing, popular education and labor movement studies. By understanding three innovative organizations, scholars, social workers and activists can gain insight into ways to promote similar values and strategies into community practice and education.

METHODOLOGY

In this study, I conducted a qualitative comparative analysis of three organizations (Schneider, 2005). The three organizations that are the focus of this research were chosen based on their engagement in economic justice work that utilized global frames. These three organizations represent a diversity of types of organizations including faith-based (American Friends Service Committee); grassroots (Highlander Center) and student-led (United Students Against Sweatshops). All three organizations would be considered "successful" in their work given their longevity.

In developing the analysis of these organizations, I drew from a range of data sources. These sources included (a) the existing scholarly data on these organizations; (b) organizational materials such as brochures, websites, workbooks and list-serves; and (c) field notes from my own personal experiences of attending workshops put on by the organizations including workshops at the U.S. Social Forum in 2007 in Atlanta, Georgia and workshops held at the Highlander Center's 75th Anniversary Celebration in 2007 in New Market, Tennessee.

In the following sections, after describing the organization, I attempt to answer the research questions and discuss the global justice frame of the organization in relation to a mainstream frame and the activities and practices that facilitate the re-framing.

HIGHLANDER CENTER

The Highlander Center is a support organization that conducts trainings and workshops to build the capacities of organizations and coalitions to effect social change. Beginning in the 1930s, the Highlander Folk School (now called the Highlander Center) was founded in Tennessee as a school of adult popular education offering trainings for workers and labor organizers. These organizers came from rural mining and milling towns, as well as from urban industrial settings where workers were affiliated with the Congress of Industrial Organizations (CIO) (Peters & Bell, 1989). One of the founders of the Highlander Center, Miles Horton, had come to realize that traditional teaching methods influenced by formal school systems did not work with rural workers and other laborers living in poverty. He therefore utilized alternative pedagogical methods as well as innovations appropriate to the setting in the rural South.

The teaching at Highlander would be guided by the problems brought forth by the students and included learning experiences that valued culture and expression such as improvisational drama, song-writing, and singing (Peters & Bell, 1989). Horton and his cohorts came to believe in the axiom that the people themselves are the authorities on their experiences and thus on their own learning needs and educational agendas. A reflection of his commitment to democracy, he emphasized that education should be grounded in the learner's experiences and included the use of questions to stimulate self-examination as well as an examination of social systems.

Highlander's Frame

The Highlander Center's frame can be captured by considering some key language expressed on their website:

> There is a growing gap in the distribution of wealth available to the rich and the poor, both nationally and internationally. Many wealthy individuals and companies promote systematic changes that increase their wealth while pushing low-income people, communities, and governments further and further into poverty. . . . Policies of structural adjustment and decreasing taxes on corporations and the wealthy are lowering government tax revenues, resulting in less access to social services and decreased government power. Corporations increased their influence over governments through campaign contributions, paid lobbyists and pushing through international trade policies to protect corporate interests . . . (http://www.highlandercenter.org/r-global-economic.asp)

Frames tend to "identify injustices, attribute blame, and suggest solutions"; indeed, Highlander's frames are doing just that. Clearly, they identify injustice and attribute blame from a neo-Marxist perspective, emphasizing the injustice of worker-owner disparities. They place explicit blame for the injustices primarily on corporations; governments appear to be culpable as well. This Marxist analysis of the political economy employs a critical analysis of top-down, neoliberal globalization policies and practices of governments, corporations and trade organizations. The frame critiques the system of campaign finance and acknowledges that lawmaking is often driven by corporate agendas.

The Highlander Center has a resonant frame around economic justice, suggesting solutions geared toward worker's rights and solidarity organizing. They emphasize grassroots action for global change through the establishment of what they call "economic democracy." Globalization itself has triggered innovative framing practices in recent years as the Center casts an even wider net to accommodate expanding migrant populations displaced from the Global South and a greater awareness of the intersectionality of oppression. They emphasize a wide frame of liberation through racial justice, environmental justice, LGBT rights, international peace, and criminal justice reform. They are also concerned with the shared fate and solidarity of the Global South and thus center their own work in the United States on issues of concern to Appalachia and the South. The increase of immigrants into the U.S. South and practices such as mountain-top removal and movement of industry from the U.S. North to the U.S. South, has triggered broader, more resonant framing in Tennessee and beyond. Building solidarity across the common theme of global justice has become a necessity.

Framing Practices

The work of the Highlander Center is unified around a common belief in "constructing democracy" which is achieved by creating democratic spaces that seek to build a base of global justice activists. The Highlander Center believes that building the base happens in environments where constituents and leaders can re-frame the dominant discourse of globalization in their own language. Holding firm to its roots of tapping into the wisdom of the mountain cultures of Tennessee, workshops are conducted in circles sitting in rocking chairs. Besides dialogue, the creative arts, especially music, have been central mechanisms for facilitating frames and enhancing solidarity. Creating specialized programs for specific populations, such as youth and Latinos, they proactively facilitate an organizational culture that actualizes dialogue across races/ethnicities and issues. Their multi-lingual capacity-building program is an example of an innovative initiative that facilitates these re-framing practices. By developing the capacities of individuals to be able to articulate themselves in their native languages, critical questioning and empowerment possibilities are strengthened. As Horton believed and the Highlander Center practices, these democratic spaces appear to be necessary conditions for and directly associated with the ability to re-frame and ultimately mobilize.

AMERICAN FRIENDS SERVICE COMMITTEE - PRAXIS/ECONOMIC JUSTICE PROJECT

The American Friends Service Committee is a Quaker organization founded in 1917 that is committed to peace, development and social justice work in local and global contexts. Their mission statement affirms: "We are called to confront, nonviolently, powerful institutions of violence, evil, oppression, and injustice" (http://www.afsc.org/about/mission.htm). The Praxis/Economic Justice Project began its work in 1994 in association with the American

Friends Service Committee in Chicago with the goal of developing leadership within labor, community, and student groups. Working on local and global economic justice issues this organization engages in popular education initiatives, helping groups of individuals to connect their personal experiences in local economies with larger global economic trends (Zerkel, 2001).

Praxis' Frame

The frame used by Praxis can understood through an analysis of ideas expressed on their website:

> In today's global economy, many people are experiencing hunger, hardship, and the impact of a growing inequality of wealth, power, and access to basic resources. Around the world, 1.2 billion people live in "extreme" poverty . . . The total net worth of America's 400 wealthiest individuals reached $955 billion, while the median weekly wage for an American worker was $625 . . . Economic justice means building a fair economy that works for everyone. It means fair trade policies that protect workers' rights to organize and to receive a living wage for their work at home and abroad . . . It means calling for new national priorities that reduce wasteful military spending and redirect tax dollars to helping our children, elders, and communities meet their needs. (http://www.afsc.org/economic-justice/LearnAbout.htm).

Praxis works to transform poverty and oppression drawing from a frame that conceptualizes these problems as emerging from institutions. This critique of the economy places blame on corporations and governments for perpetuating the divide between the rich and poor. They draw attention to the impact that the practices of governments and corporations have on human well-being. Their vision for economic justice emphasizes the role that governmental interventions can play in fulfilling the social contract.

Framing Practices

In an effort to foster sustainability and depth of critical consciousness, Praxis works with groups over several years. For example, they worked with a public sector union local that included public school janitors, teachers' aides, park district workers, and county hospital workers. Praxis employs the practice of *coyuntural* analysis which has its roots in the work of Freire and critical theory (Zerkel, 2001). This technique facilitates the understanding and critique of the historical moment emphasizing the personal experiences of individual members and collective analysis. Their workshops involve hands-on activities that are democratically run and tap into the wisdom and creativity of participants.

UNITED STUDENTS AGAINST SWEATSHOPS

The United Students Against Sweatshops (USAS) was founded in the late 1990s as an avenue to support the work of college students in the United States who were organizing to oppose the manufacture of college apparel in sweatshop conditions. These students developed alliances with workers in China, Guatemala, and New York City; the students developed solidarity alliances with these workers as they discovered that they were people their own age working in factories in inhumane conditions. The sweatshop movement came to be a response to the increased corporatization of universities as well as a raised consciousness about the ways in which consumers contribute to the problem (Featherstone, 2002).

USAS's Frame

USAS frames their issues and work around "economic justice," pointing to "corporate power" and the "global economy" as sources of oppression. They believe that the global economy creates sweatshops and working conditions that violate human rights. Examining the literature used in the Sweat-Free Campus Campaign is also helpful for illuminating their frames. They identify "the problem" as (a) sweatshop conditions and poverty wages of workers making university apparel; (b) illegal repression of workers attempting to organize; and (c) the race to the bottom which multinational corporations are running. They identify the "solutions" as (a) a voice on the job; (b) a living wage; and (c) an alternative to the Wal-Mart model.

Framing Practices

USAS developed their frame in response to outrage at the long hours, low wages and poor conditions that young factory workers experienced to make college sweatshirts and other products that they were buying. The USAS were also "moved by a sense that their own desires were being manipulated, that the glamorous advertising aimed at youth markets was a cover-up meant to distract from corporate wrongdoings" (Featherstone, 2002, p. 10). In addition, with strong leadership from students of color, including Latino and other immigrant students whose families work or have worked in sweatshop conditions, they are able to draw, to some degree, from the wisdom and lived experiences of these families.

USAS utilizes liberation methods of self-governance that promote a frame of intersectionality, or the philosophical position that oppressions such as classism, racism and sexism are interconnected. Their decision-making is made by members of their four identity causes–Womyn/Gender Caucus; People of Color Caucus; Queer Caucus; and Working Class Caucus.

One of the mechanisms that USAS builds into their work is that of an Alliance Building Committee that "works to ensure that USAS is an actively anti-oppressive organization, both in the work we do and the way we work" (http://www.studentsagainstsweatshops.org/index.php?option=com_content&task=view&id=24&Itemid=88888916). Ross (2004) surmises the reasons for this approach:

> Perhaps as a result of the influence of a kind of seasoned feminism, USAS meetings are characterized by teaching and emulation of fairly sophisticated techniques of group discussion and leadership. Repeated observation of USAS meetings at local and regional levels demonstrated their painstaking efforts to include all participants in discussion and active care to insure that women were selected as discussion leaders or representatives and spokespersons. This is reflected substantively in USAS Code of Conduct campaigns and WRC [Worker Rights Consortium] inspections: treatment of women workers is specifically focused upon (in an industry in which the vast majority of workers are female). (p. 307)

LIMITATIONS

This research is limited by the fact that formal interviews were not conducted with participants. A more in-depth study that includes sustained observation and interviews would likely yield more insight, including further reflection on similarities and differences of the organizations. Indeed, such an inquiry could further amplify the voices of the organizations' participants. Other studies could also focus on the relationship between frames and specific organizing strategies as well as the impact that frames have on outcomes. Nonetheless, this study is important because the literature on framing is relatively undeveloped and the growing importance of transnational and global justice organizing is critical to economic justice practice.

DISCUSSION

USAS employs their frames to engage in community organizing campaigns, while Highlander and Praxis mostly employ their frames in their work as support organizations offering popular education trainings and movement building activities. All the groups studied here have similar issue frames, pointing to the culpability of corporations and economic globalization policies and practices as the source of economic injustice. Though the groups recognize that governments have the ability to take action against corporations, the primary target, especially for USAS, is corporations. Recent research on social movements and community organizing have noted that organizers are focusing on corporate targets more often than governmental targets as has been the case in the past (Michelleti & Stolle, 2007). Today, the three global economic justice activist groups analyzed here appear to understand that targets of social action in a globalizing economy also include financial institutions, such as the World Trade Organization, International Monetary Fund and World Bank, which are key sources of power and thus must be key targets of change.

Though all three groups are aware of multiple oppressions, Highlander and USAS are especially interested in framing their work from an intersectionality perspective, making explicit connections between economic oppression and other forms of oppression in their frames and practices. What is particularly noteworthy about this global economic justice organizing is that these groups are concerned with issues beyond class and are making the connections to race and gender. While the labor movement has its origins in patriarchal, male-dominated analyses and structures, this new movement seems to have the inclination and skills to transcend these old exclusionary approaches. The global justice movement that is taking place in the context of a globalizing world incorporates changing norms and roles for women and the realities of increasingly multicultural contexts.

All the groups value and engage in some form of critical consciousness raising and/or popular education strategies as a precursor and ongoing component of their framing practices. In addition, all the organizations tend to emphasize process-oriented social change activities, whereby the means of social change are as important as the ends. Highlander and Praxis affirm the role of process in their popular education techniques; USAS especially emphasizes social change in the way in which they organize themselves. This finding raises a critical question: Can these global justice frames be constructed separately from these democratic practices (constructing democracy, popular education, coyuntural analysis, democratic organizational structures, etc.)? I hypothesize that they cannot, at least not in a way that would allow an organization to be both sustainable and deeply accountable to the base grassroots. Traditional educational and training approaches in development, advocacy, and social service organizations do not tend to utilize such democratic approaches nor do they employ global justice frames that question capitalism and globalization in such fundamental ways. The practices of the organizations studied here go beyond mere critique and instead problematize economic relations drawing from the lived experiences of base constituents creating sustainable social change organizations.

It is also important to note the divergent demographics, that is, social standpoints, of its leaders and members. While USAS includes individuals that are of diverse racial and ethnic origins, as college students they certainly have a degree of economic privilege in society. Their frames tend to emphasize "solidarity" with global workers since the student organizers themselves are not necessarily constituents. The Highlander Center is a

Southern organization that identifies themselves and strategically allies with other countries of the Global South whose citizens tend to be marginalized in the global economy. Their staff, volunteers, and constituents are primarily living in the South of the United States.

All the groups recognize that there is something about the global economy that is disrupting democratic practices and silencing citizens. Their frames and analyses are directly related to their practices that emphasize popular education, democracy building and process-oriented organizational management. The ability of community organizers to critically reframe disempowering media messages and false assumptions about institutions, economic policies and clients of social services is arguably the most important skill that practitioners and educators can develop and nurture.

Though social work scholars have critiqued economic globalization and written about the impacts of neo-liberal ideologies on social welfare extensively, there has been little in the U.S. literature focusing on liberation practice interventions such as that engaged in by global economic justice activists (Dominelli, 1999; Midgley, 2007; Polack, 2004). Actualizing a vision of social and economic justice entails going beyond disembodied critiques of the global economy to real life engagement in global economic justice activism. This activism has great potential when it is grounded in critical consciousness raising practices that are based on lived experiences, empowering citizens to act in the world.

REFERENCES

Armbruster-Sandoval, R. (1999). Globalization and cross-border labor organizing: The Guatemalan maquiladora industry and the Phillips Van Heusen workers' movement. *Latin American Perspectives, 26*(2), 109–128.

Armbruster-Sandoval, R. (2005). Workers of the world unite? The contemporary anti-sweatshop movement and the struggle for social justice in the Americas. *Work and Occupations, 32*(40), 464–485.

Beausang, F. (2002). Democratising global governance: The challenges of the World Social Forum. *Management of Social Transformations Discussion Paper Series, 59*, 1–27. Paris: UNESCO.

Bobo, K., Kendall, J., & Max, S. (2001). *Organizing for social change: Midwest Academy manual for activists.* Santa Ana, CA: Steven Locks Press.

Chandler, S. K., & Jones, J. (2003). 'You have to do it for the people coming': Union organizing and the transformation of immigrant women workers. *Affilia, 18*(3), 254–271.

Dominelli, L. (1999). Neo-liberalism, social exclusion and welfare clients in a global economy. *International Journal of Social Welfare, 8*(1), 14–22.

Featherstone, L. (2002). *Students against sweatshops.* London: New Left Books.

Ferguson, I., & Lavalette, M. (2006). Globalization and global justice: Towards a social work of resistance. *International Social Work, 49*(3), 309–318.

Ferree, M. M., & Hess, B. B. (2000). *Controversy and coalition: The new feminist movement across three decades of change*. New York: Routledge.

Finnegan, W. (2003). Affinity groups and the movement against corporate globalization. In J. Goodwin & J. Jasper (Eds.), *The social movement reader: Cases and concepts* (pp. 210–218). Oxford: Blackwell Publishing.

Fort, M., Mercer, M., & Gish, O. (Eds.). (2004). *Sickness and wealth: The corporate assault on global health*. Cambridge, MA: South End Press.

Freire, P. (1970). *Pedagogy of the oppressed*. New York: Seabury Press.

Gadotti, M. (1994). *Reading Paulo Freire: His life and work*. Albany: State University of New York Press.

Gilligan, P. (2007). Well motivated reformists or nascent radicals: How do applicants to the degree in social work see social problems, their origins and solutions? *British Journal of Social Work, 37*, 735–760.

Goodwin, J., & Jasper, J. (Eds.). (2004). *Rethinking social movements: Structure, meaning and emotion*. Lanham, MD: Rowman & Littlefield.

Jasper, J. (1997). *The art of moral protest*. Chicago: University of Chicago Press.

Katsiaficas, G. (2004). Seattle was not the beginning. In E. Yuen, D. Burton-Rose & G. Katsiaficas (Eds.), *Confronting capitalism* (pp. 3–10). Brooklyn, NY: Soft Skull Press.

Klein, N. (2002). *Fences and windows: Dispatches from the front lines of the globalization debate*. New York: Picador USA.

Lakoff, G. (2004). *Don't think of an elephant! Know your values and frame the debate*. White River Junction, VT: Chelsea Green Publishing.

Lechner, F. J., & Boli, J. (Eds.). (2004). *The globalization reader*. Malden, MA: Blackwell Publishing.

Mander, J. (2001). Facing the rising tide. In J. Mander, & E. Goldsmith (Eds.), *The case against the global economy and a turn toward the local* (2nd ed., pp. 3–19). London: Earthscan.

Micheletti, M., & Stolle, D. (2007). Mobilizing consumers to take responsibility for global social justice. *Annals of the American Academy of Political and Social Science, 611*, 157–175.

Midgley, J. (2007). Perspectives on globalization, social justice and welfare. *Journal of Sociology and Social Welfare, 34*(2), 17–36.

National Labor Committee (2004). *Trying to live on 25 cents an hour*. Retrieved July 15, 2009, from http://www.nlcnet.org/campaigns/archive/chinareport/costoflivingdoc.shtml

Noakes, J. A. & Johnston, H. (2005). Frames of protest: A roadmap to a perspective. In H. Johnston & J. A. Noakes (Eds.), *Frames of protest: Social movements and the framing perspective* (pp. 1–29). Oxford: Rowman & Littlefield.

Peters, J. M., & Bell, B. (1989). Horton of Highlander. In J. M. Peters & B. Bell (Eds.), *Highlander Research and Education Center: An approach to education* (pp. 34–64). New Market, TN: Highlander Research and Education Center.

Polack, R. J. (2004). Social justice and the global economy: New challenges for social work in the 21st century. *Social Work, 49*(2), 281–290.

Pyles, L. (2009). *Progressive community organizing: A critical approach for a globalizing world*. New York: Routledge.

Reisch, M., & Andrews, J. (2001). *The road not taken: A history of radical social work in the United States*. New York: Brunner-Routledge.

Ross, R. J. S. (2004). From antisweatshop to global justice to antiwar: How the new New Left is the same and different from the old New Left. *Journal of World-Systems Research, 10*(1), 287–319.

Schneider, C. (2005). Political opportunities and framing Puerto Rican identity in New York City. In H. Johnston & J. A. Noakes (Eds.), *Frames of protest: Social movements and the framing perspective* (pp. 163–181). Oxford: Rowman & Littlefield.

Shepard, B., & Hayduk, R. (2002). *From ACT-UP to the WTO: Urban protest and community building in the era of globalization*. Brooklyn, NY: Verso.

Shor, I. (1993). Education is politics: Paulo Freire's critical pedagogy. In P. McLaren & P. Leonard (Eds.), *Paulo Freire: A critical encounter* (pp. 25–46). London: Routledge.

Shiva, V. (2005). *Earth democracy: Justice, sustainability, and peace*. Cambridge, MA: South End Press.

Specht, H., & Courtney, M. E. (1994). *Unfaithful angels: How social work has abandoned its mission*. New York: Free Press.

Staggenborg, S. (2005). Social movement theory. In G. Ritzer (Ed.), *Encyclopedia of social theory* (pp. 753–759). Thousand Oaks, CA: Sage Publications.

Streeten, P. (2001). *Globalisation: Threat or opportunity?* Copenhagen, Denmark: Copenhagen Business School Press.

Wapner, P. (2003). Transnational environmental activism. In J. Goodwin & J. Jasper (Eds.), *The social movement reader: Cases and concepts* (pp. 202–209). Oxford: Blackwell Publishing.

Zerkel, M. (2001, Winter). Demystifying global economics: Making the local/global connection. *Radical Teacher*, 1–7.

LABOR-COMMUNITY PARTNERSHIPS FOR ECONOMIC JUSTICE

The Politics and Practice of Economic Justice: Community Benefits Agreements as Tactic of the New Accountable Development Movement

VIRGINIA PARKS

School of Social Service Administration, University of Chicago, Chicago, Illinois, USA

DORIAN WARREN

Department of Political Science and School of International & Public Affairs, Columbia University, New York, New York, USA

A tactic recently deployed by economic-justice community campaigns has been the negotiation of Community Benefits Agreements (CBAs). CBAs are legally binding agreements between a private developer and a coalition of community-based organizations in which community members pledge support for a development in return for benefits such as living wage jobs, local hiring, and affordable housing. We elucidate key employment-related features of CBAs, and argue that the strongest CBAs result from organizing campaigns which utilize a range of political tactics including the dissensus organizing power of labor-community coalitions. We discuss how CBA campaigns often lead to broader economic justice strategies aimed at public regulation.

The authors wish to thank all individuals interviewed for this article. This research was funded in part by a Junior Faculty Grant from the School of Social Service Administration, and approved by the SSA-Chapin Hall IRB of the University of Chicago (Protocol #06-073).

INTRODUCTION

One of the most significant challenges currently facing urban communities of color is increasing economic inequality. Unlike past economic devastation wrought primarily by de-industrialization, rising inequality within many urban economies has resulted from new structural conditions of growth rather than abandonment (Sassen, 1998). Polarization within the labor market driven by the rise of low-wage work has been a central feature of this new growth regime, attended by community-level effects of gentrification, displacement, and increased poverty. In a number of cities experiencing a resurgence in development, low-income communities of color have challenged the new growth regime by embarking upon innovative campaigns that demand growth with equity. Among the many tactics deployed by this new accountable development movement, one of the most innovative and successful has been the negotiation of community benefits agreements (CBAs). Though not limited to employment, a concern for living-wage jobs has been at the center of such agreements.

Community Benefits Agreements (CBAs) are legally binding agreements between a private developer or governmental body and a coalition of community-based organizations, labor unions, environmentalists and other advocacy groups. In the agreement, community members pledge support for a development in return for tangible benefits such as living wage jobs, local hiring agreements, green building practices, funds for parks, affordable housing, and child care. Through the use of community benefits agreements as the most recent of several tactics and the focus on high-road, quality jobs as a key component of urban development, the new accountable development movement brings economic inequality and redistribution claims to the center of contemporary urban politics. Strategically, this new accountable development movement exploits the geographic constraints of a post-industrial, service-sector economy (hotel beds cannot be globally outsourced to be made, sports arenas demand real bodies to fill their seats, retailers increasingly seek the purchasing power of urban consumers) and the political process that attends these geographic constraints: service-sector enterprises that are the hallmark of new urban development *need* the city, securing the special purchase that urban politics and governance provides grassroots actors for contesting corporate power.

In this article, we elucidate key features of CBAs and assess their utility as a strategic mechanism through which to achieve the goals of equitable community development. We first situate CBAs as the latest among several tactics in the strategic repertoire of the new accountable development movement (NADM) aimed at transforming low-wage work, redistributing resources to and expanding the political voice of residents in disadvantaged communities. We then discuss how CBAs reflect as well as contest local regulatory norms and broader neo-liberal dynamics. Though CBAs rest on privately negotiated agreements rather than on public regulation, they sometimes, but not always, move forward economic justice strategies focused on public regulation.

The key focus of our discussion is the central role of organizing and politics in winning and monitoring CBAs. While CBAs are often seen as either an innocuous policy outcome or technocratic solution to inequitable development, we argue that the strongest and most effective CBAs result from carefully crafted organizing campaigns that engage both "insider" and "outsider" political tactics. Although research in this area is only beginning to emerge, what is missing from the extant scholarship on CBAs is the fact that the strategic politics behind a successful CBA campaign centers on the dissensus organizing power of community and labor in order to secure a concessionary agreement with developers. We conclude by arguing that the utility of CBAs is best assessed relative to their immediate organizing contexts: the strongest, most effective CBAs are employed as part of a larger accountable development and economic justice movement, not as one-off campaigns or as technocratic mechanisms driven primarily by developers or elected officials.

Our research draws primarily upon in-person interviews with key actors involved in securing CBAs in Los Angeles, Denver, and with leaders of a new national network of labor and community coalitions engaged in accountable development campaigns.

BACKGROUND

Over the last decade, a new accountable development movement (NADM) has emerged in cities and states across the country. In a context of extreme economic inequality and federal inaction in response, coalitions of labor and community activists have pushed for economic justice at the local level (Orr, 2007; Turner & Cornfield, 2007). Starting with living wage campaigns in the mid-1990s, NADM actors have deployed a wide range of redistributive mechanisms and tactics to address decades of increasing income inequality and inequitable development, particularly in urban communities of color. These include living wage ordinances;[1] expansions of many of these living wage ordinances to cover greater numbers of workers; state-level minimum wage campaigns;[2] labor peace agreements; superstore ordinances, which open up the planning and political process of retail development to local community residents; and campaigns around CBAs (Luce, 2004; Martin, 2001). Community benefits agreements, in particular, are part of this larger strategic repertoire of redistributive tactics advanced primarily by community-labor coalitions within the larger NADM with the long-term purpose of redistributing the benefits of new urban development to less-advantaged communities, residents, and workers.

The conventional wisdom in the scholarship on urban politics is that development is central to the function of cities as growth machines (Logan & Molotch, 1987; Mollenkopf, 1983). Urban development is uneven at best, and often reproduces racial, class and place-based inequalities; when development does occur, the benefits are spread unevenly and usually benefit business and other developer-related interests (Squires, 1994). As such, the general consensus is that cities do not redistribute to lower-income and disadvantaged communities—whether around development or broader issues of economic inequality. Because of their structural constraints in a federal political system with few mechanisms for redistribution vis-à-vis the national government, cities generally are not viable locations for political actors and ordinary people to make redistributive claims (Peterson, 1981).

The new accountable development movement challenges this scholarly consensus. CBA campaigns in particular have quickly become one of the most prominent community mobilization responses to new urban development. An effort to ensure growth with equity, a CBA is a legally enforceable contract between a developer and a coalition of community and labor groups that stipulates the provision of a host of community benefits as part of a development project (see Gross, LeRoy, & Janis-Aparicio, 2005, for a comprehensive description of CBAs). In exchange, the community-labor coalition pledges to support the project, providing developers with important public backing during approval processes when government bodies consider permits or subsidies for the project. As key CBA innovators and advocates stress, CBAs are only one of many concrete policy tools that can be used to advance the goals of a community benefits agenda—"the simple proposition that the main purpose of economic development is to bring measurable, permanent improvements to the lives of affected residents, particularly those in low-income neighborhoods" (Gross et al., 2005, p. 5).

Since the signing of the nation's first CBA in 1997 (the Hollywood and Highland CBA in Los Angeles), between 17 and 50 self-proclaimed CBAs have been negotiated in the United States (Partnership for Working Families, 2008; Salkin & Lavine, 2007). As recently as late 2008, three new CBAs were negotiated in San Francisco, Pittsburgh, and Seattle. Fourteen CBAs currently in effect have been negotiated with the technical assistance of a national network of labor-community coalitional partners called the Partnership for Working Families (hereafter, the "Partnership"). These CBAs share much in common both substantively and politically—most involve a labor-community coalition that predominantly represents residents and workers of color and that engages grassroots organizing as its *modus operandi*. Now with affiliates in 18 cities, the Partnership is an outgrowth of the work of the Los Angeles Alliance for a New Economy (LAANE) and other Los Angeles community organizations responsible for innovating, organizing, and negotiating the country's first CBAs.

As these are model CBAs in terms of both their technical innovation and political strength, we focus in this paper on Partnership CBAs—those agreements negotiated by Partnership affiliates or that have received Partnership assistance (see the Partnership's website for information about its affiliates' current CBA campaigns at www.communitybenefits.org). We distinguish Partnership CBAs from all others based on three key criteria: scope, transparency, and oversight. Scope refers to whether or not a CBA specifies a broad range of benefits that accrue to the broader community, as opposed to narrow and particularistic benefits that go to just the signatories to the agreement. Transparency refers to whether the agreements themselves are transparent and made available to the public. Finally, oversight refers to the monitoring and enforcement procedures included within the agreements. These three core features separate strong from weak CBAs. A broad scope, high level of transparency, and explicit and robust monitoring and enforcement mechanisms are the core characteristics of strong CBAs. Non-Partnership CBAs include those negotiated in New York, such as the Atlantic Yards and Yankee Stadium CBAs, and New Jersey; all qualify as weak CBAs by these criteria (see Gross, 2007/2008 for an analysis of these CBAs).

While CBAs stipulate a range of community benefits, the extant CBA literature largely overlooks the fact that employment-related provisions sit at the center of all strong CBAs currently in effect. Key community organizations involved in the innovation of CBAs, such as LAANE, explicitly articulate employment concerns as central to their economic justice agenda and share a history engaging employment as an area of focus and activity. These community organizations looked to CBAs as one way to address two problems that have long plagued community efforts focused on job-centered development: job access (getting residents into jobs) and job quality (making sure those jobs pay decently).[3] All Partnership CBAs are crafted to guarantee both. Provisions stipulating job training, targeted hiring, living wages and labor peace are key to achieving these guarantees. We briefly review these below.

Job Training

Getting residents into jobs requires both "job-readiness" on the part of the resident and "hiring-readiness" on the part of the employer. Job training provisions address the former, targeted hiring the latter. CBAs with job training provisions stipulate that the developer provides funds to be used for training impacted residents, often for specific development jobs. These funds may be directed toward established training programs (e.g., those overseen by a Workforce Investment Board) or to the creation of new programs that tailor training to the needs of employers associated with the development. Impacted residents can be defined a number of ways. Residents living in neighborhoods adjacent to the proposed development are usually included, but most CBAs broaden the reach of CBA benefits and programs beyond this single category of geographically impacted individuals to include low-income residents, dislocated workers, and special needs individuals, such as those who are ex-offenders, homeless, chronically unemployed, or who have received public assistance within the last two years (Gross et al., 2005, pp. 57–8). These provisions are an example of the ways in which strong CBAs specify benefits to a broad group of disadvantaged residents, rather than to a narrow signatory constituency.

Targeted Hiring

Targeted hiring provisions are perhaps the most distinctive employment component of CBAs currently in effect. As many disillusioned community organizations can attest, job training initiatives often leave residents empty handed—trained but without a job (Lafer, 2002). Targeted hiring provisions address this critical labor market disconnect by providing concrete steps that ensure workers in the community are hired into development jobs—the most touted benefit of new development. The concept of targeted hiring inheres within other government policies, such as HUD's Section 3 program, but the specificity of many CBA provisions and their application to *private* development is unprecedented. (HUD Section 3 "requires that recipients of certain HUD financial assistance, to the greatest extent possible, provide job training, employment, and contract opportunities for low- or very-low income residents in connection with projects and activities in their neighborhood;" U.S. Department of Housing and Urban Development, 2008). Further, most CBAs explicitly incorporate community-based organizations as part of targeted hiring programs, a proven strategy of successful employment programs but missing from many Section 3 implementation strategies (Caftel & Haywood, 1994; Melendez & Harrison, 1998).

Recruitment and referral processes as part of targeted hiring programs can be structured in a number of ways (e.g., requiring that employers post job notices in a certain manner), but most CBAs incorporate "first source" hiring. First source provisions mandate that the developer and other employers associated with the project must interview job applicants referred from specified "first sources" such as community training centers or programs (for information on the use of first source hiring in local development programs across the United States, see Molina, 1998). Lastly, targeted hiring provisions stipulate performance goals, often as a percentage of all jobs filled with targeted job applicants, and enforcement procedures. The Staples CBA in Los Angeles, for example, calls for 50% of all posted jobs within a six-month period to be filled with targeted hires (see Gross et al., 2005, pp. 108–112, for text of the First Source Hiring Policy included within the Staples CBA).

Living Wages

Building off the success of the living wage movement, most CBAs call for development and development-related jobs to pay living wages. In a few cities, CBAs may not need to include living wage provisions because the local living wage ordinance already covers all jobs related to a development (e.g., San Francisco and Toledo). In cities with less comprehensive living wage ordinances, CBAs can extend the benefits of the ordinance to a larger set of workers, i.e. those employed by tenants of a development. In cities without living wage ordinances, a living wage provision within a CBA becomes all the more valuable as a tool to ensure the benefit of quality jobs as a result of new development.

Labor Peace

Finally, community benefits agreements often include "labor peace" requirements. These provisions (often called "right to organize" agreements, neutrality agreements, and card-check/majority sign-up procedures for workers to choose unionization) make it easier for workers employed by the development to unionize, thus transforming non-union, low-wage jobs into living wage jobs with benefits. Workers attempting to organize unions today face increased employer hostility in organizing campaigns; a range of studies have found that employers illegally fire workers in anywhere from 24–32% of union election campaigns (Bronfenbrenner & Juravich, 1995). In this context of employer opposition to unionization and illegal conduct in union organizing campaigns, National Labor Relations Board elections are being abandoned as the dominant mechanism used to determine whether or not workers want to be represented by a union (Brudney, 2005). Instead, labor peace agreements have become much more of the norm.

Often negotiated alongside community benefits agreements, these labor peace side agreements come in several variants, including neutrality agreements and majority sign-up procedures. *Neutrality agreements* are agreements between employers and unions in which employers agree to remain neutral on the question of unionization during an organizing campaign. These types of agreements set restrictions on the kind of conduct, such as speech, in which employers and unions can engage during a specified length of time. *Card check or majority sign-up procedures* allow workers to decide on union representation by signing a union authorization card. In these cases, an employer agrees to recognize a union as the exclusive representative of employees if a majority of workers sign authorization cards. Usually, a mutually agreed-upon neutral third-party counts the cards and makes a determination as to their legitimacy. Neutrality, card-check and labor peace agreements diminish employer hostility and opposition and enable workers a fair and hostile-free environment for freedom of association. Thus far, variants of labor peace agreements have been included in dozens of community benefits campaigns affecting over 150,000 workers (L. Moody, personal communication, July 18, 2008).

Beyond these core employment-related provisions, CBAs vary from development to development, reflecting both the specific impact of the development on its surrounding communities (e.g., sound-proofing provisions as part of the Los Angeles Airport CBA) and the particular needs of the communities involved (e.g., affordable housing, downtown parking, and green space as part of the Staples Center CBA). What is common about this diversity, however, is the holistic approach to community benefits that these CBAs reflect. For example, many CBA coalitions have rallied around both economic and environment issues, eschewing what they view as a false divide between jobs or the environment. This approach reflects, in large part, the experience of many coalitional members' past and ongoing involvement with environmental justice campaigns (e.g., an ongoing project of AGENDA, a South Los Angeles community organization and LAX CBA coalitional member organization, focuses on developing green jobs for inner city communities of color). Not simply satisfied with training for and placement into living wage jobs, community residents have demanded that developers address the various ways in which development should benefit the community while minimizing its negative impacts.

ANALYZING COMMUNITY BENEFITS AGREEMENTS

Regulatory Context and CBAs

In a context of neo-liberalism, what mechanisms are available for ordinary people to have a voice in what happens in their lives, especially in their workplaces and communities? In the case of neighborhoods and communities, Gilda Haas, Executive Director of Strategic Alliance for a Just Economy (SAJE), argues that residents can influence community development in three ways: they can do it themselves, they can look to the public sector, or they can negotiate directly with the private sector (personal communication, June 17, 2006). In the context of the workplace, workers can influence their wages and working conditions in similar fashion: through syndicalist enterprises, state regulation, and collective bargaining. As a tactical mechanism, CBAs primarily reflect the third approach: they rest on a private negotiation with employers and developers rather than on public regulation. As such, CBAs as legal contracts rely upon tort law for their enforceability and "teeth." The legal specificities of CBAs are a critical factor of their success, and we direct readers to an emerging legal literature on CBAs for an in-depth discussion of these specifics (to date, most of this scholarship has been authored by lawyers directly involved in crafting Partnership CBAs, e.g., Beach, 2007/2008 and Gross, 2007/2008).

Nonetheless, CBAs are not simply legal contracts nor policy outputs that stand alone, apart from a political or regulatory context. CBAs reflect larger political dynamics of neo-liberalism even as they challenge these dynamics. They are influenced by local contexts of public regulation, and they sometimes complement and help move forward economic justice strategies focused on public regulation, such as improved public oversight of development projects. These regulatory dimensions of CBAs and their campaigns illustrate how political and regulatory contexts condition tactics and strategies available to economic justice activists, but also how activists can wield these same tactics and strategies to re-shape political and policy contexts. In addition to leveraging immediate change, such outcomes of CBA campaigns often lay the groundwork for more expansive change in the future.

Much like the advent of environmental "good neighbor agreements," CBAs were developed by activists in the context of few regulations on private capital and nearly no redistributive mandates for urban development (Lewis & Henkels, 1996). Though scholars describe the current and recent era of urban development as neo-liberal (Hackworth, 2007; Harvey, 2005), it shares much with past cycles of urban growth and capital accumulation (Sites, Chaskin, & Parks, 2007; Teaford, 1990). As in the past, city governments continue to demand little of developers. Tax breaks and subsidies are often no-strings rewards to private capital for projects that would have been built anyway. Past efforts to use subsidies as an incentive to support development with redistributive outcomes have largely fallen by the wayside, or sit idly on the books with no political will to back their implementation (Smith, 1988; Weber, 2002).

Given the herculean task of passing new regulation in such a climate, community and labor activists turned to a strategy of direct negotiation: this delimited the arena of political contestation and involved community members most directly impacted by a proposed development, and thus most willing to engage in a protracted organizing campaign. Because CBAs are privately negotiated legal contracts between a circumscribed group of actors (ultimately the contract signatories), CBAs resemble independent, privatized market mechanisms. As such, they can be described as neoliberal, market-based and decidedly non-public policies. Yet CBAs have been utilized in organizing campaigns in such a way as to challenge the idea that development is autonomous from a larger socio-political context. This involves conceptualizing the idea of development as dependent upon communities and the city, which deserve concrete benefits in return. Further, most CBA organizing campaigns articulate the impact of development as stretching beyond a specific site and its adjacent neighborhoods, a sentiment reflected in targeted hiring definitions that include all low-income residents of a city as eligible beneficiaries. Thus, while CBAs have emerged within constraints dictated by the larger political dynamics of a neo-liberal development environment and federal inaction around broader issues of inequality, key CBA components tend to challenge those constraints by broadening beneficiaries and mandating equity-oriented returns.

Though CBAs are, at their core, private contracts, they nonetheless are influenced by local contexts of public regulation. Living wage provisions readily illustrate this point: in cities with living wage ordinances, CBAs reinforce the implementation of the ordinance and sometimes build upon its precedence to extend living wage coverage to a broader set of workers. In Denver, a CBA campaign never resulted in a CBA because community demands were directly incorporated into public regulation of the proposed Gates development (L. Moody, personal communication, July 18, 2008). In this way, the idea and organizing behind a CBA led directly to changes in public regulation and policy, though the extant regulatory mechanism shaped how and what demands were ultimately incorporated. Even the general outcome of the Denver CBA campaign was dependent upon the local regulatory context. Denver activists were able to push for the incorporation of community demands into a development agreement between the city and the developer because Colorado state law allows such agreements. Many states, however, do not authorize local municipalities to enter into developer agreements (Salkin & Lavine, 2007, p. 131, fn. 5).

More influential than these substantive regulatory influences, however, is the tactical leverage that the public regulatory apparatus provides CBA activists in their organizing campaigns. In Los Angeles especially, activists have learned to leverage technocratic planning processes to build political bargaining power with developers. Public participatory planning forums allow CBA activists to speak as impacted community members and to articulate their demands for community benefits. Rather than simply providing feedback to city planning staff, CBA activists utilize such forums as public claims-making spaces, as organizing venues, and as political pressure points.

Importantly, the environmental impact review process required by California state law creates some transparency around the development process often not available in other cities or states (such as Chicago, Illinois) by providing public access to information about a proposed development. By making plans available to the public, environmental review functions as an often critical source of information for community residents. CBA activists can utilize the process to slow up the development review process, thereby gaining more time in which to develop an organizing campaign. Environmental review can also be utilized to gain political power: CBA activists may raise legitimate environment concerns through the process, signaling their technical ability and capacity to engage the developer on all fronts—a show of their strength as a formidable political opponent, or ally. In these ways, CBA activists utilize urban governance processes and the local regulatory context as points of purchase upon which to leverage their public, and thus political, power as citizens—one of the very few resources available to community groups when taking on resource-rich developers (see Beach, 2007/2008, for more examples specific to the regulatory code of California and Los Angeles that provide leverage over new development decisions for community actors).

Often the short-term focus of such tactics is to bring the developer to the (private) negotiating table. But CBAs sometimes complement and help move forward economic justice strategies focused on public regulation, such as improved public oversight of development projects. One of the most significant examples to date is the passage of the Los Angeles Superstore Ordinance in 2004 that mandates a community economic impact review for every proposed "big box" retail development in economic assistance zones (M. Janis, personal communication, June 17, 2006). This ordinance stipulates that building approval be given only if a store "would not materially adversely affect the economic welfare of the Impact Area" (Ord. No. 176,166 at www.lacity.org/council/cd13/houscommecdev/cd13houscommecdev239629363_05042005.pdf). This review process provides yet another window upon development before it receives political approval and codifies expectations of beneficial development into the local regulatory context.

Leslie Moody, executive director of the Partnership for Working Families, describes how other Partnership affiliates have moved from CBA to public policy campaigns:

> Most of these groups started doing community benefits campaigns, that was the sort of founding and it's a great way to build the coalition in a city that can think about power differently. So we still really stick to community benefits as a launch pad for our new organizations because they pull people together, help them understand how development decisions get made, how the city is structured, who really has power and influence. It's a really good tool for building the coalition. But a lot of the groups then moved on to do bigger policy campaigns. The Denver community benefits campaign turned into a city-wide prevailing wage reform coalition that a lot of rank-and-file construction workers got involved in. We've also been involved in the city's housing task force to ramp up affordable housing investment on the part of both the public and private sectors. (personal communication, July 18, 2008)

In these instances, community groups were able to expand their political domain of engagement from the delimited arena of a single development to the broader arena of public regulation and more expansive terrain of urban politics. These CBA campaigns functioned as stepping stones, albeit critical power building events, to bigger and somewhat more universalistic policy campaigns.

Though political contexts condition tactics and strategies available to economic justice activists, these CBA campaigns indicate how activists can wield such tools to re-shape political and policy contexts. In addition to leveraging immediate change, such re-shaping often lays the groundwork for more expansive change in the future (but see Gornick & Meyer, 1998, for a discussion of how policy victories can also curtail movement activities). The factor common to these cases of political domain expansion, however, is that all occurred in contexts of sustained grassroots organizing.

Organizing, Politics, and CBAs

CBAs are most significantly *political* outcomes that rely centrally on the organizing power of the community for their emergence, implementation, and enforcement. Strong CBAs result from carefully crafted organizing strategies that bring together community and labor constituencies with overlapping interests and that engage both "insider" and "outsider" tactics (Luce, 2004). These CBA campaigns represent an innovative hybrid form of community action, one in which social action tactics are utilized in conjunction with research and community development expertise (Sites, Chaskin, & Parks, 2007, p. 535). For example, CBA activists may leverage technocratic planning processes by both contributing expert research and by flooding a city planner's office with community members in order to raise awareness and gain support for their demands. The success of Partnership CBAs derives in part from this strategic model and the effective coordination of the disparate tactics and skill sets that such a hybrid model demands.

The model's success, however, hinges on both the ability of coalitional partners to organize and "turn out" their members, whether to a community meeting, a protest, or the ballot box. Ultimately, the strategic politics behind a CBA campaign centers on the dissensus organizing power of community and labor in order to secure a concessionary agreement with developers (Cloward & Piven, 1999). Though negotiating the CBA requires an altogether different mode of engagement that is much more deliberative in nature (Baxamusa, 2008; Fung & Wright, 2001), the political power behind the CBA campaign rests in residents' organized dissent. In short, a CBA as a redistributive mechanism is only as good as the organizing behind it.

At the center of most Partnership CBAs is an alliance between community organizations and labor unions, often aided in coordination by the city's central labor council (CLC). Leslie Moody, the Partnership's current executive director and former president of the Denver Area Labor Federation, argues that labor brings an established political repertoire to CBA campaigns that is often instrumental to gaining political support within city government. Tactically, such political support often provides the critical point of leverage that a CBA coalition has over a developer—a project must obtain land use and other public approval in order to be built. Additionally, labor functions as a critical mobilization partner, ready and able to turn out its members in large numbers. "On the whole, if they [unions] have a progressive vision and a membership base that reflects the community, they can be a really responsive organization with a built-in base that's self-funding" (L. Moody, personal communication, July 18, 2008).

Though labor unions play an important political and mobilization role in winning CBA campaigns, they often are not the lead actors within a coalition. Because labor law disallows a CBA to address employment concerns of workers covered by a collective bargaining agreement, unions participate in CBA coalitional organizing efforts for a number of reasons unrelated to the direct benefit of their members. Though unions may participate out of self-interest in order to pressure employers on contract issues, they often use their power to influence these same employers to negotiate a CBA in order to win better working conditions for workers who are not union members. For example, Miguel Contreras, former president of the Los Angeles Labor Federation, stopped short of signing negotiated labor agreements on behalf of five unions with the Staples Center developers until they signed off on the Staples CBA (Meyerson, 2006). In such examples, labor's efforts are largely solidarity efforts in support of community residents (often union members' families) and other workers, but solidarity efforts that nevertheless help build labor's power politically. In terms of urban politics, labor can then look to allied community organizations and residents for support in local electoral and policy efforts (Eimer & Ness, 2001).

The political organizing power of the labor-community coalition behind a CBA campaign is perhaps most critical to the implementation and enforcement of a CBA. To paraphrase the research findings of Weber (2002), CBAs as "better contracts" do not in themselves make better community benefits a reality. But strong political backing behind a good CBA can make these benefits a reality. Such a situation is hardly a surprise, as extensive policy implementation research predicts just such a scenario (e.g., Brodkin, 1990; Luce, 2004). Given the private nature of most CBAs, community-driven oversight of a CBA's implementation is essential as no other actor, such as the public sector, has any regulatory power to direct implementation.

Yet the work of monitoring a CBA differs little from what community organizations often have had to do to ensure implementation of public policies. Many community groups involved in CBAs draw upon their experience monitoring city living wage ordinances to develop a finely honed monitoring strategy around their CBA (see Luce, 2004, for an illuminating analysis of how community groups have participated in the implementation of living wage ordinances across the country). LAANE, for example, has successfully employed both insider and outsider tactics to oversee enforcement of Los Angeles' living wage ordinance, such as participation on the city's living wage task force and protest rallies at noncompliant employers. This experience has contributed significantly to the implementation acumen evident within LAANE-negotiated CBAs, as well as LAANE's external monitoring activities. As the convener of the Figueroa Coalition for Economic Justice, SAJE (Strategic Actions for a Just Economy) has been especially involved in the implementation process surrounding the Staples CBA, going so far as to help craft the job training program in partnership with Los Angeles City College (G. Haas, personal communication, June 17, 2006).

Crucially, implementation and enforcement of a CBA depends upon the continued organizing strength of the CBA coalition and its partners. In the end, CBA campaigns cannot be one-off organizing drives—the real success of a CBA lies not in its winning but in realizing its benefits. The long, often mundane, process of implementation depends upon the continued efforts of community residents and the maintenance of the CBA coalition. This sustained engagement obtained when CBAs come out of organizing efforts driven by coalitions that view a CBA not as a strategy in and of itself, but as one tactic within a broader strategy for accountable development and economic justice. A model example, SAJE and the Figueroa Coalition engage a comprehensive strategic approach that "combines changing policies, negotiating agreements, and developing alternative institutions," all premised upon a singular commitment to community organizing (Leavitt, 2006, p. 258). Ultimately, CBAs derive their effectiveness from a larger accountable development movement grounded in sustained community action and organization.

ASSESSMENT & CONCLUSION

Through the use of CBAs and their focus on high-road, quality jobs as a key component of urban development, the new accountable development movement brings economic inequality and redistribution claims to the center of contemporary urban politics. CBAs do, however, have weaknesses and limitations. They sacrifice scale for scope—they specify a broad range of benefits for a relatively small number of beneficiaries. CBAs rest primarily on politics rather than the law to monitor and enforce implementation, and by doing so, burden community organizations with the tasks of monitoring and implementation for which they often are ill-equipped or under-resourced to tackle alone. Significantly, CBAs sidestep the regulatory power of the state that may be most necessary to make development accountable to low-income communities of color (Scholz & Wang, 2006).

And because CBAs are only as good as the organizing behind them, CBAs are at great risk of being wielded as tools of cooptation by developers and elected officials. Developer- and elected official-led CBAs, while not inherently bad, are suspect in that the developer or elected official is able to exercise control over who gets to negotiate the CBA—even selecting upon a criterion of minimal feasible participation—and its terms from the beginning. These CBAs also tend to be weaker based on the criteria discussed earlier. Developer- and elected official-led CBAs tend to be narrower in scope, have lower levels of transparency (often they are not available to the public), and have little oversight mechanisms for monitoring and enforcement (see Gross, 2007/2008, for a discussion of three such CBAs in New York). Organizing post-hoc is difficult; CBAs "won" with little mobilization on the part of the community itself lack sufficient political power to meet the developer at the negotiating table on equal footing and to engage in deliberative, participatory decision making (Fung & Wright, 2001). Successful implementation under such conditions of asymmetrical power is questionable (Shapiro, 1999).

Economic context largely determines the use of CBAs: they work only under conditions of economic and urban growth. CBAs depend upon the political leverage afforded to community residents through the planning process—developers need zoning permits, and sometimes subsidies, to move forward. Community actors can hold up this process—their key point of political leverage—but only *before* the development is built. Bluntly put, this leverage only exists because new development is being proposed at all. Thus, in contexts of disinvestment and economic decline characterized by the absence of new development (i.e., most low-income urban neighborhoods of color), CBAs are not a viable community development strategy. CBAs are structured specifically in relation to development and were designed with the express purpose of holding new development accountable.

Even under conditions of economic growth, CBAs may be limited, strategically, in their applicability to all new development. CBAs particularly suit unique, high-value development projects such as sports stadiums (e.g., the Staples Center in Los Angeles or the Penguins Arena in Pittsburgh) and other specialized entertainment venues (e.g., the Academy Awards theater that anchors the development attached to the Hollywood and Highland CBA). Locations suitable for such development are of special value relative to other sites in the city or locale, providing activists with unusual leverage through which to exact extractions on capital through a CBA. This means that CBA campaigns have less political leverage and are less likely to succeed around proposed developments of a more mundane nature for which special locational criteria are minimal (e.g., multiple locations in a city may equally meet the requirements for a grocery store).

At their best, CBAs challenge the public regulatory apparatus to do more, as long as that message is explicitly part of the campaign through which the CBA is advocated. If not, then a CBA risks being no more than a privatized mechanism through which some residents can gain highly individualized benefits with little to no claims made to public policy and public oversight. Operating as a kind of NIMBYism in reverse (benefits "only in my backyard"), such use of a CBA fails to function even as "neo-syndicalist" (Sites, 2007, p. 2645) given its ad hoc, one-off nature that foregoes the enforcing power of a CBA—the continued threat of organized political resistance.

The ongoing campaign led by LAANE against the British grocery conglomerate, Tesco, illustrates this point. In confronting the prospect of Tesco moving into the Los Angeles region, LAANE initially led a coalitional CBA campaign that demanded a commitment from Tesco to locate new grocery stores in "food desert" neighborhoods. Tesco refused to sign a CBA with the coalition. The tactical move away from a site-specific negotiated CBA to a sector- or company-specific CBA (Tesco is not simply seeking to locate one store in Los Angeles, but many) may expand the political terrain of conflict too far for the purposes of a privately negotiated CBA. But LAANE has persevered by engaging the policy arena in its bid to ensure equitable grocery development that addresses the grocery needs of Los Angeles' lower-income residents. As Elliott Petty, LAANE's Retail Project Director, explains:

> They [Tesco] were saying good things to the community. We said this should be the easiest community benefits agreement in the world. . . . Tesco promised to talk about their community benefits program, talk about making their commitments real. After we did our action [in November 2007 when the coalition presented its CBA demands], that agenda completely changed . . . [With no CBA] we strategically decided that we were going to engage with them on the political level. (personal communication, June 20, 2008)

LAANE is currently organizing in support of a city ordinance that would require a grocery development impact review for all new proposed stores, similar to the superstore ordinance passed by Los Angeles City Council in 2004.

While the Tesco campaign reveals the limits of CBAs in some cases of new development, we end on this example to stress the importance of CBAs as a tactic best employed as part of a larger accountable development and economic justice movement and one that ultimately looks to institutionalize community benefits as "non-negotiable rights" within the public regulation of urban development (Lewis & Henkels, 1996). When initially defeated in its CBA campaign with Tesco, the community coalition in Los Angeles quickly turned to other tactics, particularly those within the sphere of public regulation, in its effort to gain equity for Los Angeles's most disadvantaged residents and neighborhoods. Such a strategic move is indicative of the dynamism of the new accountable development movement and its commitment to the larger goals of economic justice through broad scale organizing rather than through a narrow allegiance to a single technocratic approach or tactic. Recent evidence of such a commitment indicates that under the right conditions, ordinary people can, indeed, make development equitable and bring about economic justice in their communities.

In this article, we have described key features of community benefits agreements, highlighting their employment-related provisions while situating them as part of a larger strategic repertoire of redistributive tactics advanced by labor-community coalitions within the larger new accountable development movement. In response to growing inequality, the proliferation of low-wage jobs, and patterns of uneven development in disadvantaged communities, CBA campaigns have emerged as the latest tactic of the NADM to redistribute the benefits of new urban development to less-advantaged communities, residents and workers. We explicated three key regulatory dimensions of CBAs: they rest on privately negotiated agreements with employers and developers rather than on public regulation but are nonetheless influenced by local regulatory contexts; they reflect the larger political dynamics of neo-liberalism even as they challenge these dynamics by mandating the redistributive outcomes; they sometimes move forward economic justice strategies aimed at public regulation and oversight of development project. Finally, we argued that the strongest CBAs result from strategic organizing campaigns that utilize a range of political tactics including the dissensus organizing power of labor-community coalitions.

NOTES

1. Over 140 local jurisdictions have passed living wage ordinances since 1995. See, http://www.livingwagecampaign.org, for the most up to date number.

2. Twenty-three states currently have minimum wage standards higher than the federal rate. See, http://www.dol.gov/esa/minwage/america.htm, for the most up to date number.

3. For more analysis on the two issues of lack of jobs and job quality in Black communities, see, Steven Pitts, 2008, "Job Quality and Black Workers: An Examination of the San Francisco Bay Area, Los Angeles, Chicago and New York," UC Berkeley Labor Center, http://laborcenter.berkeley.edu/blackworkers/blackworkers_07.pdf

REFERENCES

Baxamusa, M. H. (2008). Empowering communities through deliberation: The model of community benefits agreements. *Journal of Planning Education and Research, 27*(3), 261–276.

Beach, B. S. (2007/2008). Strategies and lessons from the Los Angeles community benefits experience. *Journal of Affordable Housing, 17*(1–2), 77–112.

Brodkin, E. (1990). Implementation as policy politics. In J. Palumbo & D. Calista (Eds.), *Implementation and the policy process: Opening up the black box* (pp. 107–118). New York: Greenwood Press.

Bronfenbrenner, K., & Juravich, T. (1995, February). The impact of employer opposition on unioncertification win rates: A private-public sector comparison (Working Paper No. 113). Washington, DC:. Economic Policy Institute.

Brudney, J. J. (2005). Neutrality agreements and card check recognition: Prospects for changing paradigms. *Iowa Law Review, 90*, 819–886.

Caftel, B., & Haywood, A. (1994). Making Section 3 work: Employment training and job opportunities for low-income people. *Clearinghouse Review, 27*, 1336–1341.

Cloward, R. A., & Piven, F. F. (1999). Disruptive dissensus: People and power in the industrial age. In J. Rothman (Ed.), *Reflections on community organization: Enduring themes and critical issues* (pp. 165–193). Itasca, IL: Peacock.

Eimer, S., & Ness, I. (2001). *Central labor councils and the revival of American unionism: Organizing for justice in our communities.* Armonk, NY: M. E. Sharpe.

Fung, A., & Wright, E. O. (2001). Deepening democracy: Innovations in empowered participatory governance. *Politics & Society, 29*(1), 5–41.

Gornick, J., & Meyer, D. (1998). Changing political opportunity: The anti-rape movement and public policy. *Journal of Policy History, 10*(4), 367–398.

Gross, J. (2007/2008). Community benefits agreements: Definitions, values, and legal enforceability. *Journal of Affordable Housing, 17*(1–2), 35–58.

Gross, J., LeRoy, G., & Janis-Aparicio, M. (2005). *Community benefits agreements: Making development projects accountable.* Los Angeles: Good Jobs First and the California Partnership for Working Families. Retrieved June 1, 2008, from http://www.laane.org/docs/research/CBA_Handbook_2005.pdf

Hackworth, J. (2007). *The neoliberal city: Governance, ideology, and development in American urbanism.* Ithaca, NY: Cornell University Press.

Harvey, D. (2005). *A brief history of neoliberalism.* New York: Oxford University Press.

Lafer, G. (2002). *The job training charade.* Ithaca: Cornell University Press.

Leavitt, J. (2006). Linking housing to community economic development with community benefits agreements: The case of the Figueroa Corridor Coalition for Economic Justice. In P. Ong & A. Loukaitou-Sideris (Eds.), *Jobs and economic development in minority communities* (pp. 257–276). Philadelphia, PA: Temple University Press.

Lewis, S., & Henkels, D. (1996). Good neighbor agreements: A tool for environmental and social justice. *Social Justice, 23*(4), 134–151.

Logan, J. R., & Molotch, H. L. (1987). *Urban Fortunes: The Political Economy of Place.* Berkeley: University of California Press.

Luce, S. (2004). *Fighting for a living wage.* Ithaca: Cornell University.

Martin, I. (2001). Dawn of the living wage: The diffusion of a redistributive municipal policy. *Urban Affairs Review, 36*(4), 470–496.

Melendez, E., & Harrison, B. (1998). Matching the disadvantaged to job opportunities: Structural explanations for the past successes of the Center for Employment Training. *Economic Development Quarterly, 12*(1), 3–11.

Meyerson, H. (2006). No justice, no growth: How Los Angeles is making big-time developers create decent jobs [Electronic version]. *American Prospect, 17*(11), 39–42. Retrieved August 5, 2008, from http://www.prospect.org/cs/articles?article=no_justice_no_growth

Mollenkopf, J. H. (1983). *The contested city.* Princeton: Princeton University Press.

Molina, F. (1998). *Making connections: A study of employment linkage programs.* Washington, DC: Center for Community Change.

Orr, M. (Ed.). (2007). *Transforming the city: Community organizing and the challenge of political change.* Lawrence, KS: University of Kansas Press.

Partnership for Working Families. (2008). Retrieved December 15, 2008, from http://www.communitybenefits.org/article.php?list=type&type=46

Peterson, P. E. (1981). *City limits.* Chicago, IL: University of Chicago Press.

Salkin, P., & Lavine, S. (2007). Negotiating for social justice and the promise of community benefits agreements: Case studies of current and developing agreements. *Journal of Affordable Housing, 17*(1–2), 113–144.

Sassen, S. (1998). *Globalization and its discontents.* New York: New Press.

Scholtz, J. T., & Wang, C. L. (2006). Cooptation or transformation? Local policy networks and federal regulatory enforcement. *American Journal of Political Science, 50*(1), 81–97.

Shapiro, I. (1998). Enough of deliberation: Politics is about interests and power. In S. Macedo (Ed.), *Deliberative politics: Essays on democracy and disagreement* (pp. 28–38). Oxford, UK: Oxford University Press.

Sites, W. (2007). Beyond trenches and grassroots? Reflections on urban mobilization, fragmentation, and the anti-Wal-Mart campaign in Chicago. *Environment and Planning A, 39*(11), 2632–2651.

Sites, W., Chaskin, R., & Parks, V. (2007). Reframing community practice for the 21st century: Multiple traditions, multiple challenges. *Journal of Urban Affairs, 29*(5), 519–541.

Smith, M. P. (1988). The uses of linked development policies in U.S. cities. In M. Parkinson, B. Foley & D. Judd (Eds.), *Regenerating the cities: The U.K. crisis and the American experience*. Manchester, UK and Boston, MA: Manchester University & Scott Foresman.

Squires, G. D. (1994). *Capital in communities Black and White: The intersections of race, class and uneven development*. Albany: SUNY Press.

Teaford, J.C. (1990). *The rough road to renaissance: Urban revitalization in America 1940–1985*. Baltimore, MD: Johns Hopkins University Press.

Turner, L., & Cornfield, D. (Eds.). (2007). *Labor in the new urban battlegrounds: Local solidarity in a global economy*. Ithaca, NY: Cornell University Press.

U.S. Department of Housing and Urban Development (2008). Retrieved on December 15, 2008, from http://www.hud.gov/offices/fheo/section3/section3.cfm

Weber, R. (2002). Do better contracts make better economic development incentives? *Journal of the American Planning Association, 68*(1), 43–55.

Evolving Strategies of Labor-Community Coalition-Building

DAVID DOBBIE

*Labor Studies Center, Wayne State University, Detroit, Michigan,
and Building Partnerships, USA*

*Multiracial labor-community coalitions have attracted considerable
attention from scholars and activists based on their potential to
rebuild local working-class movements, but we lack a systematic
understanding of their emergence and evolution. This article
explores the divergent development of collaborative efforts in
Chicago, Milwaukee, and Pittsburgh following successful campaign
to pass a living wage ordinance in each city during the late 1990s.
Activists' capacity to bridge cultural differences and develop new
structures and strategies within an intermediary organizational level
is the key factor in explaining the emergence of durable coalitions.*

INTRODUCTION: FRAGMENTED WORKING CLASS MOVEMENTS IN THE AGE OF NEOLIBERALISM

Economic justice movements have endured many setbacks over the last
thirty years as reenergized corporate elites have pushed governments
toward a neoliberal version of capitalism. Movements rooted in working-
class communities have pushed back against the erosion of social rights and

This research was supported by National Science Foundation Dissertation Improvement
Grant #0623084, as well as the University of Michigan School of Social Work, Department of
Sociology, and Rackham Graduate School.

I received tremendous feedback and support on this project from activists in Pittsburgh,
Chicago, and Milwaukee, as well as Michael Reisch, Howard Kimeldorf, David Reynolds, Ian
Robinson, Julia Paley, Rachel Meyer, Greg Pratt, and Alice Gates.

marketization, but their success has been limited by internal fragmentation. Particularly in wealthy countries like the United States, most organizing has been contained in "silos" restricted by organizational type, neighborhood, race or ethnicity, or specific issue. From community organizing to labor, movements have experienced decreasing power and influence over this period as their ability to coalesce around common goals has atrophied.

Still, there are signs of change in the air. New alliances of movements are increasingly emerging around the world. The sense of neoliberal inevitability that led Margaret Thatcher to claim that "there is no alternative" in the 1980s has foundered amidst mounting signs of economic and social meltdown, but it remains uncertain how resistance to the crumbling "Washington consensus" will develop, or what will replace it. While the legitimacy of neoliberalism has been shaken at the international level, regional economic development discussions in the United States remain dominated by corporate interests. The left has largely ceded this ground, leaving conversations of regional planning focused on enhancing the "business climate" rather than equity and social justice. This has become increasingly significant in recent decades as decentralization of government power has combined with economic trends to make regions an ever more important level of intervention.

Many local organizers are trying to climb out of this rut and build the power to reshape their regions along more equitable lines. Innovative strategies have emerged from experimentation across the country, including an upsurge in labor-community coalition building since the 1980s. The first widely noted sign of this trend came in the early 1990s, when a Service Employees International Union local in Los Angeles made up of largely undocumented immigrant janitors pulled off a historic victory by utilizing community networks and creative tactics to put direct pressure on building owners. Over the next decade, this emerging movement has demonstrated a new willingness to treat members of the working class as "whole people" with multiple, interlocking interests. Churches have become more willing to take a stand on behalf of their members' work conditions; community organizations to look beyond neighborhood boundaries; and unions to use their political clout to address members' interests in clean air, affordable housing, and public transportation (Waldinger et al., 1996). While labor and community organizing are often separated from each other, internally divided, and struggling to adjust to the context of neoliberal capitalism, alliances of unions and community organizations remain the most viable potential foundation of economic justice struggles in the United States.

This article compares emerging working-class movements[1] in three deindustrializing U.S. cities: Pittsburgh, Milwaukee, and Chicago. Following a string of ad hoc mobilizations against plant closings and other crises in the 1980s, activists in each region tried to "get out in front" of issues by building a broader base of power through labor-community coalitions. As part of this effort, multiracial labor-community coalitions came together to pass living wage ordinances in the mid-1990s, but the trajectories of the three regions have since diverged. Similarly to other regions across the country, these efforts ranged from ambitiously broad coalitions to more loosely linked intermediary organizations playing a coordinating and consolidating role between campaigns (Tattersall & Reynolds, 2007).

Their relative success in achieving policy victories is of course due to variations in political and economic context between regions, but also to their adaptations to that context. This article documents strategic evolution in three key spheres of activity: organizational structures, movement cultures, and political strategies.

Overview of Cases

Although Chicago is much larger than the others, these regions are similar in many ways. Both Chicago and Milwaukee are the dominant cities in primarily rural and suburban states, nestled in the corner of their states along the shores of Lake Michigan (and Pittsburgh is so far from Philadelphia that it plays a similar role as the de facto capital of Western Pennsylvania). Each continues to rely heavily on manufacturing to drive their regional economies, though the number of jobs in the sector has declined sharply. As shown by Table 1, deindustrialization has led to similarly high levels of unemployment and poverty in each region.

All three are racially segregated and have similar proportions of residents renting their homes, leading to roughly similar economic geographies. Pittsburgh is less racially diverse than the other two cities, where white residents make up only a bare plurality. And while Milwaukee and Chicago have gained many Latino immigrants in recent decades, Pittsburgh has remained basically biracial. While local variations exist, organizers in these cities and across the country have followed a broadly similar process in building a regional working-class power base:

TABLE 1 Economic Indicators by Region, 2006

Region (MSA)	Unemployment rate	Poverty rate
Milwaukee	6.1%	13.0%
Pittsburgh	5.9%	11.7%
Chicago	7.5%	11.9%

Note. From American Communities Survey 2006. Retrieved March 12, 2009, from http://www.factfinder.census.gov.

1. "Map out" the local movement infrastructure and diagnose gaps.
2. Knit together a diverse core group of leaders with a shared vision.
3. Create bridging institutions to serve as network hubs and provide technical assistance.
4. Seek out economic justice campaigns to help fuse together a broad constituency.
5. Link these campaigns to electoral politics and a long-term vision (Dobbie, 2009).

Numerous opportunities for labor-community collaboration have presented themselves in recent decades. These include large, publicly-subsidized construction projects; private sector workers facing aggressive employer campaigns and public sector workers fending off privatization, outsourcing, and cutbacks; companies demanding concessions and public subsidies; and campaigns to pass living wage ordinances and other proactive economic justice initiatives. I spent several months in each city during 2006 doing archival research and interviews with coalition participants[2]. Their stories reflect efforts to adapt their organizing models to changing circumstances and emerging needs, and thus provide lessons to generalize other regions.

As shown by Table 2, Pittsburgh and Milwaukee seemed to have a head start on Chicago, forming broad and vibrant coalitions in the early 1990s. Both the Campaign for a Sustainable Milwaukee (CSM) and Pittsburgh's Alliance for Progressive Action (APA) united a broad swath of the local left under one roof and ran several successful campaigns. Both the CSM and APA sought to use living wage campaigns to deepen relationships between unions and community groups in the late 1990s. Around the same time, Chicago organizers pulled together a living wage coalition. Only Milwaukee was immediately successful, passing a string of ordinances and tackling even larger projects. Pittsburgh and Chicago both suffered painful losses in their living wage campaigns; Chicago's coalition bounced back to win a city living wage the following year while the issue (and the APA) died in Pittsburgh. Chicago's Jobs and Living Wage Coalition not only produced a campaign victory, it also led to the formation of the Grassroots Collaborative and a string of increasingly ambitious campaigns. In 2006, they took on Wal-Mart, the Chamber of Commerce, and Mayor Daley in an effort to create a "Big Box Living Wage" and are now challenging the Mayor again over development plans for the 2016 Olympics.

Discussion: Evolving Strategies to Facilitate Movement Emergence

Chicago's relatively quick progress from fragmented parochialism to such broad and powerful campaigns show that coalition-building requires more than just accumulated effort—Milwaukee and Pittsburgh's head start would otherwise have translated into a continuing advantage. While it would also

TABLE 2 Major Collaborative Efforts in Each City

City	Name	Dates	Key partners	Major campaigns
Pittsburgh	Alliance for Progressive Action (APA)	1991–2002	SEIU, Mon Valley Unemployed Committee, United Electrical Workers	Citizens Police Review Board, Living Wage
	Pittsburgh UNITED	2007–present	SEIU, Mon Valley Unemployed Committee, Northside Common Ministries, ACORN, PIIN, UNITE HERE!	Community benefits agreements for stadiums and related developments
Milwaukee	Campaign for a Sustainable Milwaukee (CSM)	1993–2000	Labor Council, UW-Center on Wisconsin Strategy, Esperanza Unida, Laborers Union, Transit Union	Living Wage, Convention Center, Jobs Initiative
	Good Jobs and Livable Neighborhoods (GJLN)	2003–present	MICAH, Painters Union, 9 to 5 (National Association of Working Women), UW-Center for Urban Economic Development	Park East Development Community Benefits Agreement
Chicago	Chicago Jobs and Living Wages Coalition/ Grassroots Collaborative	1997–present	SEIU, ACORN, Chicago Coalition of the Homeless, IL Hunger Coalition, UFCW, Metro Seniors, Chicago Federation of Labor, UNITE HERE!	Living Wage, immigrant drivers' licenses, state minimum wage, KidCare, Big Box Living Wage

be reasonable to suggest that economic conditions created different pathways for organizing, Chicago's unemployment and poverty rates are comparable to, if not higher than, Milwaukee and Pittsburgh's. These three cities have weathered deindustrialization more successfully than places like Detroit, where the degree of capital flight significantly impedes such organizing efforts.

If the differing trajectories of each region cannot be explained away by past events or the regional political economy, it suggests that their approach to coalition building played some role. These cases show that working-class organizers are faced with the daunting task of coordinating activity within three interrelated spheres to foster strong local movements:

1. Building a strong organizational infrastructure,
2. Developing a transformative culture of solidarity, and
3. Melding together several different tactical forms of political power.

There has been a well-documented decline in membership organizations (whether workplace- or community-based) bringing working-class Americans together. Even fewer intermediary organizations link such groups together. In fact, relationships are often shaped by mistrust across racial, neighborhood, or organizational boundaries, with a particularly long history of conflict between unions and communities of color. Within labor-community coalitions, community organizations often feel taken for granted while unions are frustrated by the lack of clear structure and authority (Krinsky & Reese, 2006). Political strategies have also become more narrowly delimited since the 1970s, as many unions and community organizations came to define themselves solely as "insiders" or "outsiders." Political interventions tend to be focused on short-term goals and remain within narrow strategic repertoires.

In sum, working-class organizing has generally become confined within silos and has weakened over the past several decades. Amenta (2006) claims that organizers' ability to match their organizational forms and political strategies to the context is the most important variable explaining differential movement outcomes, suggesting that this narrowing has been one factor limiting the success of the U.S. left. It thus follows that recent signs of rebirth have resulted from efforts to rebuild and reconnect unions and community organizations.

SPHERE 1: EVOLVING FORMS OF ORGANIZATIONAL INFRASTRUCTURE

Local working-class movements include three main types of structures: membership-based organizations, networks that link these organizations together, and intermediary organizations that provide technical assistance. Working class residents of these cities belong to organizations in three main sectors: unions, churches, and community groups. Coalitions in each city were most successful when they included at least one organization within each sector actively engaging its members in broad economic justice campaigns. Since such ready-made coalition partners often do not exist in a region, the reform of existing bodies and/or new organizing is crucial.

In the 1960s and 1970s, community groups in all three cities retreated into parochialism under a variety of funding and political pressures. The increasing professionalization of "community development" as a field pulled organizations away from conflict approaches (Stoecker, 2003). Many became dependent on government and foundation dollars and adjusted their missions to keep the money coming, including cooperating in right-wing efforts such as welfare reform and privatization of public services. Even when not directly co-opted, many organizations retreated into narrow definitions of issues or communities they worked with, resulting in what one Chicago organizer remembered as a "wasteland in terms of organizing, with everyone trying to be the next Alinsky instead of actually putting in the work . . . all these letterhead coalitions where a few people'd get together and then 20 other individuals sign on and you end up with this laundry list of issues" (Anonymous Interviewee 1, personal communication, August 20, 2006). More recently, organizing has been rejuvenated in Chicago, with revived neighborhood groups and vibrant ACORN and Gamaliel chapters.

Similarly, the U.S. labor movement has fallen a long way from its peaks of energy in the 1930s and membership density in the 1950s. The early organizing efforts of the Congress of Industrial Organizations (founded in Pittsburgh in 1935) combined workplace and community-based organizing on a class basis, but this approach was almost completely lost following World War II. Most unions gave up trying to organize new workers and the labor movement withdrew from its role leading a broad working-class movement striving to achieve union representation for every worker. This led the labor movement to focus narrowly on winning better contracts for members, who began to see themselves as paying a fee for service rather than as members of a social movement. Unions have begun to return to an organizing model in fits and starts; none more successfully than SEIU Local 880, which has grown to become Illinois's largest local by creatively organizing homecare workers.

Although there are seldom enough core activist organizations available, most regions have even fewer "bridging organizations" to bring together disparate activist groups and provide a point of focus for pressuring elites (Lawrence & Hardy, 1999). Central labor councils vary in effectiveness across the country, from loose agglomerations of locals to something deserving of the name *labor movement*. At times, the Milwaukee County Labor Council has fused together such a shared vision and resources, particularly around electoral organizing. Interfaith justice coalitions like Milwaukee's MICAH exist across the country, but also often struggle to engage more than a handful of congregations. Neighborhood organizations are even more separated by turf battles and parochialism. Chicago's Grassroots Collaborative is the only example of a network of membership-based community organizations dedicated to building power arising from these cases.

Strong cross-sector networks are even more rare, meaning community activists, union leaders, and progressive people of faith seldom share the same spaces or get to develop relationships. This fragmentation makes coalition campaigns, leadership institutes, and groups like Jobs with Justice very valuable spaces for bringing people together across differences. Technical assistance intermediaries also provide movement support in policy analysis, leadership development, and political action. Two national networks, Building Partnerships USA and the Partnership for Working Families, focus on supporting regional "think-and-do tanks" like Pittsburgh UNITED and Milwaukee's Good Jobs and Livable Neighborhoods and encouraging the evolution toward more effective organizational structure. A good first step for organizers is assessing the strength of their local organizational capacity across the dimensions in Figure 1.

1. Organizational building blocks
   a. Local unions
   b. Grassroots organizations
   c. Activist congregations

1. Networks
   a. Central labor council
   b. Grassroots organizing network
   c. "Religious Left" network
   d. Diverse cross-sector core of leaders

1. Technical assistance
   a. Research and policy development
   b. Independent political apparatus
   c. Leadership development and training

FIGURE 1 Key elements of regional organizing capacity.

SPHERE 2: EVOLVING CULTURES OF SOLIDARITY

These organizational elements are intimately connected to the cultural and community-building work of movements. The assumptions of our pluralist political discourse can work against challenging groups by treating them as "interest groups" parallel to corporations or the military industrial complex. Offe and Wiesenthal (1980) argue that working-class organizations must not only *aggregate* the interests of members, but also *transform* these interests through a dialogical process. Only through such cultural transformation of their constituencies can challenging groups generate enough power to break down the status quo and create the possibility of fundamental structural change.

Coalitions and intermediary organizations provide spaces for local activists to come together, develop trust and better understandings of each other, and begin to form common goals. Working class movements in the United States have often stumbled while trying to bring people together across differences, particularly race. These repeated frustrations have contributed to tendencies to slide into single-issue organizing silos and increased fragmentation. Indeed, strained relationships between unions and communities of color have held back movement-building in each of these three cities, prompting organizers to proactively confront divisions between groups as they attempt to construct broader movement identities and solidarity.

Bridge-building coalition leaders have tried to make themselves and their organizations reflect the norms and structural relationships they would like to see, while recognizing that most others are operating according to different logics. Individually, these leaders try to model practices of forthrightness and trust, "swallowing hard" during conflicts, and creating space for new relationships to develop by absorbing negative energy. A Milwaukee labor leader described this as "webslinging"—proactively searching out and repairing weak spots in networks (Anonymous Interviewee 2, personal communication, October 9, 2006). Such leaders also try to create organizational structures that foster cooperative norms and realistic expectations between partners, and then extend these new norms beyond the initial core group of leaders through mentorship and clear communication.

The most successful collaborative efforts created formal structures with attention to the differences between participants. For example, the Grassroots Collaborative requires organizations to commit resources and turn out members at events in order to be involved in strategic decisions, which clarified the system and brought things out in the open for discussion. In contrast, the Pittsburgh Living Wage Campaign's efforts to maintain strict equality between partners proved difficult to maintain in the heat of a campaign. Several organizers reported that such idealistic efforts often seem to slide into informal systems whereby a few key organizations make important decisions, creating a situation of "false equality" that poses more risks of internal conflict than the structural differentiation of the Grassroots Collaborative model.

These cases also demonstrate that developing new cultures is a fragile process of building new relationships over a series of interactions. Along the way, participants must break old habits reinforced by broader social structures and elite interventions. While people can be transformed by collective action—as in Chicago, where activists reported a dramatic increase in levels of trust and openness during the final weeks of the Big Box Living Wage campaign—bad interactions can also quickly set back an effort, as people find their pessimistic expectations confirmed. The relative absence of class-based discourse and history of white working-class racism in this country make working-class movements vulnerable to racial splits. Coalitions in Milwaukee and Chicago were able to survive concerted elite efforts to split them along racial lines because they had fostered a diverse core group of leaders who shared a vision and bonds of trust.

These activists seek to intervene in this complex system in ways that strengthen the local working-class community's ability to wield power in the broader society. Bate, Khan, and Pye (2000) frame organizational change as a process of restructuring by deliberately breaking and refashioning prevailing cycles. Most change efforts focus on either structure or culture, rather than fostering the development of a learning community that integrates the coevolution of structures and cultures. Such integrated change efforts provide the added benefit of developing consensus and a core leadership group through a transformative cycle of action and dialogue—what Paulo Freire (1970) called *praxis*. This transformation of interests and identities marks a moment in which local coalitions move beyond additive logics of collective action to become "more than the sum of their parts." One longtime Chicago organizer described how the Big Box Living

Wage campaign was "critical to solidifying relationships . . . in the heat of battle we found ourselves sharing things that just a few weeks before we would have hidden" (Anonymous Interviewee 3, personal communication, August 5, 2006).

Many of the most effective leaders of labor-community coalitions have come out of a community organizing background where they have developed relationship-building methods like "one-on-ones." Milwaukee's Gamaliel affiliate MICAH could model the process of intentionally setting up a series of one-on-ones with coalition partners where leaders sit down and ask each other questions, each doing more listening than talking during their turn. The resulting basic understanding of where other coalition leaders are coming from can help people find common ground and proactively intervene in conflicts.

Sphere 3: Evolving political strategies

Campaigns are the galvanizing events of movement-building, providing opportunities to win concrete changes and plough the ground from which movements emerge by building organizational infrastructure and promoting cultural change. They help organizers discover new possibilities, develop new relationships, and experiment with new strategies. When placed within a broader strategy, such campaigns hopefully build the strength of the movement going forward.

In their efforts to wrest control over local policy-making away from the corporate elites who dominate each region, these local movements pursue a variety of goals. Their greatest impact has come through combining insider (e.g., lobbying) and outsider (e.g., protests) forms of power, particularly in conjunction with an independent electoral capacity to "reward friends and punish enemies." Such balance is facilitated by effective bridging organizations, which can help diverse coalition members coordinate their strengths. When unions and community groups develop the ability to mobilize their constituents to vote, take direct action, and lobby, local politicians find it difficult to resist their demands, even in the face of large financial interests (Ganz, 2005).

While these efforts have been able to sustain (and even benefit from) short-term losses, organizers should avoid catastrophic losses that harm the long-term health of the movement. Strategic choices within campaigns thus should be made with long-term goals in mind, and maintaining key relationships should be prioritized over short-term victories. In this spirit, the community organizations involved in the Good Jobs and Livable Neighborhoods coalition refused to entertain proposed community-benefits agreements that would have more fully addressed their demands for affordable housing and local hiring because it likely would have limited their ability to work more closely with the building trades unions.

By taking this long term-perspective on campaigns, organizers hope to:

- Strengthen the core group of bridge-building leaders by incorporating new activists, deepening bonds of trust, and developing shared norms and vision;
- Develop cultures of solidarity within the broader membership of the organizations involved that expands their collective identities and connects to a broader vision of social justice; and
- Build the organizational infrastructure that will continue bringing people together across differences and support future campaigns.

CONCLUSION: LEARNING ORGANIZATIONS, URBAN FARMING, AND MOVEMENT-BUILDING

Ideally, successful evolution within each of these spheres of practice is reinforced through a virtuous cycle in which well-selected issue campaigns provide the opportunity to recruit new partners, experiment with new intermediaries and strategies, and deepen cultures of solidarity. Down times between campaigns allow the chance to institutionalize the most successful of these experiments and set the stage for emerging issues. As opponents adapt and the political-economic context evolves, it is more than a truism that movements must keep evolving or die.

Urban farming provides a potential metaphor for the craft of local movement-building. Community gardens are collaborative efforts to reclaim some slivers of our deindustrialized cities for the production of immediately useful goods. As in organizing, context matters—the gardens are built on the history of what came before, often requiring the cleanup of contaminated soil, just as coalitions must proactively confront legacies of racism and mistrust. Some gardens are just an agglomeration of individual plots, but others reflect the development of deeper relationships and synergies between participants. A good gardener tests the soil and understands the growing season, but also accepts that only experience can show what the exact best strategy for that plot of land will be. Rotating crops, fertilizing, and mulching enable a gardener to grow things that would have been impossible when they began, much as coalition work builds on itself and expands possibilities by creating cultures of solidarity and expanding political opportunities.

The most realistic prospect for the transformative and complex systems change desired by groups like these working-class organizers lies in the development of "learning organizations" that are able to evolve and continue to increase their strategic capacity over time. Working-class organizers face an unfriendly environment and the challenge of balancing multiple logics of action—requiring them to both bring people together and help them change simultaneously. These cases provide a glimpse of the process through which movements can grow and evolve as participants learn from their experiences.

Marshall Ganz (2005) has argued that the strategic capacity of a leadership team—their ability to recontexualize and synthesize data in fashioning new approaches—is the key variable in understanding why challenging groups sometimes win. Planning for this sort of "knowledge work" is quite inconsistent in regions across the country, suggesting that it should be a focus of capacity-building interventions. Smart and committed organizers brought good ideas to their work in each of the three cities. However, some of the organizations they created have been more able to adapt to changing circumstances than others, leading to more longevity and success. The ability to perform such strategic diagnosis develops within "movement halfway houses" like coalitions and training centers that also play a central role in forging common frameworks and transforming groups into "more than the sum of their parts" (Morris, 1984).

To bring such processes of innovation more to the center of regional movement-building, the *thinking* and *doing* need to be more closely linked. A cadre of activist-intellectuals—people doing the real work of organizing but also thinking about the bigger picture—could be tied together within an intermediary layer of bridging organizations. By virtue of their central positions within local networks, such leaders are well placed to function as webslingers surveying local movement infrastructure, diagnosing weak points, and proactively creating new intermediary organizations or connections. By analyzing past campaigns and efforts in other regions, this core group could play a lead role in consolidating local knowledge and strategic innovations, catalyzing change within existing organizations, and facilitating communication across divides.

National movement-building networks and university-based allies could play an important role in linking these activist-intellectuals together across regions and developing their capacity to make grounded generalizations across contexts. Through the comparative process of trying to translate their experiences into recommendations, those involved would hopefully develop a deeper understanding of their local efforts and begin to isolate the common threads that emerge across cases. Over time, these activist-intellectuals might come to see their organizing work like farming—an ongoing process embedded in a complex system, with no hard and fast rules, but with many relatively consistent patterns, a rich trove of folk wisdom, and the certainty that one's work will never end. With such a perspective, they might very well navigate a variety of locally-specific paths toward strong working-class movements, build alternative structures while also forcing existing bodies to change, and begin to explore the routes connecting their local movements across regional and national boundaries.

NOTES

1. Defining class boundaries, particularly drawing a line between the working and middle classes in the United States, plunges one into longstanding political debates. In this article, I describe these organizations and movements as "working class" because they represent primarily low- and moderate-income memberships and focus on economic justice.

2. My research process is described in more detail elsewhere (Dobbie, 2008, 2009).

REFERENCES

Amenta, E. (2006). *When movements matter: The Townsend plan and the rise of social security*. Princeton, NJ: Princeton University Press.

Bate, P., Khan, R., & Pye, A. (2000). Towards a culturally sensitive approach to organization structuring: Where organization design meets organization development. *Organization Science, 11*(2), 197–211.

Dobbie, D. (2008). *More than the sum of their parts? Labor-community coalitions in the Rust Belt*. Unpublished doctoral dissertation, University of Michigan, Ann Arbor.

Dobbie, D. (2009). From coalitions to movements: Realizing the promise of regional power building. *Working USA, 12*(1), 57–71.

Freire, P. (1970). *Pedagogy of the oppressed*. New York: Continuum.

Ganz, M. (2005). Why David sometimes wins: Strategic capacity in social movements. In D. M. Messick & R. M. Kramer (Eds.), *The psychology of leadership* (pp. 209–238). Mahwah, NJ: Lawrence Erlbaum.

Krinsky, J., & Reese, E. (2006). Forging and sustaining labor–community coalitions: The workfare justice movement in three cities. *Sociological Forum, 21*(4), 623–658.

Lawrence, T. B., & Hardy, C. (1999). Building bridges for refugees: Toward a typology of bridging organizations. *Journal of Applied Behavioral Science, 35*(1), 48–70.

Morris, A. D. (1984). *The origins of the civil rights movement: Black communities organizing for change*. New York: Free Press.

Offe, C., & Wiesenthal, H. (1980). Two logics of collective action: Theoretical notes on social class and organizational form. *Political Power and Social Theory, 1*, 67–115.

Stoecker, R. (2003). Understanding the development-organizing dialectic. *Journal of Urban Affairs, 25*(4), 493–512.

Tattersall, A., & Reynolds, D. B. (2007). The shifting power of labor-community coalitions: Identifying common elements of powerful coalitions in Australia and the US. *Working USA, 10*(1), 77.

Waldinger, R., Erickson, C., Milkman, R., Mitchell, D., Valenzuela, A., Wong, K., et al. (1996). Helots no more: A case study of the justice for janitors campaign in Los Angeles. In K. Bronfenbrenner, et al. (Eds.), *Organizing to win: New research on union strategies* (pp. 102–120). Ithaca, NY: Cornell.

Organizing Community and Labor Coalitions for Community Benefits Agreements in African American Communities: Ensuring Successful Partnerships

BONNIE YOUNG LAING

Department of Social Work, Youngstown State University, Youngstown, Ohio, USA

Community benefits agreements are a relatively new tool in the economic justice movement. This article discusses community-labor partnerships in efforts to win community benefits agreements in African American communities, with implications for other communities of color. Union and African American organizing strategies are explored and two community benefits campaigns are examined: the Figueroa Corridor Coalition for Economic Justice and the One Hill Community Benefits Coalition. Clashes emerging around divergent world views are reviewed along with strategies to address potential challenges in order to build and maintain successful cross cultural coalitions.

The United States is experiencing a "back to the city movement" that is fueling redevelopment efforts in disadvantaged communities across the country (Janis, 2008). Because disadvantaged African American and other communities of color are likely to have large percentages of vacant land or land and buildings with low market value, these communities have become ripe with opportunities for land banking by developers, who seek to create new housing and retail spaces close to central business districts (Gibbons & Haas, 2002). These urban re-development efforts promise to revitalize communities by reducing vacant housing, fostering new businesses and increasing the local tax base (Janis, 2008).

Yet many activists, academics, and neighborhood residents are concerned that these revitalization efforts will mean the economic exploitation and displacement of low-income, disenfranchised African, Latin, Asian and Native American (ALANA[1]) people (Anthony, 2008; Clarke, 2008; Fullilove, 2004). Many of those concerned are troubled by the fact that the displacement and exploitation of poor people of color are being subsidized by municipalities, via the gift of public land and public dollars (Baxamusa, 2008; Clarke, 2008; Cummings, 2006; Gross, Leroy & Janis-Aparicio, 2005; Leavitt, 2006).

For labor unions and community groups, community benefit agreement (CBA) campaigns have become important tools for combating the use of public dollars to support resident and worker exploitation (Partnership for Working Families, 2008). These campaigns have also provided opportunities to highlight the mutual interest of workers and community residents in improving quality of life in the work place and in the neighborhoods in which workers live (Haas, 2002). The potency of labor-community collaboration for economic justice has been shown in the community benefits agreements won by disadvantaged ALANA communities from Los Angeles to Washington, DC (Baxamusa, 2008; Cummings, 2006) and in mid-sized cities such as Pittsburgh, Pennsylvania. Yet, several critical questions emerge around how to build strong and effective labor-community partnerships in African American and other ALANA communities. What happens to coalitions if ALANA community groups and labor unions clash around the goals and strategies to be employed in CBA efforts? What are the foreseeable disagreements? How can organizers avoid potential challenges in forming or maintaining labor-community partnerships, or correct problems that develop (Arguelles, 2005; Bronfenbrenner &Warren, 2007; Fletcher & Hurd, 2000). This article answers these questions by presenting a review of literature describing (a) CBA campaigns, (b) labor-community partnerships in CBAs, (c) organizing perspectives of unions and African American community groups and (d) strategies for successful partnerships in CBA campaigns; along with (e) the application of these strategies to an examination of two CBA campaigns.

LITERATURE REVIEW

Community Benefits Agreement Campaigns

Across the country community benefits agreements campaigns typically begin when community or labor organizations become aware of proposed developments that will be sited in or near residential communities, and that will have a significant negative impact on their target constituency, as in workers and/or residents (Cummings, 2006; Gibbons & Haas, 2002; Gross et al., 2005; Haas 2002; Leavitt, 2006). CBA coalitions gain the leverage to protect workers and community residents by taking advantage of the opportunity structure (Sellers, 2007) created by municipal policies, which mandate public hearings around large commercial projects involving the use of public funds and/or public land (Baxamusa, 2008; Gross et al., 2005). Labor and community partners use their leverage through the threat to mobilize *en masse* to oppose the approval of developments during these public processes (LeRoy & Purinton, 2005). Via these means, disadvantaged African American and other ALANA community residents, and their labor allies, have forced municipalities and developers to make formal commitments that guarantee measurable contributions to workers and communities. Such agreements between developers and communities have come to be known as community benefits agreements (CBAs), which are legally enforceable contracts between commercial developers and community coalitions. The following section will discuss labor-community partnerships in CBAs.

Labor-Community Partnerships in CBAs

Emergence

Typical labor-community CBA partnerships emerge as fairly broad coalitions, as organizations recognize the opportunity created by a development and launch an effort to ensure that the members of their bloc benefit. The primary goal of the labor and community partners is to form a cooperative agreement with the developer, in exchange for their support, e.g. lack of opposition, during the public approval process (Gross et al., 2005). Members of CBA coalitions must begin by exploring municipal timelines, and possible leverage points in the public approval process for the proposed development. At the same time, the coalition must work to communicate their efforts to the community members, union members and the general public in order to mobilize support. Labor and community partners also work in concert to identify, vet and otherwise prioritize the constituent issues that will form the basis of the CBA. In most cases, labor-community coalitions are obliged to complete their CBA proposal and present it to the developers and local redevelopment planning bodies for vetting. All the while, the coalition must pressure developers to formally agree to the CBA proposal within the timeframe set by municipal guidelines which steer the public approval process. Moving from discussing the process coalitions undergo to win concessions in CBA campaigns, it is important to explore the internal process of coalition formation.

Internal processes

To begin, a core strength of labor-community partnerships is that each group brings to the table a desire to promote economic justice and social change. In addition, both labor unions and community groups bring a specialized savvy about how to achieve social justice. These groups must work expediently to establish a working partnership that pulls together this savvy, in a manner that avoids forming an amalgamation of groups with disparate missions and foci (Frege, Heery, & Turner, 2003). Because of the time demands placed on coalitions to form and take action, coming together flawlessly can be a real challenge. When labor and community groups join together with little time to understand each other, they may operate with divergent views on the goals and strategies each intends to use to structure and carry out the CBA campaign (Arguelles, 2005; Dubro & Feller, 2005; Miller, 2004). Rivas (2006) explains that such challenges may be due, in part, to an overreliance on assumed commonality.

Types of Coalitions

Although labor and community groups seek partnerships, in many cases, organizers have not thought through how the partnership should be constituted. To clarify coalition formation options, Rivas proposes a classification typology, as Table 1 illustrates.

Table 1 shows Rivas's conceptualization of the core issues shaping labor-community partnerships. These include relationship building, common interests and partner dominance. Rivas concludes that only those coalitions that (a) provide for long-term relationships, (b) have formally developed shared interests and (c) have mutually beneficial campaign objectives are true labor-community partnerships. For Rivas, relationship building refers to whether the focus of the coalition is to foster long-term or ad hoc associations between the coalition partners; whereas dominance is conceptualized as the degree to which one partner's interests dominate the alliance. Under her typology, dominance is empirically reflected by determining who sets the coalition agenda. Dominance also refers to which partner controls the resources supporting a coalition.

TABLE 1 Rivas' (2006) Typology for Labor-Community Coalitions—Modified

	Focus on building relationships and achieving objective	Relationships ignored/focus on achieving objective
Partners share interests	*Partnership coalition* Community and labor organizations have developed shared interests. The coalition is structured to provide for long-term relationships.	*Ad hoc coalition* Community and labor organizations have shared interests, but relationships are not seen as important or are taken for granted. The coalition works toward the goal.
One partner's interest dominates	*Support committee coalition* Relationship is cultivated; Subordinate partner interests are not taken for granted.	*Letterhead coalition* Subordinate partner endorses dominant partner's agenda, but provides limited support.

Rivas (2006) points out that partnership coalitions provide the strongest foundation for social movement unionism, as such coalitions foster the shared interests, equality and power sharing necessary to keep partners motivated to work together over the longer periods of time typically necessary to promote social change. She asserts that because many true partnership coalitions have not been formed, additional work is needed to uncover strategies for developing this type of coalition. Seemingly, an important area to explore surrounding her first criteria, shared interests, would be an examination of the potentially differing perspectives labor unions and community groups bring to coalitions.

Labor and Community Organizing Perspectives

Community organizations and labor groups share an orientation toward social justice yet, beyond this, may hold divergent perspectives on organizing in terms of goals, strategies and power. When adding the dynamic of culture (race), additional differences may emerge. The following section provides some detail on labor union and community organizing perspectives with emphasis on African American community organizing.

Union Organizing

Unions have tended to focus on "bread–and-butter" issues in the work place (Fletcher & Hurd, 2000) such as the right to organize, wage increases or affordable health benefits. Yet, as union membership has dropped nationally, progressive union organizers have begun to explore innovative approaches to reaching out to communities (Frege et al., 2003). Labor scholars identify these two approaches as business unionism (focusing on the bread-and-butter issues), and community unionism (incorporation of community issues), respectively (Kelber, 2003; Tattersall, 2007; Turner & Hurd, 2001).

In business unionism, organizing has been characterized as efforts of union leadership to work out a package of worker privileges and benefits with the employers using the "carrot" or inducement of non confrontational union tactics, along with the "stick" or implied threat of mass mobilization and disruption of the work environment. Under this organizing model negotiations take place between labor representatives, who are professional organizers from a similar class background and/or status, as corporate representatives (Kelber, 2003; Milkman & Voss, 2004; Sellers, 2007; Tatterstall & Reynolds, 2007). Business unionism has avoided worker mobilization; where mobilizing workers becomes necessary, those unions with a business unionism approach are more likely to use professional organizers, who are less likely to have direct experience as workers in the target industry (Lopez, 2004). Because this organizing model focuses primarily on the work place, purveyors are considered less likely to become involved in community coalitions (Lopez, 2004; Tattersall & Reynolds, 2007). When business unionists do become involved in community efforts, they view labor-community coalitions purely in terms of short-term opportunities for growing union membership and or increasing negotiating power at the bargaining table (Frege et al. 2003; Rivas, 2006). In this regard, labor-community coalitions built on a business unionism model may be likely to function as letterhead coalitions as described by Rivas (2006).

In contrast, Milkman and Voss (2004) posit that community partnerships seem to fit best with unions embracing missions centered on the promotion of social justice. This union organizing approach is labeled community unionism. According to Tattersall (2006),

> community unionism is defined as the range of strategies that involve unions "reaching out" to the community. These include labor-community coalitions [reaching out to community groups], broadening the frame of union campaigns to embrace "community concern" [reaching out to community issues], and campaigns that seek to control place [reaching out to local communities]. (p. 1)

Community unionism also involves capacity building efforts that empower workers to take active roles in organizing for both work-place and community-based economic justice. Unions which take a membership growth view of CBAs, may focus their efforts on partnering with communities to increase their leverage for ensuring that developers and succeeding hiring organizations commit to card check neutrality (not opposing a unionize labor force), yet may struggle to partner beyond worker issues (Arguelles, 2005; Bronfenbrenner & Warren, 2007; Sellers, 2007; Tattersall, 2006). Coalitions using less ambitious forms of community unionism may be likely to act as support committee coalitions or ad hoc coalitions.

A third union organizing model is social movement unionism. Some scholars see community unionism and social movement unionism as synonymous (Milkman & Voss, 2004), while others see the focus on social justice, grass roots organizing and worker empowerment beyond the work place as distinct (Frege et al., 2003; Rivas, 2006; Worthen, 2004). Social movement unionism uses a capacity building focus targeted at building workers' and community residents' capability to combat oppression on their own behalf (Turner & Hurd, 2001). Because this model targets social injustice, the organizing strategies employed are more likely to have a long-term focus indicative of a true partnership. Of the three types of unionism described, social movement unionism may correspond best with the empowerment and self-help focus, which has characterized much of organizing in urban, disadvantaged ALANA communities. The following section highlights some cultural dynamics which may impact labor-community partnership building with African American community groups.

AFRICAN AMERICAN COMMUNITY ORGANIZING

Countering oppression and realizing social and economic justice has been the *raison d'être* of African American organizing (Akbar, 1984; Kelley, 2005; O'Donnell & Karanja, 2000; Schiele, 2005; Young Laing, 2009a). This is reflected in examinations of African American community organizing in the progressive era (Burwell, 1995; Carlton-LaNey, 1999; Carlton-LaNey & Burwell, 1995; O'Donnell, 1995), as well as those of key social movement organizations (Young Laing, 2009a) and in contemporary organizing in disadvantaged urban African American communities (O'Donell & Karanja, 2000; Young Laing, 2003). The anti-oppression/pro-justice stance of Black organizing is based in the fact that the subjugation of African Americans has occurred from all levels of American society from governmental institutions, (Davis & Bent-Goodley, 2004; Rasheed & Rasheed, 1999; Young-Laing, 2003) to workplace groups such as unions (Kelley, 2005; Fletcher & Hurd, 2000).

Examinations of effective efforts to counter oppression have shown that African American organizing has included some of the following six components: (a) world views acknowledging the impact of racism on African American's psyche, social reality and economic opportunities; (b) problem definitions that reflect a conflict oriented perspective on the macro social environment; (c) an orientation to transformative macro-level social change; (d) efforts to increase personal efficacy, cultural esteem and critical consciousness, (e) assets-based efforts to promote collective self help by identifying and employing community strengths; and (f) the development of community-based and controlled institutions that address community defined needs (Young Laing, 2009b). These foci are reflected in the following contemporary models of African American community organizing.

Young Laing (2003) uncovered three core organizing models that are being used in contemporary progressive African American community organizing. These may help labor partners better understand community organizing perspectives in this milieu, i.e., political action, resource and capacity development and cultural empowerment.

Political action organizing is centered on drawing power and resources into the community. Purveyors of this model view African American communities as resource deficient in regard to remediating community problems, but as resource rich in terms of the power to apply social pressure to force external systems to take action to address community needs. Political action organizers see force as a necessary tool in community problem solving and may come to labor-community partnership desiring to have their organization in a lead role. Thus, the political action organizer may be most amenable to serving in a partnership coalition or in an ad hoc labor-community coalition as described by Rivas (2006). Political action organizers may also be comfortable in steering coalition or letter head coalition where they are the dominant partner.

Resource and capacity development organizers focus on developing community based intuitions to address community needs, thereby limiting dependence on hostile or indifferent macro institutions. Adherents of this model assume that community power lies within the collective resources and capacities of community members to address their own needs; and in drawing in economic or educational resources from supportive external organizations. Yet, resource and capacity development organizers have an ultimate goal of self-reliance. Promoting mutual aid among community members and formalizing relationships into institutions is the chief change strategy used by resource and capacity development organizers. Additional strategies would include collaboration and coordinated community problem solving, community education, technical assistance, philanthropy and leadership development. In terms of participating in labor-community partnerships, the type of coalition these organizers would be most comfortable with might primarily be influenced by the degree to which the partnership would foster institution building and community autonomy. Partnerships would also be influenced by the level of trust, connection and mutual interest held in common with a labor union partner. Thus, resource and capacity development organizing may be best suited for a partnership coalition or steering committee coalition.

Cultural empowerment strategies have centered on countering internalized oppression, as in self blame and self hate, through cultural consciousness building initiatives. The goal of cultural empowerment organizing is to build critical consciousness. For cultural empowerment organizers, power lies in individual and communal efforts to resist denigrated and powerless stereotypes of African descended people. Thus, change strategies center around exploring African and ALANA history to build cultural appreciation. Cultural empowerment organizers use culture as a tool for fostering resistance and liberation. Of the three approaches to community organizing, this one may present significant challenges to labor-community coalition building, unless a significant number of the union members and organizers are culturally similar.

In all cases, labor-community coalitions will be influenced by the history of labor unions in African American and other ALANA communities. This may be of concern, as Kelley (2005) points out that unions have at times played a key role in African American worker oppression, as a both foe and an ally. In his review of literature on unions and African American communities, he details ongoing discrimination against Black workers and reticence to address African American community issues. At the same time, he describes powerful partnerships to organize majority Black locals and highlights efforts such as the Service Employees International Union's (SEIU) Justice for Janitors campaign.

In sum, Kelley and others (Benson, 2008; Fletcher & Hurd, 2000; Himeda, 2006; Hunter, 1997) observe that Black communities may have ambivalent perceptions of unions that should be explored in coalition building efforts. Fortunately, various practitioners working in cross-cultural community/ union milieus have provided insights on key considerations and strategies for coalition building. The following section details such strategies.

Strategies and Tactics for Effective Cross-Cultural Labor and Community Partnerships

As shown in Table 2, a review of literature offering practice wisdom for strengthening cross-cultural labor-community partnerships yields five key factors: (a) assessing community strengths (Kretzmann & McKnight, 1993; Young Laing, 2003); (b) developing a shared vision, shared goals and strategies (Arguelles, 2005; Baxamusa, 2008; Sellers, 2007; Tattersall, 2007); (c) establishing a basis for long-term relationships (Cummings, 2006); (d) discussing and addressing conflict (Arguelles, 2005, Gibbons & Haas, 2002); and (e) sharing power and responsibility (Arguelles, 2005; Cummings, 2006).

TABLE 2 Strategies for Building Partnership in African American and Other ALANA Communities

Strategy	Guiding question(s)	Actions
Assess partner strengths. (Kretzmann & McKnight, 1993; Worthen, 2004; Young Laing, 2003)	What do unions bring to the table? What do community groups bring to the table? (Worthen, 2004)	Focus group. Community assets map.
Develop shared perspectives, shared vision, and strategies. (Cummings, 2006)	How has this community been challenged? Did unions play a role (helping/ hurting)? What do unions want? What do community groups want? (Worthen, 2004)	Visioning session. Focus group. Appreciative inquiry.
Establishing a basis for long-term relationships. (Arguelles, 2005; Gibbons & Haas, 2002)	How can we learn each other better? How can we build relationships beyond an active campaign?	Training across expertise, e.g., Union train community in negotiation. Community trains unions in community dynamics or diversity.
Discussing and addressing conflict. (Arguelles, 2005; Gibbons & Haas, 2002)	Are we in agreement? Are any unaddressed issues simmering in the coalition?	Planned open discussions. Checking in around conflict. Mediation. Conflict resolution.
Sharing power and responsibility. (Arguelles, 2005; Cummings, 2006)	How is power shared? What mechanism allows all voices to be heard? How is input valued? What resources can we share?	Executive committee. MOUs. Mini grants. In-kind support. Staff sharing.

Table 2 shows five core coalition building strategies derived from some of the collective wisdom of organizers involved in cross-cultural community-labor coalitions and/or CBA campaigns. Overall, these authors' recommendations suggest that CBA coalition building can be a very complex task, which demands more than a passion for social justice. Organizers working to craft successful coalitions will need to attend to the issues of dominance, conflict and power by promoting equality, mutual respect, shared influence and shared resources. To facilitate the practical application of these insights, Table 2 includes questions to guide organizers' thinking around the coalition building process that might be used in discussions with partnership members. Also included in the table are general action steps that can be undertaken to facilitate coalition building. This table represents only a beginning framework for developing a model for labor-community partnerships. Additional detail on each strategy is provided next.

Assess Community Strengths

Unions seeking to enter communities to build relationships or launch an organizing initiative should know community strengths and resources. Likewise, community organizations should know their own strengths and those of the labor partner. This could be accomplished by using such techniques as assets mapping and interviews with key informants (Kretzmann & McKnight, 1993).

Developing a Shared Vision, Shared Goals and Shared Strategies

Baxamusa (2008) recommends discussion between divergent groups forming coalitions to develop shared vision and shared goals to aid coalitions in becoming more cohesive. Baxamusa also recommends holding open discussions to help community and labor groups forge common perspectives. Other authors recommend including discussions regarding (a) issues (Tattersall, 2007), (b) values (Sellers, 2007), and (c) strategies (Baxamusa, 2008; Tattersall, 2006) and resources. In terms of cross-cultural coalitions, gaining shared perspectives may also involve exploring the history of oppression of or within the target community. Likewise, it may be helpful for union coalition partners to understand internal community conflicts, so that these can be addressed as part of developing a shared vision.

Establish Basis for Long-Term Relationships

A key lesson learned by Cummings (2006) from his work in an Los Angeles CBA coalition is that labor-community partnerships are strengthened where community and labor have had an established relationship prior to the CBA effort, and where the coalition plans to stay together over the long haul. In this coalition, unions developed relationships with Latino workers in the neighborhoods where they lived (Gibbons & Haas, 2002; Haas, 2002). Thus, at the time when the community benefits opportunity presented itself relationships had already been established and familiarity and trust had been built.

DISCUSS AND ADDRESS CONFLICT

Gibbons and Haas (2002) suggest that it is critical to the success of the coalition for leaders to have open discussions of hot-button topics. For Arguelles (2005), such issues include race/culture, class and power/ownership issues. Baxamusa (2008) recommends that when differences emerge in CBA coalitions partnering organizations should shift focus to broader more generally agreeable goals. Alternately, groups with divergent foci may choose to work together where there is agreement and undertake separate efforts where there is no consensus. With this choice, partners can still increase their power on issues of agreement, while having other avenues to address what they see as critical issues.

SHARED POWER AND RESPONSIBILITY

Arguelles (2005) discusses the importance of shared power:

> The relationships between union and community can be very strong, but I think that an impediment to becoming a real alliance has been that labor sometimes . . . imposes something new instead of making alliances with groups that have already been recognized and worked for many years on that issue. That is one of the major tensions. (p. 1)

It is important that coalition building begin with all partners at the table to shape the agenda and that partners share resources to support their work in the campaign, such resources could include money or in-kind support, such as staff.

Moving beyond hypothetical discussions of labor-community partnerships, the following section, examines two actual coalitions-the Figueroa Corridor Coalition for Economic Justice and One Hill CBA Coalition to illustrate the realities of labor union partnership strategies in implementing CBA campaigns. Descriptions of One Hill CBA Coalition were garnered through personal communications, meeting minutes, records from One Hill's on-line discussion group, as well as via participating as a member/organizer of the coalition. Accounts of the work of FCCEJ were gathered from primary and secondary sources rather than through first-hand knowledge of the coalition building process. Yet, the description of the work of FCCEJ is instructive for similar efforts across the country, and is derived from sources including documents on the FCCEJ website, case studies, and articles written by key organizers in academic literature on the work of the coalition.

The Figueroa Corridor Coalition for Economic Justice

The first labor-community partnerships for community benefits agreements came together under the umbrella of the Figueroa Corridor Coalition for Economic Justice (FCCEJ) in Los Angeles, California. The Figueroa Corridor is a 40-block neighborhood that houses the University of Southern California (USC), entertainment venues such as the Staples Center, cultural institutions, and residential neighborhoods with long histories of blight (Cummings, 2006; Haas, 2002; Leavitt, 2006). Residents are primarily poor working Blacks and Latinos, significant numbers of whom work in service positions at USC and in the hospitality, entertainment, and cultural institutions surrounding the corridor (Haas, 2002; Figueroa Corridor Coalition for Economic Justice [FCCEJ], 2008).

The CBA won by the FCCEJ remains the most comprehensive agreement won in the country. The FCCEJ CBA coalition was initiated by community groups and was the outgrowth of a previous effort to address worker rights and residential displacement issues at the University of Southern California. In that effort, community groups partnered with the unions that represented many of the community residents working at USC to use coordinated pressure tactics, under separate negotiating efforts, to win just salaries and a university expansion policy that minimized the displacement of community residents. An FCCJE organizer, Enrique, recalls the early days of the coalition:

> I remember when we started this Staples campaign, and I learned who the owners were [Rupert Murdoch]. In the back of my head I said, "These are the people who are really responsible for the displacement- we have to get more than relocation benefits for the community." (FCCEJ, 2003, p. 16)

The Figueroa Corridor encompasses a number of groups of organized residents, particularly tenants rights groups (FCCEJ 2003; Haas, 2002). These groups mobilized to empower themselves to control revitalization efforts affecting their lives (Cummings, 2006; Haas, 2007) and to ensure that residents would have influence at the table where developers, redevelopment organizations and construction unions have often shut out meaningful community input (Goodno, 2004). Here we see the value of groups having a shared vision and long-term relationships. Because the coalition that formed was built upon previous efforts, labor and community partners in this coalition had a strong sense of what each partner was brining to the table in terms of assets. Unions knew who the active community groups were, and visa versa. The mutual awareness of assets was strengthened by the fact that the coalition also consisted of many residents who were also union members.

Consequently, it may have been easier for community and union part-ners to see their mutual assets and interests. The union member/community resident connection was also important in helping coalition members to feel connected beyond the immediate effort. Community members were also likely to be familiar with the unions, their goals and strategies. Conversely, the union organizers may have been better able to connect with the issues of the community, because their members shared the same cultural back-ground and were directly affected by the displacement, environmental pollution and other issues that surfaced in the neighborhood.

The connection also aided the coalition in sharing power and avoiding conflict. Another critical feature of the Figueroa Corridor for Economic Justice Coalition was the shared power and control dynamic. The members of coa-lition first came together around a mutual interest in proposed USC food service layoffs (Cummings, 2006). Union collaborators who entered the coa-lition advocated *with* the community groups and not *for* them. Thus in this coalition, power relationships were balanced.

In regard to addressing conflict, within the coalition community partners found they had some interests which were uniquely community issues, such as asbestos and vermin in housing (FCCEJ, 2003). Instead of broadening the focus of the coalition efforts to address community concerns beyond the CBA, FCCJE convened meetings to address issues of import to community members. In addition, the SEIU and HERE formed the Los Angeles Alliance for a New Economy (LAANE), an organization focused on labor concerns in regard to the CBA. The two separate organizations were able to pursue divergent foci, while still jointly serving as members of the original coalition.

Although race was not analyzed in several examinations of the FCCEJ, authors noted Mexican immigrant rights as a core theme to empower workers and community residents. As a result, FCCEJ saw negotiating successes as skir-mishes in a long term battle for social change that would need to go far beyond the CBA campaign (Cummings, 2006; Gibbons & Haas 2002; Leavitt, 2006).

Unfortunately, not all coalitions come together smoothly, as the One Hill case shows.

One Hill CBA Coalition

The One Hill CBA Coalition formed in the Hill District, a predominately African American disadvantaged neighborhood in Pittsburgh, Pennsylvania. The Hill District has high rates of vacant land abutted by the University of Pittsburgh and the city's central business district, and thus has been a target for residential and commercial development. Interestingly, the Hill District has been portrayed as an exemplar for redevelopment done poorly due to the displacement of some 8,000 Hill District residents and dozens of busi-nesses in an earlier development effort, which extended the central business district into the Hill District (Murphy, 2004).

A key challenge in the One Hill CBA coalition building effort was that it was formed amidst a contentious environment between community groups, which extended into the association with their labor partners. Fortunately, the coalition held together and later learned to work together effectively. Part of the contention can be explained by the fact that this labor-community partnership was preceded by community organizing around a casino which was planned to be located in the neighborhood. A small set of neighborhood groups launched, then won, a campaign to block the casino to the dismay of a larger set of community groups who wanted the Casino and the resources its developer promised to the community. Friction emerged between these neighborhood factions and created ongoing intra-community conflict. After the casino development was rejected, a development project for building a new arena for the Pittsburgh's hockey team received preliminary approval. The Penguins received a large donation of public land and a $300 million subsidy to build the new arena. Some members of the Hill District factions agreed that a CBA campaign needed to be launched. However a high degree of jockeying took place around who would lead the CBA organizing process.

Around the same time, SEIU Local 3 became interested in launching a CBA campaign-via a newly formed community unionism arm of the local called Pittsburgh United. Pittsburgh United was awarded a CBA organizing grant by local foundations and took on the task of trying to mediate the neighborhood's intra-community conflict. Pittsburgh United was unsuccessful in its mediation efforts. The effort to build a CBA coalition went forward with one CBA faction (One Hill) aiming to build a very broad coalition of community members and allies to in order to win a CBA. The broad coalition effort was also used to counter the influence of the group which formed to thwart the casino. This group, which became known as the Hill Faith and Justice Alliance, was also working to win a CBA by using small group of highly influential community members and political leaders to win community benefits.

One Hill's campaign strategy was designed to foster trust and dispel some of the conflict around the CBA organizing effort. Pittsburgh United decided to support the effort of One Hill by partnering and sharing resources. Yet conflict soon emerged between Pittsburgh United and One Hill. One Hill organizers viewed mobilizing residents to turn out *en masse* to support the CBA negotiating efforts as the key campaign strategy. Pittsburgh United focused on using SEIU Local 3 members and their allies from sister unions to fill out mobilizations. SEIU organizers also felt they could win community benefits on the strength of the union's political power. In early mobilizations at public meetings, One Hill members turned out in large numbers, while Pittsburgh United's union representation was very small. This eroded community confidence in both the competence and veracity of Pittsburgh United union staff.

Further conflict emerged around the control of the resources to support the campaign, with One Hill seeking to control its own resources to wage the campaign. Pittsburgh United denied this request. One Hill organizers viewed this as an assault on their autonomy and Pittsburgh United came to be seen as inhibiting community empowerment.

This conflict provides an example of the central importance of shared vision and shared power. Access to resources was a critical tension point between Pittsburgh United and One Hill. Some community members resented the level of power afforded to Pittsburgh United, because of its control of funding resources. Key community members saw the denial of the request for direct access to resources as evidence of paternalism and an orientation to exploit community disadvantage for the advantage of the union. This perspective was voiced openly to Pittsburgh United and was the subject of much community discussion. But without mediating and problem solving discussions, the partnership never arrived at an acceptable resolution and the conflict became an ongoing source of distrust and hostility. Fueling this conflict was some anti-union sentiment derived from African American men's experience of being discriminated against by building trade unions. These unions are perceived as racist, thus some community partners expected Pittsburgh United staff to be so as well. An open discussion of the conflict may have brought resolution to this issue.

Adding fuel to this fire was a seemingly lack of understanding of the African American focus on empowerment. Pittsburgh United seemed to enter the partnership to act as a steward. This may have been fueled by viewing the community as "disadvantaged". An assessment of strengths may have given Pittsburgh United staff a more positive sense of community capacity. For instance, One Hill's membership possessed a wealth of community organizing and organizational management experience and understood the importance of developing a sense of empowerment as part of African American community organizing approaches. Pittsburgh United staff had primarily organized in the workplace and brought these sensibilities to their community organizing.

Conversely, One Hill members' lack of full awareness of Pittsburgh United's skills in negotiation, and the discounting of their political and philanthropic clout caused the community members to attempt to minimize the role of the unions in the negotiation process. Community members chose negotiators they felt comfortable with, which resulted in One Hill failing to have the most experienced and proven negotiators fighting to gain community benefits. If Pittsburgh United and members of One Hill would have had the opportunity to assess each other's strengths and needs, and to use these assessments as the basis for developing a shared vision and strategy, some of the conflict that characterized the coalition may have been avoided. In this case, a core part of Pittsburgh United's vision and strategy was to become a recognized resource for forming and implementing CBA campaigns.

While some community members saw Pittsburgh United's effort to take a visible leadership as solely patriarchy or internalized dominance, Pittsburgh United's approach was motivated by the need to fulfill its commitments to funders and other stakeholders. If Pittsburgh United staff had been more aware of the assets of the community organizations they were partnering with, they may have found ways to adjust their campaign vision and strategies to operate on the basis of their mutual interests.

This approach to gain shared understanding and mutual respect might have aided in identifying and addressing potential conflict and in forming power sharing strategies to minimize conflict. It is essential that mainstream (predominately White middle/upper class) institutions develop an assets-based mutual respect orientation when entering ALANA communities. This case example shows how critical it is to recognize assets and needs, a shared vision, goals and strategies, as well as shared power. Fortunately, as Pittsburgh United and One Hill CBA Coalition move to the implementation and monitoring phase of the CBA campaign, power sharing mechanisms have been formed. The coalition is moving to a becoming a true partnership coalition and now meets to discuss goals and strategies.

It is fortunate that despite the high level of contentiousness within the coalition, One Hill was eventually able to win a CBA with the support of Pittsburgh United. The coalition is still together, as it moves to the implementation and monitoring phase of the CBA process. With lessons learned, and staff/membership changes, this labor-community partnership has begun working together more effectively.

CONCLUSION

Many scholars of unionism see the future of labor organizations as intimately connected to social movement organizing and community benefits agreements as valuable tools for bringing labor and communities together in the advancement of social justice. In order to be effective, both labor and community partners must think critically about the CBA coalition building *process* to the same degree as they do the intended *outcome*. This examination should begin with recognizing the perspectives each partner brings to the coalition, as well the various types of coalitions that are possible. The coalition building process should continue by assessing the strengths and assets each partner brings to the coalition and continue with the development of common vision, strategies and structures for sharing the work of the CBA and ensuring equitable access to power and resources. As labor and community partners work together they must also search for and address conflict.

Equally important, considering that a core component of social justice is equalizing power and privilege, is that labor organizations will need to consider the influence of issues of racism, dominance and power in coalition building. This should include being openly self-critical about the ways in which union power and privilege may be used in ways that become (or are perceived as) oppressive to community partners in African American and other ALANA communities. To thwart unintended dominance, labor partners in CBA coalitions should embrace an empowerment orientation to organizing in CBA coalitions, whereby they aim to recognize community strengths and assets, while also addressing power differentials, by transferring portions of their knowledge, financial and human resources, along with some of their accrued political influence to ALANA community groups. Empowerment organizing efforts would pair well with the long standing African American tradition of struggle and self help, aimed at having Black and other ALANA communities be sufficiently resourced to become non-dependant on external help. On the whole, there is a need for continuing examinations of the complex dynamics at play in CBA coalitions, in order to advance our understanding of best practices for labor-community partnerships in CBA coalitions. In closing, taking the FCCEJ as an exemplar, it seems that ultimately, labor community partnerships seem to work best where unions and community residents use social movement unionism strategies.

NOTE

1. ALANA is a term gaining usage in non-White communities across the United States. It is meant to capture more specifically the ethnic and cultural affiliations of non-White Americans (Oslin, 2004). ALANA is meant to be synonymous with, or to replace, the more generic term *people of Color*.

REFERENCES

Akbar, N. (1984). *Chains and images of psychological slavery*. Jersey City, NJ: New Mind.

Anthony, C. (2008). Livable communities. *Race, Poverty & Environment, 15*(1), 9–11.

Arguelles, P. (2005). *Unions are from Mars, community groups are from Venus: Does that mean we are all aliens?* Retrieved January 12, 2008, from http://www.thepraxisproject.org/toolkit/labor/mars.html

Baxamusa, M. (2008). *Beyond the limits to planning for equity: The emergence of community benefits agreements as empowerment models in participatory processes*. Unpublished dissertation. Available from the University of Southern California. Retrieved July 24, 2008, from http://www.onlinecpi.org/downloads/CBA%20Dissertation.pdf

Benson, H. (2008). Black and White can unite vs. construction discrimination. *Union Democracy Review, 171*, 9–12.

Bronfenbrenner, K., & Warren, D. (2007). Race, gender and the rebirth of trade unionism. *New Labor Forum, 16*(3–4), 142–148.

Burwell, N. Y. (1995). Lawrence Oxley and locality development: Black self help in North Carolina 1925–1928. *Journal of Community Practice, 2*(4), 49–70.

Carlton-LaNey, I., & Burwell, N. Y. (1995). African American community practice models: Historical and contemporary responses. *Journal of Community Practice* 4(2), 1–6.

Carlton-LaNey, I. (1999). African American social work pioneers' response to need. *Social Work, 44*(4), 311–32.

Clarke, J. (2008). In this issue. *Race, Poverty & Environment, 15*(1), 3–4.

Cummings, S. (2006). Mobilization lawyering: Community economic development in the Figueroa Corridor. In A. Sarat & S. Scheingold (Eds.), *Cause lawyers and social movements* (pp. 302–336). Stanford, CA: Stanford University Press.

Davis, K., & Bent-Goodley, T. (2004). *The color of social policy.* Alexandria:VA: CSWE.

Dubro, A., & Feller, K. (2005). Working with labor, a primer, a history, a guide. Retrieved January 12, 2008, from http://www.thepraxisproject.org/toolkit/labor/whyunions.html

Figueroa Corridor Coalition for Economic Justice (FCCEJ). (2003). *We shall not be moved: Posters and the fight against displacement in L.A.'s Figueroa Corridor.* Retrieved January 30, 2009, from http://www.saje.net/atf/cf/%7B493B2790-DD4E-4ED0-8F4E-C78E8F3A7561%7D/Weshallnotbemoved.pdf

Fletcher, B., & Hurd, R. (2000). Is organizing enough? Race, gender, and union culture. *New Labor Forum, 6*(Spring-Summer), 59–70.

Frege, C., Heery, E., & Turner, L. (2003). Comparative coalition building and the revitalization of the labor movement. *The Proceedings of the 55th Annual Meeting of the Industrial Relations Research Association.* Retrieved February 5, 2008, from http://www.press.uillinois.edu/journals/irra/proceedings2003/frege.html

Fullilove, M. T. (2004). *Root shock: How tearing up city neighborhoods hurts America and what we can do about it.* New York: Ballantine Books.

Gibbons, A., & Haas, G. (2002). Redefining redevelopment participatory research for equity in the Los Angeles Figueroa Corridor. Retrieved August 19, 2008, from http://www.saje.net/atf/cf/{493B2790-DD4E-4ED0-8F4E-C78E8F3A7561}/redefineredevelopment.pdf

Goodno, J. B. (2004). Feet to the fire: Accountable development keeps developers and community groups talking—and walking. *Planning.* Retrieved February 16, 2009, from http://www.laane.org/pressroom/stories/ad/ad0403planning.html

Gross, J., LeRoy, G., & Janis-Aparicio, M. (2005). *Community benefits agreements: Making development projects accountable.* Los Angeles, CA: Good Jobs First.

Haas, G. (2002). Economic justice in the Los Angeles Figueroa Corridor. In L. Delp, M. Outman-Kramer, S. Schurman & K. Wong (Eds.), *Teaching for change: Popular education and the labor movement* (pp. 90–100). Los Angeles, CA: UCLA Center for Labor Research and Education.

Haas, G. (2007). Community benefits and community control? What we really want. Retrieved September 11, 2008, from http://www.saje.net/site/c.hkLQJcMUKrH/b.2615505/k.13C4/Community_Benefits_or_Community_Control.htm

Himeda, K. (2006). *White wall.* Real Change News. Retrieved September 19, 2008, from http://www.realchangenews.org/2006/2006_11_29/whitewall.html

Hunter, R. P. (1997, September). Union racial discrimination is alive and well. *View points on public issues*. Mackinac Center for Public Policy. Retrieved July 9, 2008, from http://www.mackinac.org/article.aspx?ID=325

Janis, M. (2008). New movement for equitable urban development. *Race, poverty and the environment, 15*(1), 73–75.

Kelber, H. (2003). New game plan for union organizing. *Labor Educator*. Retrieved August 5, 2008, from http://www.laboreducator.org/gamplan1.htm

Kelley, R. (1999). Building bridges: The challenge of organized labor in communities of color. *New Labor Forum, 5*(Fall/Winter), 42–58.

Kretzmann, J. P. & McKnight, J. L. (1993). *Building communities from the inside out: A path toward finding and mobilizing a community's assets*. Evanston, IL: Institute for Policy Research.

Leavitt, J. (2006). Linking housing to community economic development with community benefits agreements: The case of the Figueroa Corridor Coalition for Economic Justice. In P. Ong & A. Loukaitou-Sideris (Eds.), *Jobs and economic development in minority communities: Realities, challenges, and innovation* (pp. 257–276). Philadelphia: Temple University Press.

LeRoy, G., & Purinton, A. (2005). *Community benefits agreements: Ensuring that urban redevelopment benefits everyone*. Washington, DC: Neighborhood Funders Group.

Lopez, S. (2004). Overcoming legacies of business unionism: Why grassroots tactics succeed. In K. Voss & R. Milkman (Eds.), *Rebuilding labor: Organizing and organizers in the New Union Movement* (pp. 114–32). Ithaca, NY: Cornell ILR Press.

Milkman, R., & Voss, K. (Eds). (2004). *Rebuilding labor*. Ithaca, NY: Cornell ILR Press.

Miller, Y. (2004). *Organizers of color seek collaboration*. Retrieved November 11, 2008, from http://www.baystatebanner.com/archives/stories/2004/Feb0504-2.htm

Murphy, P. (2004). *The housing that community built*. Retrieved July 15, 2008, from http://www.nhi.org/online/issues/138/bedford.html

O'Donnell, S. (1995). Urban African American community development in the Progressive Era. *Journal of Community Practice, 2*(4), 7–26.

O'Donnell, S., & Karanja, S. (2000). Transformative community practice: Building a model of developing extremely low-income African American communities. *Journal of Community Practice, 7*(3), 67–84.

Oslin, R. (2004, November 14). The staying power of AHANA [Electronic version]. *Boston College Chronicle, 13*(6). Retrieved April 30, 2009, from http://www.bc.edu/bc_org/rvp/pubaf/chronicle/v13/n18/ahana.html

Partnership for Working Families. (2008). *Victories*. Retrieved September 30, 2008, from http://www.communitybenefits.org/article.php?list=type&type=8

Rasheed, J., & Rasheed, M. (1999). *Social work practice with African American men: The invisible presence*. Thousand Oaks: Sage.

Rivas, L. (2006). The limits of the service employees' international union's social movement unionism. *Proceedings of the Annual Meeting of the American Sociological Association,* August 11, 2006. Retrieved February 5, 2009, from http://www.allacademic.com//meta/p_mla_apa_research_citation/1/0/4/7/4/pages104748/p104748-1.php

Schiele, J. (2005). Cultural oppression and the high-risk status of African Americans. *Journal of Black Studies, 35*(6), 802–826.

Sellers, J. M. (2007). Unions and the strategic context of local governance. In L. Turner & D. Cornfield (Eds.), *Labor in the new urban battlegrounds: Local solidarity in a global economy* (pp. 21–34). Ithaca, NY: Cornell University Press.

Tattersall, A. (2006). *Solidarity whenever? A framework for analyzing when unions are likely to practice collaboration with the community.* Ithaca, NY: Cornell University, School of Industrial and Labor Relations, International Programs. Retrieved July 9, 2008, from http://digitalcommons.ilr.cornell.edu/intlvf/23/

Tattersall, A. (2007). Coalitions and community unionism: Using the term community to explore effective union-community collaboration. Retrieved July 9, 2008 from http://www.communityunionism.org/nucleus/index.php?itemid=29

Tattersall, A., & Reynolds, D. (2007). The shifting power of labor-community coalitions: Identifying common elements of powerful coalitions in Australia and the USA. *Working USA: The Journal of Labor and Society, 10*(1), 77–102.

Turner, L., & Hurd, R. (2001). Building social movement unionism. In L. Turner, H. Katz & R. Hurd (Eds.), *Rekindling the movement: Labor's quest for relevance in the 21st century* (pp. 9–26). Ithaca, NY: ILR Press.

Worthen, H. (2004). *Unions, community-based organizations and pre-apprenticeship programs: Partners respond to the question, what brings these partnerships together?* Unpublished manuscript.

Young Laing, B. (2003). *African American models of community organizing: Toward a culturally competent theory.* Unpublished doctoral dissertation, Virginia Commonwealth University, Richmond.

Young Laing, B. (2009a). The Universal Negro Improvement Association, Southern Christian Leadership Conference. *Journal of Black Studies, 39*(4), 635–656.

Young Laing, B. (2009b). *Contemporary progressive organizing in African American communities: A theoretical model.* Manuscript under review.

Critical Pedagogy as a Tool
for Labor-Community Coalition Building

ROLAND ZULLO

*Institute for Research on Labor, Employment, and the Economy,
University of Michigan, Ann Arbor, Michigan, USA*

GREGORY PRATT

AFT Michigan, Detroit, Michigan, USA

*Conditions are ripe for a reunion between organized labor and
progressive social activists. Nonetheless, experiments in labor-
community coalitions offer few examples of lasting collaborations.
We report on a pilot project that uses critical pedagogy to create
ongoing, region-based labor-community coalitions. We discuss
context, theory, process, and outcomes in order to offer a model for
replication.*

Scholars concerned about the declining status of wage earners have
engaged in a dialogue over the barriers to rebuilding the union movement,
and the proper strategic course that organized labor should take to reverse
current trends. A critical view posits that unions erred by evolving into institutions that pursue narrowly defined economic interests—specifically, better
conditions and compensation for members—through the mechanism of
contract negotiations, while abdicating a commitment to broader social
causes or community needs (Buhle, 1999; Moody, 1988). As such, the idea
of labor-community coalitions, a model reminiscent of the burst of union

The University of Michigan's Institute for Research on Labor, Employment, and the
Economy is a newly formed institute which includes the former Institute of Labor and Industrial
Relations.

organizing that took place during the Great Depression era, has emerged as a recommendation for union revitalization (e.g., Brecher & Costello, 1990; Reynolds, 2004; Sciacchitano, 1998).

Recent efforts, however, provide no assurance that such a strategy will bear fruit. Collaborations are often single-issue initiatives that dissipate once the mobilizing phase has passed. To the consternation of non-union partners, reciprocal support from unions for community causes can be weak. And too often, a "coalition" amounts to a handshake among institutional leaders, lacking any genuine collaboration from an integrated team of rank-and-file activists. For these reasons, labor-community projects of late tend to be ephemeral pacts that fail to blossom into sustainable movements.

In this article, we report on a pilot project initiated by the University of Michigan's Labor Studies Center that is designed to avoid these pitfalls and facilitate ongoing and effective labor-community coalitions. What distinguishes this effort is the use of critical pedagogy to establish the laboratory conditions for collaboration. Critical pedagogy has shown to be effective at union leadership development (Zullo & Gates, 2008). We extended this application by using critical pedagogy to assemble and nurture leadership from the nonunion members of the community and foster partnerships with labor union activists within the Detroit Metropolitan area.

The project, titled "Labor & Community," was an education program that began in September 2007, produced a conference on April 26, 2008, and will resume in 2009. The pedagogical approach is straightforward: identify union activists with a passion for a community or public cause, pair them with activists belonging to non-union organizations fighting a similar cause, and have these like-minded social agitators co-instruct a class of peers on the urgency of the cause and map a remedial plan of action. In the discussion that follows, we sketch the contextual trends favoring labor-community coalitions, present a theory for why critical pedagogy can fill this purpose, and describe the organizing process, forms of resistance, outcomes, and opinions of the 2008 Labor & Community activists. Our data for this case study is based on participation observation, project documents such as attendance records and correspondence, and responses to a survey by the persons involved in planning the conference (see Appendix). Our hope is to stimulate experimentation with this education method by practitioners interested in mobilizing labor and community resources for sustainable and inclusive social and economic justice movements.

LABOR'S TRANSFORMATION

Mills (1963) emphasized that from the post-Depression institutionalization of labor relations emerged union leaders who assimilated many of the characteristics and behavior of their corporate counterparts. The radical-led organizing fury of the 1930s was quickly followed by a period of tripartite wartime compromises, and after World War II, the purging of communist-branded activists from union leadership. Those remaining earned legitimacy as powerbrokers adept at managing wage-earner discontent for the purpose of achieving gains through contract negotiations. Labor unions and their leaders secured an economic foothold in society, and the "system" went largely unchallenged because unions collectively and members individually benefited materially. Shared prosperity tamed radical impulses: union halls that were centers for debating the virtues of socialism during the 1930s became places for casual socializing by the 1950s. Political mobilizing languished, although parochial, closed-door maneuvering was undertaken to support economic aims. From the end of World War II to the stagflation years of the 1970s, union leaders largely complied with, as John Dunlop (1958) would phrase it, the "web of rules" and forsook broader political reform.

Complacency with a contract-centered model was by no means universal. Leftist labor organizations, such as the Industrial Workers of the World (IWW), agitated for local and community-based forms of radicalism, and viewed contracts as acquiescence to an inherently unjust system. Even leaders in conventional roles, such as auto workers leader Walter Reuther, understood the limitations of what became pejoratively tagged as "business unionism," and remarked on the potential for unions to become vehicles for progressive social change (Bok & Dunlop, 1970).[1] Nonetheless, as Reuther discovered, orienting a labor union to spearhead lofty ideals is a risky mission. The legal structure and incentives of the U.S. industrial relations system operate against strategies that redirect union resources away from tangible payoffs to be had at the bargaining table in a play for dubious gains through community activism. Union members certainly factor into this preference. Large numbers of unionists, as Perlman (1928) long ago observed, are politically and socially conservative. As long as the rules enable labor to re-expropriate some share of U.S. business earnings into the pockets of dues-paying members, those members would elect leaders skilled at negotiating labor's fairest share. In such a world, bargainers are wanted, not radicals envisioning dramatic social change.

Unfortunately for labor, those conditions have unraveled. De-industrialization since the 1980s eviscerated the ranks of manufacturing unions,[2] incremental changes in labor law have burdened the task of organizing new workers,[3] and trade policies protect and encourage the relocation of capital to lower-wage nations. As a result, union density in the private goods-producing sector has declined from the post-World-War-II apex of nearly 35% to around 7%. Union growth is currently limited to public services, or non-tradable private services, such as health care. Even here, however, employers mount obstacles and work the political system to circumscribe union power.[4] Labor's role as an economic agent for the wage-earning class has clearly diminished.

The failed gambit of business unionism was that labor would retain its role as a junior partner to industry if labor leaders championed the spread of American capitalism. At the plant level, this meant labor-management cooperation and collective restraint; at the national level, it meant discrimination against minorities, endorsing anti-immigrant policies and laxity toward the plight of the working poor. Internationally, it meant countenancing military and covert efforts to destabilize socialist regimes, secure energy and other raw materials, and to protect the expatriated assets of U.S. corporations. Business unionism was a critical misjudgment that alienated organized labor from left-progressive political movements (Buhle, 1999; Zullo, 2007). For much of the political left, organized labor was part of the problem, on the wrong side of anti-war, immigration, and emergent environmental causes. Moreover, pro-business posturing led many unions to lower their guard against tactics by business to escape from their obligations to organized labor, and implement a union-free strategy (Kochan, Katz, & McKersie, 1986).

However, it was long-term neglect in the area of political mobilization that produced the gravest disappointments. Labor's hope for a return to pluralism under President Bill Clinton, as repayment for financial and volunteer support in the 1992 election, was doused by Clinton's half-hearted pitch for striker replacement legislation, which would have augmented labors' strike power by banning the use of permanent replacements during a strike, and enthusiasm for the North American Free Trade Act, which was designed to protect corporations that relocated operations in Mexico and Canada.[5] The fact that the Democratic Party could so easily fob off the grievances and demands of union leaders underscored labors' increased irrelevancy.

Out of necessity, organized labor upgraded its organizing and political programs. By the late 1980s, with the junior partnership defunct, labor placed renewed emphasis on organizing, as symbolized by the creation of the American Federation of Labor–Congress of Industrial Organizations (AFL-CIO) Organizing Institute in 1989. To augment their political capacity, labor is reaching out for political allies. Recent positions by the AFL-CIO on internal and national policy are conspicuous attempts to establish bona fides with the left. In 1997, the AFL-CIO removed language in its constitution barring communists from holding office. In 2005, after pressure from a campaign by U.S. Labor Against the War, the AFL-CIO supported the rapid withdrawal of U.S. troops from Iraq. Finally, in 2003 the AFL-CIO embraced immigrant rights to citizenship; a historic reversal indicating a heightened awareness that lifting the "bottom" of the labor market is a precondition for reversing the decline in union membership. The loss of influence in the economic sphere has forced labor to become more effective in the political sphere, which in turn means establishing coalitions with left-progressive movements. In order to recruit sympathetic allies, labor is transforming into a more progressive entity.

A POTENTIAL REUNION OF LABOR AND SOCIAL WORK ACTIVISTS

The modern labor movement and the profession of social work were both a response to the great inequality and poverty brought about by the industrial revolution. Long before the founding of social work schools, activists for the poor understood the link between gainful, safe employment for the adult members of the household and family well-being. As such, early social workers collaborated with, and often identified with, union activists. Prominent early reformists, such as Jane Addams and Florence Kelley, conspired with leftist union leaders, such as Eugene V. Debs, Mary "Mother" Jones, and Rose Schneiderman, to push for the passage of laws that protected the most vulnerable from harsh corporate policies (Reisch & Andrews, 2001; Simon, 1994). Reformers established the National Consumers' League in 1899 to pressure corporations by sensitizing consumers to the unfair labor conditions within the factories. With support from the American Federation of Labor, social activists founded the Women's Trade Union League in 1903 to educate female workers on the benefits of unionization. Such high-profile ventures inspired and were inspired by lesser-known collaborations between organized labor and social reformers at the state and local levels (Axinn & Stern, 2001; Reisch & Andrews, 2001).

The labor-social work nexus cooled, however, as the two fields institutionalized. Unions sanctioned by the state came to represent the voice for all things related to labor. Meanwhile, social work evolved into a formal profession, and schools hired instructors and adopted curricula that focused on preparing students for careers in expanding public service agencies or as private clinicians; both of these social work trajectories involved a focus on casework and individualized solutions for social inequality (Axinn & Stern, 2001; Lubove, 1965). Thus, business unionism solidified just as social work retreated from radical advocacy on behalf of wage earners. Consequently, collaborations between labor and social work activists have nearly disappeared (Reisch & Andrews, 2001; Simon, 1994).

Nonetheless, a reunion is feasible. Labor's travails have opened the door for collaboration on progressive causes, a role that social workers, with their longstanding advocacy of social justice, can potentially fill (Karger, 1989). And the need is great: the decline in union coverage means that large swaths of wage earners are unprotected. As was the case a century ago, the most vulnerable populations—immigrants, the young, minorities, single parents—have the least power in society. The allies for whom labor is searching are those who can encourage unionization, or secondarily, improve conditions for oppressed populations and thus indirectly relieve unions from downward labor market pressure (Piven & Cloward, 1995; Scanlon & Harding, 2005). However, while labor appears open to partnerships with non-union organizations, methods for achieving lasting coalitions are underdeveloped. The process needs "bridge builders," trusted brokers of collective aspiration, to facilitate inter-organizational collaboration (Brecher & Costello, 1990). Social workers who choose to be social activists can be credible bridge builders, and one promising tool for this purpose is critical pedagogy.

CRITICAL PEDAGOGY AS A TOOL FOR COALITION BUILDING

In making the case for using critical pedagogy to unite labor and community efforts, it is useful to state the assumptions that drive this model and describe why such a model is appropriate for these times.

A major assumption, implicit in the title of Paolo Freire's *Pedagogy of the Oppressed* (1970), is that the superstructure is unjust. If the starting premise is that the rules are stacked to favor the powerful, then it follows that traditional education, designed to convey the rules and the boundaries the rules impose, would only reinforce the caste structure and perpetuate injustice. Critical pedagogy invites an interrogation of the rules, and further, provokes the oppressed to establish their own rules. It does so by rejecting the traditional educational approach whereby the professional teacher stands before the pupils, imparting knowledge. Instead, the oppressed teach, or more accurately, facilitate a discussion on the problems within the community and their causes, and lead a remedial plan of action. Disobedience to written and unwritten rules is fully acceptable, as long as a genuine pursuit of social justice guides behavior.

A second and related assumption is that the major limitation for the oppressed is not their lack of technical knowledge, but rather a lack of awareness of their potential to confront their oppressors. To become conscious of their power, the oppressed must act collectively and achieve tangible gains. Again, traditional education methods that focus on skill transfer are insufficient. Critical pedagogy instead plunges wage earners and community members into an experiential cycle of action and reflection. Meetings take place where participants learn from each other, and reflect. Outside of the meetings, attendees are obligated to take what they learn and apply it in the field, and return to subsequent meetings to share their experiences and collectively re-strategize. Through this iterative process, wage earners and community members grow as leaders and become con-scious of their collective power. Woven throughout are cultural aspects that warm the environment; familiar symbols, contexts, and language aid in the identification of common issues and help establish long-term relations among participants.

In brief, we identify four dimensions to critical pedagogy: (a) the elimination of classroom hierarchy by removing the expert instructor; (b) sharing and developing a body of knowledge based on lived experience; (c) a programmatic dynamic of reflecting upon and then acting on acquired knowledge; (d) developing a culturally embedded learning environment, where culture serves as the collective bonding agent (Zullo & Gates, 2008). Adhering to these concepts helps ensure that activists have access to a forum where they can validate their vision before their peers, and thereby become their own examples of liberators. These concepts fit a purpose of nurturing many "small" leaders who have the capacity to provide mutual support by sharing resources through an informal network. Logistically, since critical pedagogy requires a serious time commitment from rank-and-file activists, such projects have the best chance for success if they bring together existing region-based movements.

For the educator/organizer, critical pedagogy is time-intensive. The Labor & Community project described here involved monthly planning meetings beginning in September 2007 in preparation for a training conference in the spring of 2008. We spent significant amounts of time in the first meetings explaining critical pedagogy. After a lifetime of traditional education, it was difficult for planners to conceive of an education model that does not include a certified expert as the lead character. One attendee commented, "Although at first I was unclear about the concept, I was anxious to help the AFL-CIO build leaders and broaden its base of activists." Many of those who attended the first meetings were confused or frustrated by this approach and dropped out. Nonetheless, those attending were outspoken about their dissatisfaction with the familiar conference format: a row of talking heads addressing a room of passive participants. We stressed that the conference was theirs to design. From here, a suggestion was made to include guerilla theater as part of the event. People offered ideas concerning food, entertainment, and topics. The first few meetings produced no instructor volunteers.

In critical pedagogy, it is vital for the educator/organizer to resist the temptation to step into a teaching or leadership void. Running a critical education model is analogous to producing a play. The audience pays to enjoy a performance, where the main focus is on the actors and playwrights. But a successful play also requires a stage, set production, lighting, sound, and so forth. Months before showtime there are rehearsals to perfect timing and coordination. With critical pedagogy, the rank-and-file activists are the writers and actors performing for an audience of their peers. They are responsible for script preparation, direction, and presentation and, at curtain close, bow to the applause. The educator resembles the producer, lurking in the shadows during the performance, vicariously absorbing the accolades. The bulk of his or her work took place in the preceding months, obtaining funding, organizing the group, helping individuals prepare, taking care of all the incidentals and transactions.

For Labor & Community, the strength of critical pedagogy was found in the problem solving and learning taking place in the meetings prior to the education event. Working toward a successful conference forced planners to deal with personal differences, which on an intimate level required that they reconcile conflicting positions of their organizations. It is here where bridges were built. The education event itself was a byproduct of hours of amicable negotiations by the planners. As the deadline loomed, decisions had to be made: What are our major messages? How do we present the material? Who will present? How do we handle areas where we lack a consensus? Preparing for the education event exercised the executive skills necessary for collaboration beyond the conference.

This version of critical pedagogy obligates the rank-and-file activist to take responsibility for strategy and its tactical implementation. On this point, it is valuable to distinguish this approach from the community organizing model developed by Saul Alinsky, which shares the goal of empowering lower socioeconomic persons through collective action, and stresses the importance of reaching out to working-class, blue-collar unionized workers as allies. In the Alinsky (1971) model, the professional organizer is at the center of strategic planning, helping the oppressed confront power imbalances by engineering a series of escalating victories.

More contemporary discussions on the profession of community organizing have expanded the organizer role to include teaching, coaching and facilitation (Burghardt, 1982; Mondros & Wilson, 1994; Rubin & Rubin, 2001). Yet within these frameworks organizers still retain some responsibility for vision, strategy, and tactics. For instance, Rubin and Rubin (2001) offer that the "role of an organizer is to help create a sense that change is possible and *show the way*" (p. 21, our italics). Mondros and Wilson (1994) write that "[o]rganizers bring the vision of what the organization is to become" (p. 34). Burghardt (1982), who draws heavily from Freire, constructs a trenchant analysis on how organizers engage the unorganized. Throughout, however, the organizer is the central figure, urged for instance to apply "*the use of ourselves as models of leadership*" (p. 83, italics in text).

With a coalition building project, the main concern is the engagement between activists from disparate backgrounds. Labor & Community attracted planners that were already committed to a social issue, so involvement by the educator/organizer in the area of issue identification was unnecessary. Indeed, several members of the planning group were informal leaders in their communities and unions—persons with a developed sense of empowerment. In this case, attempts by the educator or organizer to redefine the issues might have had the counterproductive effect of devitalizing this resource.

Without the professional to identify issues, develop strategy, and coordinate implementation, activists may initially stumble, but the dialectical process of action and reflection allows for the evolution of an effective strategy based on the lessons from previous actions. This is the implicit tradeoff: by placing trust in the ingenuity of the oppressed, the educator/organizer cultivates long-term dedication. As one attendee commented, "Group learning and problem solving is healthy and we should continue to try to encourage it in community and labor building. People seem to invest more in settings where they have a voice" (Zullo & Pratt, 2008).

Thus, the educator/organizer is responsible for fostering the conditions and environment by which the labor and community activists strategize. More pointedly, the educator/organizer facilitates and perpetuates periods of reflection by organizing people, marshalling resources, and dealing with nuts-and-bolts details such as facility location and food. During the planning meetings, the labor and community activists provide direction on these matters, but their main responsibility is to decide on topics, prepare for instruction, and recruit peers. The 2008 Labor & Community project did have a broad thematic umbrella, put succinctly by one activist as: "The synergy of union and community activists can bring positive change that neither can accomplish alone" (Zullo & Pratt, 2008). Guided by this general consensus for the need to collaborate, activists were empowered to identify a cause, and then use the training institute to build a miniature movement for that cause. Quite unlike traditional education, critical pedagogy is not just a study of a social problem; it is the discussion of concrete steps toward addressing a social problem, and the recruitment of sympathetic persons to implement those steps.

One task for the educator/organizer is organizing. Our initial approach was to conduct outreach to potential leaders of community organizations and unions describing the leadership development opportunities our event presented. This required one-on-one conversations that moved beyond "cold call" telemarketing and involved deeper philosophical dialogues about the potential organizational and community benefits of this project. These one-on-one conversations, in conjunction with several community and local union presentations, were the foundation upon which we were able to build a planning committee.

The planning committee was solidified in December 2007 at a pre-holiday event at which interested activists and unionists met each other and learned more about this project. This organizing event, held at a local electrical workers' union hall, struck a balance between informal mingling and didactic conversation regarding participation opportunities in the months to follow (and what exactly being a planning committee member entailed). This work resulted in commitments from about twenty-five people who volunteered for specific roles in the conference (e.g. workshop instructor, facilitator and conference coordinator). With a few exceptions, the committee formed at this initial gathering remained involved through the day of the conference. Like many community organizing projects, conflicts arose that had to be managed in order to prevent the group from disbanding.

Personality and interest differences needed to be mediated. For instance, an interest conflict came up during one of the monthly planning sessions manifest in a current local debate over whether to build an oil refinery in a particular community. Environmental activists at the meeting confronted an electrical union member over her public testimony in favor of the construction. With the depressed economic climate in Michigan, the jobs such a project would provide for union members were the primary motivation for her support of the construction project. This position was in conflict with perceived negative effects on local environmental quality. While agreement to the jobs versus environment conundrum was not reached, each planner involved in this particular conflict remained dedicated to the project and participated through the conference. Not every conflict had a positive outcome, however.

There is a risk in a labor and community event for one ideology or position to dominate, and the educator needs to work toward equal status for non-union and union activists. For example, after the first organizing meeting, one volunteer felt intimidated by the abundance of union members and believed that there was little room for her input on her chosen topic. In her prior experiences with unions, she was marginalized due to her ethnicity. Her strong feelings on this matter could not be reconciled and she dropped out of the project.

The lesson we drew from these incidents was that the educator/organizer needs to be sensitive to the power and privilege differentials among individual activists, and work toward creating an environment where people from varying backgrounds and cultures feel comfortable interacting. It is not enough to simply invite people from different social identity groups and expect that a sense of equality will automatically emerge. The educator-organizer must encourage a dialogue that acknowledges differences, and the issues arising from these differences, to encourage broad and lasting participation.

PRODUCT OF THE 2008 LABOR & COMMUNITY PROJECT

The 2008 Labor & Community conference drew approximately 90 adults and 12 children. The planning group decided to begin the conference with a plenary meeting featuring a guerilla theater skit that illustrated the problems with the U.S. health care system. In the skit, a person feigned a heart attack and a doctor and paramedics rushed in, but these health professionals withheld care because the victim had no insurance. The palpitating victim offered cash, but the health professionals instead rushed to help another, insured, person who burnt her lip on hot coffee. The actors in this comical scene served on the planning committee. After the skit, the proposed ballot measure for universal health care for Michigan was introduced, and people were asked to sign and become canvassers. For the participants, guerilla theater was a break from the usual conference format, and may become a regular cultural aspect of future conferences.

Afterward, participants broke out into workshops. Months earlier, the planning committee decided on the workshop topics, including fighting the Michigan right-to-work initiative, labor and the environment, labor and community mobilization, community cooking, and a workshop for children. Some workshop ideas, such as education policy and bringing the troops home/peace movement, were dropped due to lack of interest or lack of instructors. The session "Immigrant Rights are Human Rights" was moved to the afternoon plenary due to low enrollment. Likewise, certain topics, such as the anti-foreclosure movement, emerged late in the planning stage and were presented in the afternoon plenary. In general, workshop topics were revised depending on the composition of planning meeting members and the level of interest among registrants.

The workshops were co-instructed by a team of three to six people, union and non-union, for groups ranging from six to thirty participants. These two-hour sessions had the most intense training and cross-fertilization of opinions and plans around specific topics. As mentioned by one activist, the purpose was to remedy the " . . . misperceptions and a lack of institutional connections [that] prevent [labor and community groups] working together effectively toward shared goals" (Zullo & Pratt, 2008). The workshops extended to lunch, which was served by Detroit's Wobbly Kitchen (Detroit Branch IWW).

The afternoon plenary was reserved for community presentations. Most conference attendees were union members, so the idea was to invite community groups to discuss their efforts and ask for labor support. After each presentation, participants were offered a chance to sign onto the cause and become part of an activist network—giving opportunities, as one presenter put it, for "people searching for channels through which they might act to effect change and outcomes" (Zullo & Pratt, 2008). Figure 1 illustrates the pattern of volunteer signatures.

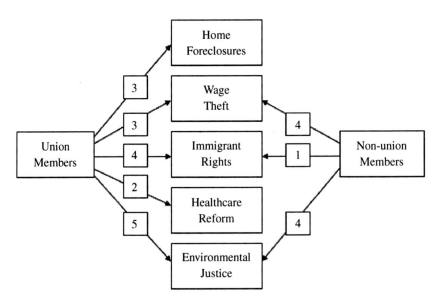

FIGURE 1 Labor & Community volunteers.

The boxes at the top of Figure 1 categorize the background of the respondent as either from a union or non-union group. Boxes at the bottom of Figure 1 give the titles of the community presentations. For instance, "wage theft" in the diagram refers to taking direct action on employers who have not paid wage-earners for work already completed. Direct action might involve, for example, camping out with a group in the bosses' office to compel him or her to pay the worker(s) in question. The arrows match the community issues with the number of volunteer signatures.

As can be seen, the interest among union members was dispersed across the five community issues. The topics that attracted the most volunteers—immigrant rights and environmental justice—had the most global themes. Environmental justice also attracted non-union volunteers, as did the issue of wage theft. What is important to note is the integration of union and non-union activists across a variety of local causes.

DISCUSSION AND RESEARCH

The initial response we received from participants, planners, and instructors indicates that most found value in convening for this day of creative hope, strategy, and camaraderie. It remains to be seen whether the relationships that came out of the process, and the product of our collective effort, will contribute to lasting movements. At this early stage in the project we can point to some encouraging signs of collaboration. In one instance, our organizing effort brought together a peace organization from Ann Arbor and one from Detroit. Previously, there had been some tension and disagreement over tactics. However, the Detroit organization now publicizes the events and actions of the Ann Arbor group. Similarly, one of the leaders of the Ann Arbor Peace organization was in attendance at a rally in Lansing to get a moratorium on foreclosures and home evictions (being promoted by the Detroit organization) passed in the Michigan Senate. In another example, a union member on our planning committee has been active in a new organization in Southeast Michigan dedicated to preventing foreclosures and helping to pass legislation that will allow homeowners in trouble to restructure their mortgages and retain their houses. In a third example, a member of our committee who has a leadership role in a statewide progressive political organization is creating space for a new restaurant workers' center to hold their own workshop as part of the policy summit his organization convenes annually in Michigan.

The next round of this ongoing project will begin with a reflection on the event itself and what has happened since then. We will try to reconvene previous participants and instructors to assess their involvement with each other and with their communities. Some of the previous participants will not return because of relocation or other priorities. Thus, organizing will be needed to counter attrition. However, we now have a core group of activists to call upon that understand the purpose of this endeavor and the operational merits of critical pedagogy. These activists will be the foundation for program growth and development.

Four questions will guide our long-term assessment of the Labor & Community project: (a) To what extent does critical pedagogy inculcate leadership traits among the activists involved in the program? (b) What is the degree to which union and community activists collaborate on strategies for social and economic change? (c) If coalitions do emerge, what form and function do those coalitions adopt? (d) Can this education model be replicated? The first three questions require a longer horizon of ethnographic analysis than was possible for this report. For the fourth question, social activists in other regions need to experiment with this method. On this final point, we invite social workers and unionists to use critical pedagogy as a tool to liberate creative and varied energies toward strengthening social and economic justice movements.

NOTES

1. Approaching the peak of UAW power, Walter Reuther is quoted in Bok and Dunlop (1970) on the importance of contributing to social growth once basic economic needs are achieved for members. History provides few examples, however, of Reuther's vision of labor as an agent for social reform in an era of prosperity and union efficacy. Rather, it seems more likely that economic hardship and union atrophy are preconditions for labor to facilitate community partnerships. As evidence, the phrase "social movement unionism" is ubiquitous today.

2. The Steelworkers, for instance, lost nearly one-half of their members during the 1980s deindustrialization period. The United Auto Workers have lost roughly two-thirds of their members since their peak in 1979.

3. Legislative revisions to labor law are infrequent. Change in labor law is largely due to federal court interpretation of the law. See Forbath (1991) for a detailed history.

4. In 2004, Indiana, Missouri, and Kentucky repealed collective bargaining rights for public employees.

5. It remains to be seen whether current legislation designed to make it easier for workers to join unions, the Employee Free Choice Act, will suffer a similar fate under the Obama administration.

REFERENCES

Alinsky, S. D. (1971). *Rules for radicals: A practical primer for realistic radicals.* New York: Random House.

Axinn, J., & Stern, M. (2001). *Social welfare: A history of the American response to need* (5th ed.). Boston, MA: Allyn & Bacon.

Bok, D. C., & Dunlop, J. T. (1970). *Labor and the American community.* New York: Simon & Schuster.

Brecher, J., & Costello, T. (1990). *Building bridges: The emerging grassroots coalition of labor and community.* New York: Monthly Review Press.

Buhle, P. (1999). *Taking care of business: Samuel Gompers, George Meany, Lane Kirkland, and the tragedy of American labor.* New York: Monthly Review Press.

Burghardt, S. (1982). *The other side of organizing: Resolving the personal dilemmas and political demands of daily practice.* Cambridge, MA: Schenkman.

Dunlop, J. T. (1958). *Industrial relations systems.* New York: Holt.

Forbath, W. E. (1991). *Law and the shaping of the American labor movement.* Cambridge, MA: Harvard University Press.

Freire, P. (1970). *Pedagogy of the oppressed.* New York: Herder and Herder.

Karger, H. J. (1989). The common and conflicting goals of labor and social work. *Administration in Social Work, 13*(1), 1–17.

Kochan, T. A., Katz, H. C., & McKersie, R. B. (1986). *The transformation of American industrial relations.* New York: Basic Books.

Lubove, R. (1965). *The professional altruist: The emergence of social work as a career, 1890–1930.* Cambridge, MA: Harvard University Press.

Mills, C. W. (1963). The labor leaders and the power elite. In I.L. Horowitz (Ed.), *Power, politics and people: The collected essays of C. Wright Mills* (pp. 97–109). New York: Oxford University Press.

Mondros, J.B., & Wilson, S.M. (1994). *Organizing for power and empowerment.* New York: Columbia University Press.

Moody, K. (1988). *An injury to all: The decline of American unionism.* London: Verso.

Perlman, S. (1928). *A theory of the labor movement.* New York: Macmillan.

Piven, F. F., & Cloward, R. A. (1995). *Regulating the poor: The functions of public welfare* (Rev. ed.). New York: Vintage Press.

Reisch, M., & Andrews, J.L. (2001). *The road not taken: A history of radical social work in the United States.* Philadelphia, PA: Brunner-Routledge.

Rubin, H. J., & Rubin, I. S. (2001). *Community organizing and development* (3rd ed.). Boston, MA: Allyn & Bacon.

Reynolds, D. B. (2004). *Partnering for change: Unions and community groups build coalitions for economic justice.* Armonk, NY: M. E. Sharpe.

Scanlon, E., & Harding, S. (2005). Social work and labor unions: Historical and contemporary alliances. *Journal of Community Practice 13*(1), 9–30.

Sciacchitano, K. (1998). Finding the community in the union and the union in the community: The first contract campaign at Steeltech. In K. Bronfenbrenner, S. Friedman, R. W. Hurd, R. A. Oswald & R. L. Seeber (Eds.), *Organizing to win: New research on union strategies* (pp. 150–163). Ithaca, NY: Cornell University.

Simon, B. L. (1994). *The empowerment tradition in American social work: A history.* New York: Columbia University Press.

Zullo, R. (2007). Labor's divided house: Contextual and theoretical terms of the U.S. divorce. *Advances in Labor and Industrial Relations, 15*, 333–358.

Zullo, R., & Gates, A. (2008). Labor education in the time of dismay. *Labor Studies Journal, 33*(2), 179–202.

Zullo, R., & Pratt, G. (2008). [Labor & Community evaluations: compilations]. Unpublished raw data, University of Michigan Labor Studies Center, Ann Arbor.

APPENDIX
LABOR & COMMUNITY EVALUATION SURVEY

1. How did you first learn about the Labor & Community conference?

- ☐ From a co-worker
- ☐ From a friend or family member
- ☐ From a union official or community leader
- ☐ From a presentation before my union
- ☐ From a presentation before my community organization
- ☐ From a presentation before the Detroit AFL-CIO
- ☐ Other (please describe)

2. How many pre-conference planning sessions did you attend?

- ☐ 0 or 1
- ☐ 2
- ☐ 3
- ☐ 4 or more

3. Why did you decide to help instruct and/or organize this event?
4. What ideas can you offer for motivating others to instruct, organize, and attend next year's conference?
6. In this conference format, we all teach and learn. First, consider your teaching role. What workshop or presentation did you help instruct?

- ☐ Labor and the Environment
- ☐ Education Policy
- ☐ Peace—Bring the Troops Home
- ☐ Immigration Rights = Human Rights
- ☐ Fighting Right to Work
- ☐ Labor and Community Development
- ☐ Community Cooking

7. What teaching techniques did your group use? Check all that apply.

- ☐ Lecture
- ☐ Group discussion
- ☐ Role play
- ☐ Quizzes
- ☐ Problem solving
- ☐ Power point presentation
- ☐ Other (please describe)

8. How do you feel you contributed to the knowledge of others in your workshop?
9. Now consider what you learned. What general lesson(s) would you draw from the conference experience?
10. After working with others, do you think differently about the topic that you instructed? If yes, please explain.
11. Now consider some other social issues discussed at the conference. Of the list below, please check whether you learned a great deal, learned something, or learned very little, about each of the topics.

Issue

Learned a great deal
Learned something
Learned very little
N/A

Immigration raids

☐
☐
☐
☐

Foreclosure crisis

☐
☐
☐
☐

Environmental justice

☐
☐
☐
☐

Wage theft – direct actions

☐
☐
☐
☐

Community youth

☐
☐
☐
☐

Health care now

☐

☐

☐

☐

Local peace movement

☐

☐

☐

☐

Blue-Green alliance

☐

☐

☐

☐

Education policy

☐

☐

☐

☐

12. If you could change one thing to improve the conference, what would it be?

ON THE FRONT LINES, IN THE CLASSROOMS

"Social Justice Infrastructure" Organizations as New Actors From the Community: The Case of South Florida

BRUCE NISSEN

Center for Labor Research and Studies, Florida International University, Miami, Florida

This article reviews the decline of U.S. unions and examines proposals for their revitalization. It also notes the emergence of new actors in working class communities to fill the void left by declining union power. Using south Florida as an example, it chronicles the growth of a "social justice infrastructure" of community organizations such as worker centers, working-class grassroots community organizing groups, faith-based worker rights groups, and labor-community coalition groups. It notes difficulties in building deep coalitions between traditional unions and such groups and explores the possibility of "networks" as a new promising organizational form. It finds limitations to the network form also, and proposes that a synergistic conjunction of various types of political and economic struggles and forms holds more promise than any one particular organizational form.

INTRODUCTION

As the U.S. labor movement continues its long decline in numbers and influence, scholarly attention has to some extent shifted to other possible avenues for working-class power to counter increasing inequality and stagnant incomes at the middle and bottom of the income spectrum. Scholars have also devoted attention to the ways in which traditional labor unions and newer social actors speaking for the interests of workers can interact for mutual benefit. In general, scholars sympathetic to working-class interests in the United States have been looking for ways in which "social justice" across class lines can be achieved when the main vehicle for its attainment appears to be mortally wounded.

One approach has been to look for ways that the labor movement can transform itself and become a different type of institution than it has been in the past. Unions are urged to become more inclusive and socially active crusaders for working-class interests in a broader sense, not merely bargainers for the economic interests of their own particular members. In short, unions are asked to transform themselves from bargaining bureaucracies primarily engaging in "business unionism" to social movement organizations leading struggles at the workplace and to some degree in the community. They are urged to transform themselves into "social movement unions" (Nissen, 2003; Turner & Hurd, 2001). A variety of other terms and related analyses have also appeared recently regarding this type of unionism, including "community unionism," "social justice unionism," and "citizenship movement unionism."

The hopes of those calling for social movement unionism in the United States have not been quickly or appreciably realized in the past 15 years, despite some high profile examples of success, such as the SEIU's "Justice for Janitors" campaign, which has used a social movement repertoire of action to win some stunning victories around the country (Albright, 2008; Fisk, Mitchell, & Erickson, 2000; Rudy, 2004). Despite the lack of widespread adoption of a social movement orientation, some observers (Johnston, 2002; Robinson, 2002) have argued that the U.S. labor movement has moved at least tentatively in the direction of "social unionism" and is beginning to coalesce around a broader vision than its primary one in the past. Despite these hopeful signs, there is no indication that wholesale internal transformation is taking root in the traditional labor unions, and this is true for both unions that stayed with the AFL-CIO during the recent split and those who left to form the Change to Win (CTW) federation.

A second avenue of investigation has looked at the possibilities for labor-community coalitions, wherein unions join forces with other worker organizing and advocacy organizations to achieve broad working class goals. There is a large literature looking at coalitional efforts, including the Jobs with Justice network and numerous other labor-community coalitional efforts around the country (Nissen, 2004). The edited volume *Partnering for Change: Unions and Community Groups Build Partnerships for Economic Justice* (Reynolds, 2004) is a mostly hopeful example of the literature on this topic. By far the most successful coalitions of this nature on a mass scale in the country have been the "living wage" efforts to require publicly-funded service providers in a number of cities and counties to pay a wage sufficient to lift a family above the poverty line (Luce, 2002; Nissen, 2000; Pollin, Brenner, Luce, & Wicks-Lim, 2008; Pollin & Luce, 1998; Reynolds & Kern, 2001–2002).

Once again, however, the hopes of labor-community coalition advocates have been only partially vindicated. While there is undoubtedly more coalition activity between labor unions and other social justice organizations than there were in earlier times, the depth and longevity of such coalitions has been questionable. Unions have a strong tendency to only seek out or accept what could be called "vanguard coalitions," where the labor movement "requires coalition partners to simply support labor-defined and labor-led activities" (Nissen, 2004, p. 72). Just as an apparent alliance between organized labor and global justice activist groups effectively collapsed shortly after the 1999 "Battle of Seattle" protests against the WTO meeting, many local labor-community coalitions turn out to be nothing more than temporary marriages of convenience. Some of the reasons for this are explored elsewhere (Heckscher & Carré, 2006; Nissen, 2004).

Another avenue of research has explored attempts by central labor councils and state federations of labor to build regional power in various cities and regions where concerted efforts are being made. A Web site (www.power-building.wayne.edu) contains studies of a number of cities where the political bodies of organized labor—state federations and local central labor councils—are systematically attempting to build political influence to shape public policy. Most instances demonstrate coalition-building, regional policy research and agenda-setting, and aggressive political action (Reynolds, 2007).

Finally, some recent investigations explore non-union formations defending workers and their communities. In some cases, traditional community organizing groups have addressed low-wage workers issues and concerns; this has been particularly true of the community organizing groups the Association of Community Organizations for Reform Now (ACORN) and the Industrial Areas Foundation (Kest, 2004; Osterman, 2006). But most of the attention has gone to new types of formations, most particularly "workers centers," which are typically community-based organizations addressing the needs of low-wage workers and their families, usually in immigrant communities. Workers centers come in many varieties, but they usually combine advocacy, organizing, and service in some proportion (Fine, 2006). Other formations, such as faith-based workers rights groups and identity-based organizations formed along racial or gender lines, are also newly active.

SOUTH FLORIDA AS AN EXAMPLE

The Miami area in south Florida (Miami-Dade County) is an excellent laboratory to examine the dynamics of groups of this nature, as well as their interaction with each other and with traditional labor unions. Ten years ago, unions in south Florida had virtually no community organizations to support their organizing efforts, and no other organizing groups directly addressing the issues of workers. One church-based community organizing group existed, but it was primarily oriented toward education, transportation, crime, and other community issues, not the issues of workers specifically. By 2008, Miami-Dade County had a wide variety of community organizations directly concerned with labor issues and a wider array of working class community issues. These organizations have been dubbed the "social justice infrastructure" of the county (Nissen & Russo, 2007). They organize workers and on behalf of workers in the county, attempting to address the imbalance in power between working class people and the local moneyed power structure.

The living wage issue began the recent growth of social justice organizing in the area (Nissen, 2004). In 1997 leaders from the central labor council, a coalition of human service providers, the NAACP, Florida Legal Services, the Gray Panthers, a tenant's council, and others formed the Community Coalition for a Living Wage (CCLW) to win a county living wage ordinance, which was won in 1999 with 500 predominantly union members applauding final passage.

But this was not a genuine social movement as has been detailed elsewhere (Nissen 2000). The living wage ordinance passed mainly because there was no organized business opposition. The CCLW subsequently won living wage ordinances in the cities of Miami Beach (2001) and Miami (2006), but at present it has no sizable base to mobilize and it relies exclusively on lobbying. One central labor council representative sits on the CCLW's steering committee, but unions play a minor role in its most current efforts, which are led by church-based or community activists.

Nevertheless, the passage of the Miami-Dade living wage ordinance had an important symbolic importance. It showed that victories can be won for working families in Miami. The national community organizing group ACORN created chapters in south Florida and throughout the state because of these living wage victories, and is now an established pro-labor presence in south Florida and statewide, broadening the social justice infrastructure.

In 1998, a local South Florida Interfaith Committee for Worker Justice (SF IFWJ) chapter was set up. This committee went through growing pains and some contentious skirmishes with an earlier generation of central labor council leaders (Nissen, 2004, pp. 75–76). But eventually it became an established organization with genuine church and synagogue buy-in to its leadership and program. In 2006, it played a major role in supporting an SEIU "Justice for Janitors" struggle at the University of Miami, and it has also run a worker's rights counseling and advocacy program to help homeless day laborers and low-wage workers enforce their rights.

The Miami Workers Center (MWC), a political education and organizing center for low-income African American communities and low-wage workers in Miami-Dade County, was created in 1999. The MWC has founded two organizing groups in the African-American and Latino communities: Low Income Families Fighting Together (LIFFT) and Miami En Acción. A somewhat similar organization, Power U Center for Social Change, exists in the African-American neighborhood of Overtown. Both MWC and Power U are primarily community organizing projects that have no direct ties to unions other than the union backgrounds of their founders. Past collaboration with organized labor has been limited, but an emerging coalition to win community benefits from development efforts containing both union-related groups and these two organizations operated for a few years prior to its demise in 2008.

In 2001, the SEIU nursing home workers union created Unite for Dignity for Immigrant Workers Rights (UFD) in order to build stronger immigrant community ties and immigrant worker leadership. UFD's signature program is the Leadership Academy, which has graduated over 150 emerging immigrant leaders (80% of them women) from a cross-section of the community. UFD strengthens labor's relations with grassroots immigrant organizations and builds mobilizing capacity for immigrant community issues.

In late 1999, South Florida Jobs with Justice (SF JwJ) was created by the local chapter of the National Association for the Advancement of Colored People (NAACP), the SEIU nursing home union, and others. SF JwJ currently has over 20 member organizations, including a cross-section of south Florida unions as well as important community groups such as the Human Services Coalition and Unite for Dignity.

South Florida JwJ has evolved into an important center of the progressive working class movement in Miami. It was founded to support workers' rights to organize, but has transitioned into a broader program agenda addressing a variety of workers rights and working class community and multicultural issues. Among other things, it has founded a community organizing group in east Little Havana and organizes residents of trailer parks in the county to defend their interests.

The research capacity needed to investigate, analyze, and validate issues raised by movements has been a weakness in the past. The Research Institute on Social and Economic Policy (RISEP) was created at Florida International University under the direction of the author in the fall of 2004. It attempts to build the capacity of this budding movement to develop and win a broader social policy agenda by researching issues raised by labor, labor-community, and working class community organizing in south Florida and Florida as a whole.[1]

One can envision the various elements needed to bring power to workers and working class communities in south Florida as pieces of a map—the "social justice infrastructure" map. Many of the pieces of the map have been developing over the past decade: leadership development (UFD,

SF JwJ, several community organizing groups); coalition-building (CCLW, SF JwJ, an attempted but ultimately disbanded Community Benefits Coalition); research (RISEP), aggressive union organizing (SEIU), community-based organizing on social policy issues (MWC, Power U, ACORN), greater conventional political activism (the union's central labor council plus newly active voter registration projects), faith-based organizing in support of workers rights (SF IFWJ), and increased interest from national unions and foundations in putting resources into the area. Table 1 shows the stark difference between south Florida's social justice infrastructure in 1998 and 2008.

Table 1 leaves out a large number of organizations that exist in south Florida in 2008 that are omitted simply because of space and focus limitations. Thus, Miami-Dade County now also houses a Florida Immigrant Coalition which foster immigrant community organizing throughout the state, a gay/lesbian rights organization called SAVE Dade, several farmworker organizations in the southern part of the county, an immigrant community organization named We Count! in the Homestead area, an active ACLU chapter, a Florida Immigrant Advocacy Center, active labor and housing programs in the local Florida Legal Services Office, several environmental groups that primarily lobby for environmental causes, progressive student organizations on college campuses where previously there were none, a new day laborer's center, an

TABLE 1 Comparison of South Florida Social Justice Infrastructure, 1998 and 2008

Type of organization or activity	1998	2008
Aggressive union organizing	Minimal; one union intently organizing – SEIU in healthcare	SEIU Healthcare; SEIU Building Services; UNITE HERE; Teamsters
Community organizing	None to little	Miami Workers Center and affiliated community groups; Power U Center for Social Change; ACORN; S. FL Jobs with Justice and affiliated community groups
Faith-based organizing	One group (PACT) with no focus on labor issues	PACT, S. FL Interfaith Worker Justice (SF IWJ)
Leadership development	No formal methods	Unite For Dignity; Miami Workers Center; Power U Center for Social Change; S. FL Jobs with Justice
Coalitions	None	Community Benefits Coalition for 4 years; other temporary ones on environmental, economic, and housing issues
Political action	Central Labor Council with minimal rank-and-file participation	Much more activated central labor council; entry of many community organizing groups in both policy and electoral campaigns
Research	None	Research Institute on Social and Economic Policy at FL International University

Hispanic voter registration project called Democracia USA, and more. In ten years, the Miami area has changed from being relatively underdeveloped in terms of social justice activism into a relatively active locale.

RECENT HISTORY IN SOUTH FLORIDA

The Miami experience to date is still a work in progress. However, a number of preliminary observations can be made. First, as has been experienced elsewhere, coalitions have been difficult, particularly between unions and community-based formations. A variety of cultural and political factors separate the typical union leader from the typical community organizer. Community organizers frequently see labor unions as exclusionary, bureaucratic, narrowly focused on their own members, and politically conservative. Labor leaders frequently see community organizers as fickle, irresponsible, overly idealistic, unanchored to or not responsible to a clear membership, politically radical, and insufferably moralistic. These differences mirror the divisions uncovered by Fred Rose in his classic book *Coalitions Across the Class Divide* (Rose, 2000).

Thus, despite temporary alliances and rhetorical claims that everybody is working for the same general goal, there has been limited coalitional work of any lasting nature in south Florida between unions and community-based organizations. For the less ideological community-based groups, such as the interfaith organization and ACORN, this is less true. But a cultural and political divide is apparent.

Nevertheless, there has been "cross-fertilization" despite the differences. The founders of the Miami Workers Center and the founders of Power U Center for Social Change all worked as organizers for the SEIU nursing home workers local in Miami before leaving to create their centers. A key organizer until recently for "Vecinos Unidos," a community group started and overseen by SF JwJ, was previously an organizer for another branch of SEIU in Miami – the "Justice for Janitors" local. One of the organizers from Power U Center for Social Change also came from this local. The head of SF JwJ was previously president of a union local in North Carolina before coming to Miami. And several community and immigrants rights organizers in Miami have backgrounds as union organizers and/or staffers. The local "fertilization" has gone only one way, however: from unions to other organizations, not vice-versa. If we expand to a national scope, however, it becomes apparent that several SEIU leaders and organizers had previous experience as student or community organizers.

It is not clear if any of the other types of formations is likely to have a longevity, stability, or impact on living standards or employment policies in any way commensurate with the major impact that unions had for decades in the United States prior to their precipitous decline. Most of these organizations depend on external funding from foundations, have unclear and small (by union standards) membership bases, and do not collect dues to sustain the organization internally. Every one of them is growing and increasing its influence, but they show limited likelihood of becoming mass organizations with significant clout in the labor market, the way unions used to.

They primarily influence public policy through mobilizations and pressure on elected officials. But their reach is far less in the private sector. While a living wage ordinance, more affordable housing, better treatment of immigrants, and the like are tangible improvements in the lives of many working class individuals and their families, it is hard to see how these groups could become a sustained presence in labor market determinations and outcomes the way unions have historically been. Geographic improvements in public policy and regulatory environment are the primary products from these groups if viewed primarily from the lens of living standards. (This is of course a restricted lens, and the groups also have important and measurable impacts on other outcomes, such as self-empowerment of low-income and minority and immigrant populations, which are also important.) But there is not yet any evidence that they can become powerful labor market intermediaries of the type that unions once were.

If the groups appear to be unlikely to "replace" the traditional labor movement, and if coalitions are important but limited in scope due to a variety of cultural, political, and organizational self-interest reasons, what are the prospects for this burgeoning "social justice infrastructure" to make a qualitative difference in the lives of working class Miamians?

Charles Heckscher and Françoise Carré (2006) have offered the intriguing argument that the solution to finding greater power lies in networks. Unable to form lasting, deep, or long-term coalitions, perhaps labor unions and social justice organizing groups aimed at improving working-class lives can link multiple organizations together in coordinated action through looser networks. Networks are more flexible; they avoid some of the contentious issues preventing easy coalition-building. Perhaps smaller, weaker organizations federated through flexible networks can accomplish more than large, strong organizations weakly federated with each other, which is the form of the traditional labor movement. They write:

> Network mobilization could help the labor movement extend across political boundaries and connect to the large number of groups that are not unions and do not intend to be, but that can sometimes exert effective pressure for workplace change. Those who have studied networks in various settings have found that their particular strength is the ability to mobilize across diverse groups and to utilize differences in capability and knowledge. (Heckscher & Carré, 2006)

There is some evidence from south Florida that this is precisely the direction that relationships between these multiple groups have been evolving. Looser networks between organizations that come and go concerning particular issues have formed and disappeared. Usually they have proved to be mutually advantageous to the participant organizations and individuals.

Some networks are longer lived than others. Many of the groups enumerated above met from 2004 to 2008 in a "Community Benefits Coalition" grouping that was trying to control rampant development. In the past, the development activities primarily benefited developers and the wealthy purchasers of condominiums while neighborhoods were gentrified and working-class and poor people were pushed to the periphery.

Repeated attempts to turn the Community Benefits Coalition into a more permanent organization repeatedly failed. Organizational autonomy of participant organizations was jealously guarded to such a degree that the "coalition" (sometimes also referred to as the "table" where groups meet) had great difficulty operating as a unit. In the end, the Community Benefits "Coalition" became simply one organizational form of a possibly-emerging "network" of these groups, combining and recombining in various ways to achieve common aims.

There was no formal hierarchy of command within this grouping. Decisions were made in periodic meetings, and generally active campaigns were taken up only by sub-sets of the entire group, which was never been able to find a common issue that all wished to address. Interdependence of the constituent group may have emerged somewhat, although the degree of such interdependence is yet unclear. The groups involved were groping their way toward shared information, shared behavioral norms, and a somewhat common mission, all key elements identified by Hecksher and Carré as essential to a successful network.

But in the end this formation proved not to be stable. A fourth necessary element identified by Hecksher and Carré never emerged: a strong mechanism of governance. Dispute resolution mechanisms, enforcement mechanisms, and similar ways to keep the organization as something more than a simple information-sharing body or meeting place for totally independent groups never developed. And it is not clear that many of the groups ever wanted them to be developed.

ANALYSIS

Organizationally, the "network" form may hold the most promise for worker justice organizations (including unions) to collaborate. But the evidence from the local Miami scene and/or the national scene gives scant verification for the belief that this will be a stable or permanent form of interaction either. Networks tend to be ephemeral even if they are powerful in specific situations or junctures. Permanent networks require more shared commonality of purpose than is readily apparent in south Florida.

This is not to say that network formations will not continue in existence—only that their power will remain quite limited and their forms constantly changing. For example, three organizations (Miami Workers Center with its related community organizations Low Income Families Fight Together and Miami en Acción, Power U Center for Social Change, and South Florida Jobs with Justice and its community organizing arm, Vecinos Unidos) recently formed a local affiliate of the new national movement "Right to the City," which aims to empower low-income residents in all spheres of life. This new network shows promise, but it is one of many constantly shifting constellations of alliances that so far have not shown great organizational stability.

Because of its national links and its origins in joint work at the U.S. Social Forum, the Right to the City may have a more permanent existence than that of the Community Benefits Coalition. The commitment of important community organizing groups like the Miami Workers Center to this formation appears to be stronger. But it is such a new formation that it is difficult to determine if it will turn out to be a permanent but flexible form of network for like-minded organizations.

The long term prospects for networks to provide the organizational form for lasting power for workers and working class communities to raise living standards are quite uncertain. It is clear that the network form coincides with the sensibilities of many of the younger activists engaged in community organizing at the present time. Compared to many of their counterparts in earlier generations, the young activists of this generation are more distrustful of bureaucracies and bureaucratized organizations than was the case with activists in the past. Ideological predispositions of many young student and other activists tends in the direction of anarchism, not "old" ideologies such as Marxism or social democracy that center on more stable bureaucratized forms of mobilization and organization. It is also clear that networks are very much in vogue in other areas of modern society in the western world, such as in the business arena.

However, the impermanence of most networks makes it likely that they too will exhibit many deficiencies as vehicles for empowerment of working class interests and communities. It would be a mistake to simply "write off" older types of bureaucratic formations such as unions or more bureaucratic types of community organizations while placing hope in networks to lead the way forward toward power.

To make an accurate assessment of the organizational forms that will best serve working class individuals and families we must make a distinction between types of power that can be exerted to protect the interests of workers and their families. Political power is one crucial type of power; another is economic power exerted in the marketplace. The two are often interrelated, as a supportive political environment is usually required to structure or shape markets in such a way that economic actors are capable of exerting market power.

Politically, the more stable and bureaucratic structures such as labor unions tend to play more of an "insider" role than do the grassroots community organizing groups. They generally endorse candidates, make political campaign contributions, engage in voter registration and get-out-the-vote efforts, and engage in conventional lobbying with politicians around legislative issues. While community groups do some of the same activities (particularly voter registration and voter turnout work), they are more likely to engage in social movement activities such as protest marches and rallies, "public accountability" meetings with elected public officials and the like than are most unions. (Exceptional unions also take on such a "social movement" orientation, but they are not typical of the bulk of unions.)

As for exerting economic power in the marketplace, most community organizing groups and various networks tying them together are severely limited in their efficacy. Unless they can spearhead an effective boycott or similar "shaming campaign" against a corporate entity (occasionally possible, but not workable in most cases), they have little marketplace power. Labor unions, on the other hand, are much more effective at exerting marketplace power through mechanisms of collective bargaining and occasional work stoppages.

The foregoing discussion shows that all types of organizations and all types of social formations have some inherent limitations. Rather than privilege any one of them as the form that provides the key to power for working class individuals, families, and communities, the most realistic understanding would see them all as synergistic rather than making any one of them dominant. Bureaucratic organizations, like labor unions and smaller more fluid social movement organizations; conventional coalitions anchored in larger more stable organizations and fluid supple networks able to shift focus rapidly; political influence through conventional political channels and influence through social movements and "outside" pressure tactics: all of these can contribute to the goal of greater influence and material concessions for working class interests.

In the end, the hope is that the various elements of the area's social justice infrastructure will all strengthen themselves. At some point in the future, a qualitative breakthrough may occur that will change the landscape and force the powerful vested interests currently running the city to make major concessions in the economic arrangements distributing wealth in the area.

If the goal is economic clout, the most likely breakthrough would entail a union or unions gaining large market share in decisive sectors of the local Miami economy (tourism-related, services, etc.). Massive organizing by a union in a more supportive environment created by multiple working-class oriented struggles from multiple fronts (the "lilliput" strategy of Brecher and Costello) could turn the tide. Of course, it is a series of networks and a growing social justice infrastructure that may provide the climate needed to make such a union organizing upsurge possible.

It is difficult to see how it could happen any other way—other groups lack the necessary labor market clout. Unions, for all their flaws, are still an essential economic mechanism for reversing growing inequality. Despite this argument for unions and their importance, it is equally clear that they are no longer the sole or even dominant force for working class betterment in the modern social and economic environment. Rather, it is the synergy of simultaneous efforts on many fronts and through multiple organizational forms that shows promise of making progress. In that sense, the network perspective has pinpointed a crucial feature of working class struggles in the modern U.S., even if some of its adherents may overstate the likely longevity or stability of emerging networks.

In south Florida, there is evidence for cautious optimism. The social justice infrastructure is growing, and most of the efforts are solid enough to survive into the future. Synergies are also making themselves evident, and although no major breakthroughs have yet occurred, limited smaller victories (too numerous to list or enumerate here) have been won in both SEIU union organizing advances and community-won measures for public commitments to affordable housing to justify tentative optimism.

NOTE

1. See the RISEP mission statement, advisory board, and numerous studies on its website: http://www.risep-fiu.org.

REFERENCES

Albright, J. (2008). Contending rationality, leadership, and collective struggle: The 2006 Justice for Janitors campaign at the University of Miami. *Labor Studies Journal, 33*(1), 63–80.

Fine, J. (2006). *Worker Centers: Organizing communities at the edge of the dream.* Ithaca, NY: ILR Press.

Fisk, C. L., Mitchell, D. J. B., & Erickson, C. L. (2000). Union representation of immigrant janitors in southern California: Economic and legal challenges. In R. Milkman, (Ed.), *Organizing immigrants: The challenge for unions in contemporary California* (pp. 199–224). Ithaca, NY: ILR Press.

Heckscher, C., & Carré, F. (2006). Strength in networks: Employment rights organizations and the problem of coordination. *British Journal of Industrial Relations, 44*(4), 605–628.

Johnston, P. (2002). Citizenship movement unionism: For the defense of local communities in the global age. In B. Nissen, (Ed.) *Unions in a globalized environmenet: Changing borders, organizational boundaries, and social roles* (pp. 236–263). Armonk, NY: M.E. Sharpe.

Kest, S. (2004). ACORN's experience working with labor. In D. B. Reynolds (Ed.), *Partnering for change: Unions and community groups build coalitions for economic justice* (pp. 29–45). Armonk, NY: M.E. Sharpe.

Luce, S. (2002). Life support: Coalition building and the living wage movement. *New Labor Forum, 10*, 81–92.

Nissen, B. (2000). Living wage campaigns from a "social movement" perspective: The Miami case. *Labor Studies Journal, 25*(3), 29–50.

Nissen, B. (2003). Alternative strategic directions for the U.S. labor movement: Recent scholarship. *Labor Studies Journal, 28*(3), 133–155.

Nissen, B. (2004). Labor-community coalition strengths and weaknesses: Case study evidence. In D.B. Reynolds (Ed.), *Partnering for change: Unions and community groups build coalitions for economic justice* (pp. 46–63). Armonk, NY: M.E. Sharpe.

Nissen, B., & Russo, M. (2007). Strategies for labor revitalization: The case of Miami. In L. Turner & D. B. Cornfield (Eds.), *Labor in the new urban battlegrounds: Local solidarity in a global economy* (pp. 147–162). Ithaca, NY: ILR Press.

Osterman, P. (2006). Community organizing and employee representation. *British Journal of Industrial Relatons, 44*(4), 629–649.

Pollin, R., & Luce, S. (1998). *Living wage: Building a fair economy.* New York: New Press.

Pollin, R., Brenner, M., Wicks-Lim, J., & Luce, S. (2008). *A measure of fairness: The economics of living wages and minimum wages in the United States.* Ithaca, NY: ILR Press.

Reynolds, D. (2007). Building coalitions for regional power: Labor's emerging urban strategy. In L. Turner & D. B. Cornfield (Eds.), *Labor in the new urban battlegrounds: Local solidarity in a global economy* (pp. 73–94). Ithaca, NY: ILR Press.

Reynolds, D., & Kern, J. (2001–2002). Labor and the living-wage movement. *Working USA, 5*(3), 17–45.

Robinson, I. (2002). Does neoliberal restructuring promote social movement unionism? U.S. developments in comparative perspective. In B. Nissen (Ed.), *Unions in a globalized environment: Changing borders, organizational boundaries, and social roles* (pp. 189–235). Armonk, NY: M.E. Sharpe.

Rose, F. (2000). *Coalitions across the class divide: Lessons from the labor, peace, and environmental movements.* Ithaca, NY: ILR Press.

Rudy, P. (2004). "Justice for janitors," no "Compensation for custodians": The political context and organizing in San Jose and Sacramento. In R. Milkman & K. Voss (Eds.), *Organizing and organizers in the new union movement* (pp. 133–149). Ithaca, NY: ILR Press.

Turner, L., & Hurd, R. (2001). Building social movement unionism: The transformation of the American labor movement. In L. Turner, H. Katz & R. Hurd (Eds.), *Rekindling the movement: Labor's quest for relevance in the 21st century* (pp. 9–26). Ithaca, NY: ILR Press.

Working Hard, Living Poor: Social Work and the Movement for Livable Wages

SUSAN KERR CHANDLER

School of Social Work, University of Nevada, Reno, Nevada, USA

In 2001, social work researchers published Working Hard, Living Poor, a living wage study for Nevada and the opening salvo in a four-year coalition effort to raise the state's minimum wage. Social work faculty and students were active participants in that campaign; their contributions included wide distribution of the study, the development of an award-winning social welfare policy unit—Nickel and Dimed: On (not) Getting by in Northern Nevada; and advocacy, including legislative testimony and media outreach, on behalf of minimum wage legislation. This article— which poses the question, what is social work's responsibility vis-à-vis the working poor?—is a case study of that effort.

There is nothing but a lack of social vision to prevent us from paying an adequate wage to every American citizen whether he be a hospital worker, laundry worker, maid, or day laborer.

Dr. Martin Luther King, Jr. (1967)

Everyone has the right to work. . . . Everyone who works has the right to just and favourable remuneration insuring for himself and his family an existence worthy of human dignity.

Article 23
Universal Declaration of Human Rights (1948)

Alma Pacheco is a janitor at one of northern Nevada's largest casinos. From 6:00 PM to 2:00 AM, five days a week, 52 weeks a year, Mrs. Pacheco cleans bathrooms and banquet rooms, for which, after eight years on the job, she's paid $8.00 an hour. At 2:00 AM, she leaves, not for home, but rather for her second job–cleaning a fast food restaurant where she earns $7.00 an hour. At 10:30 AM, Mrs. Pacheco, who is 50, returns to her modest apartment and sleeps a few hours, but by 2:00 in the afternoon she is up cooking her children's and grandchildren's dinners and helping them with homework. At 6:00 PM, she returns to the casino. Mrs. Pacheco (whose name is fictitious, but whose story is absolutely real) has worked two full-time jobs for most of the last eight years (A. Pacheco, personal communication, May 21, 2001).

What is social work's relationship, if any, with women like Alma Pacheco? Although central to the concern of early social workers like Jane Addams and Mary van Kleeck, the working poor, who stay off welfare, as a rural Utah woman put it, "by working every moment we're awake" (Gringeri, 2001, p. 3), often seem peripheral to social work, and the critical issues of their lives—wages and benefits—outside its purview. This article is a case study of how social work scholars and students in one state addressed the question of the profession's relationship to the working poor. Their efforts included the production and wide distribution of *Working Hard, Living Poor,* a living wage study that became a vital document in two Nevada campaigns to raise the state's minimum wage; development of an award-winning social welfare policy unit, *Nickel & Dimed: On (not) Getting by in Northern Nevada*; testimony on behalf of minimum wage and welfare-policy bills in the state legislature; and active participation in a four-year coalition effort to raise the state's minimum wage

SOCIAL WORK AND WAGES: LITERATURE REVIEW

Jane Addams, in her essay *The Objective Value of a Social Settlement* (1892/2002), described activities at Hull House undertaken on behalf of working men and women. She was proud that four women's trade unions met there regularly. "Recently," Addams wrote, "twenty girls from a knitting factory who struck because they were docked for loss of time when they were working by the piece" had come directly from the factory to Hull House. They had heard, Addams reported, "that we 'stood by working people'" (p. 42). Indeed, nearly all Chicago knew about the vigorous campaign against sweatshops in which Addams, Florence Kelley, Ellen Gates Starr, Mary Kenney, and other Hull House residents wholeheartedly participated.

Today, relatively few social workers, schools of social work, or social service agencies enjoy the intimacy of contact between workers and professionals that Addams captured so well in her 1892 essay. Even fewer have first-hand experience with workers' collective action for improved wages, benefits, and work conditions. This is an enormous loss for social work for, as Addams and others recognized, wages on which families can survive invariably are central to workers' and communities' well-being—no social service safety net can compensate for their absence.

Despite this absence, there has consistently existed in the profession's literature a strain that addresses itself to workplace and justice issues, one that widens and narrows as economic conditions in the country change and as progressive political movements rise and fall. In the last decade and a half, that strain has been somewhat more robust than usual. The onset of welfare reform in the 1990s spurred researchers to explore the economy and the widening gap between rich and poor in an effort to measure if the four million women about to be cast into the labor market could survive on minimum wage jobs. This has been a data-rich effort that continues (Cancian, Haveman, Kaplan, Meyer, & Wolfe, 1999; Cancian & Meyer, 2000; Gray, 2005; Lambert, 2003; Piven, Acker, Hallock & Morgen, 2002; Wu, Cancian, & Meyer, 2008). Concurrently with that effort, intellectuals and activists moved to document the cracks in an economic system that, in the midst of an enormous economic boom, left millions impoverished. Interest in work and particular groups of working people—for example, displaced workers, the rural poor, and service employees—rose (Chandler & Jones, 2003; Dawson, 1993; Gringeri, 2001; Karger, 1988; Klein, 2003; Reisch & Gorin, 2001; Rocha, 2001; Root, 1997; Schram, 2002; Sherraden, 1995; Simmons, 2004; Wagner, 1991; Zippay, 2001), as did exploration of social work's relationship to unions and other collective means to raise wages (Brooks, 2007; Donovan, Kurzman, & Rotman, 1993; Rosenberg & Rosenberg, 2006; Scanlon & Harding, 2005; Straussner & Phillips, 1988).

Outside of social work, class re-emerged in the last decade and a half as a critical issue in both scholarly and popular venues. Scholars turned considerable attention to addressing the "New Inequality" (Cavanagh & Collins, 2008) and to exploring the reality of low-wage workers' lives in both theoretical and descriptive texts, some of which explored the moral dimension of what many described as a colossal redistribution of wealth (Appelbaum, Bernhardt & Murname, 2003; Bonacich & Appelbaum, 2000; Chang, 2000; Collins & Wright, 2007; Heymann, 2000; Hondagneu-Sotelo, 2001; Rosen, 2002; Shipler, 2004; Teixeira & Rogers, 2000; Zweig, 2000). The work of Saskia Sassen (1998) stands out for its global and national perspective as well as theory building. Within popular literature, Barbara Ehrenreich's *Nickel and Dimed: On (Not) Getting by in America* (2001) remained for months on the bestseller lists. The book, dark, funny, and stunning, is one that many social work faculty have used profitably to introduce students to the class divide. Activists have documented their work as well, an example of which is Louie's *Sweatshop Warriors: Immigrant Women Workers Take on the Global Factory* (2001), which asserts women's agency in a world that too often sees immigrant women as victims.

More particular to this article, a significant body of literature, popular and academic, has grown up that both describes the living wage movement and evaluates the impact of the living wage ordinances that have been won by it. (A living wage is defined here as a wage that allows families to meet their basic needs without resorting to public assistance and provides them some ability to deal with emergencies and plan ahead. It is a basic wage, but not a poverty wage.) Economists Robert Pollin (1998) and Stephanie Luce (2004) lead progressive academics in this regard. It is on the Web sites of progressive think tanks, however, that living wage activists have been able to find the best support. The Association of Community Organizations for Reform Now (ACORN; http://www.acorn.org) and the Economic Policy Institute (http://www.epinet.org) regularly produce organizing guides and extraordinarily useful data for state activists. Their information is accurate, easily accessible, and has largely replaced the early research efforts of local living wage activists.

THE CONTEXT

Funded by a grant from the Progressive Leadership Alliance of Nevada (PLAN), the Nevada economy was studied from the point of view of working families. The report that emerged from that study, *Working Hard, Living Poor* (Chandler, 2001), which constructed multiple family budgets and measured Nevada wages against them, grew out of PLAN's and social work's concern for the position of low-wage, no-benefit workers like Alma Pacheco in the state's rapidly expanding service economy.

The Progressive Leadership Alliance of Nevada is a coalition of 43 groups representing workers, women, environmentalists, people of color, gays and lesbians, people of faith, and professionals like social workers. It is a key vehicle in Nevada for building consensus and collective strategies among progressives on a range of issues including state roles in welfare, immigration, taxes, the environment, economic justice, and reproductive choice. From PLAN's founding in 1996, the National Association of Social Work, Nevada Chapter, has worked hard to build the coalition, seeing its membership in PLAN as a means to strengthen social workers' presence in the state's policy arenas. The School of Social Work at the University of Nevada, Reno, especially has benefited from a long-standing relationship with PLAN, which provides field sites as well as work and volunteer opportunities for students, alumni, and faculty.

PLAN, like progressive organizations throughout the country, was keenly interested in the plight of low-wage workers and determined to initiate a statewide movement to improve wages. In this, Nevada activists were following the lead of the living- and minimum-wage movements that had been emerging across the country since the mid-1990s. Based on the straight-forward ideas that (a) the minimum wage should provide workers with a basic living as was intended in the Fair Labor Standards Act of 1938 that created it, and (b) businesses that win contracts or tax breaks from cities, counties, and states should pay workers a livable wage, living- and minimum-wage movements have won (by 2008) wage increases in more than 140 localities throughout the United States, and have succeeded in raising the minimum wage in 28 states and the District of Columbia (Department of Labor, http://www.dol.gov/esa/minwage/america.htm; ACORN, http://www.livingwagecampaign.org).

In 1997, Robert Kuttner, an economist and editor of *American Prospect*, called the living wage movement ". . . the most interesting (and under-reported) grass roots enterprise to emerge since the civil rights movement." He continued,

> The gross inequality of the 1990s is a national disgrace. At one extreme, some may think it shameful that Bill Gates makes more money before lunch than most people make in a lifetime. But the bigger disgrace is that amid glittering affluence, millions of Americans report punctually to work, perform conscientiously—and still don't take home enough money to escape poverty. If remedying that disgrace is truly bad for business, the flaw is not the remedy but the system (p. A25).

Living and minimum wage movements immediately distinguished themselves by the extraordinary coalitions they elicited, and by their success during a period that for social activists was depressingly bleak. Trade unionists, people of faith, the elderly, the young, people of color, people with disabilities, and women, all angered by the growing disparity between rich and poor in a time of inordinate prosperity, were more than ready to unite in support of low-wage workers. Theirs was a powerful moral imperative. As Maria Elena Durazo, a leader in the Los Angeles living wage campaign and president of Hotel Employees, Restaurant Employees, Local 11, commented:

> We cannot be isolated for the very simple reason that we are not alone. The things we are fighting for—respect, dignity, a living wage, the chance for our children to have a better future—these are things that all people want. . . . We also have justice in our corner. And patience as well (quoted in Luce, 2004, p. 207).

Critically, the movements provided the strongest challenge in decades to economic development policies that focused on building a "positive business climate" at the cost of people's needs, and reasserted the responsibility of government to ensure "that fairness and justice for all prevail in our communities" (Luce, 2004, p. 13). It was these concepts that the authors wanted to introduce to Nevada citizens through *Working Hard, Living Poor*.

WORKING HARD/LIVING POOR: RESEARCH FOR CHANGE

From the beginning *Working Hard, Living Poor* served as both a research study and an organizing tool in the statewide campaign PLAN and others hoped to build to address wage inequalities. The report—to serve those dual purposes—had to be written in straight-forward, non-scholarly language; it had to provide rigorous, geographically-specific data so as to have legitimacy in all ranges of the political spectrum; it had to be researched not in isolation, but rather with the continuing input of experts, activists, and, especially, working people; and it had to be widely distributed and discussed.

Data for the 70-page study (described later) was gathered over the course of six months, and became a community project; one of many organizing tools that steadily drew a broad range of people into the discourse and eventually into action. Researchers talked with dozens of working people (Alma Pacheco was one), state-level bureaucrats (who were cooperative across the board), agency directors (for example, of local food banks and housing coalitions), small business owners, and activists like union leaders. PLAN, which met regularly to discuss the research and build the campaign, also served to connect the researchers with many progressive organizations and elected officials. These wide-ranging relationships with everyone from dishwashers to elected officials were key in assembling the data and outlook that went into the production of *Working Hard, Living Poor,* and eventually to building a movement to raise Nevada's minimum wage.

Working Hard, Living Poor asked three questions:

1. How much does it cost families to live in Nevada?
2. What wage do workers need to earn in order to provide the basics for themselves and their families—that is, how much is a living wage? and,
3. Are there enough living-wage jobs in Nevada?

The report also examined long and short range trends in the Nevada economy, which, over three decades of boom, left 80% of Nevada's families in about the same place or behind where they had been before the boom, and 20% (and especially the top one percent) much wealthier.

Working Hard, Living Poor estimated the cost of basic needs for five different family units in the Reno and Las Vegas Metropolitan Statistical Areas, in rural Nevada, and for the state as a whole. These family budgets measured expenses in eight areas (food, rent and utilities, health care, transportation, childcare, household and personal expenses, savings, and taxes) using data from public agencies (local whenever possible) like the Nevada Department of Human Resources and Housing and Urban Development. (The report and its methodology are available online at http://www.plane-vada.org/working1202.htm.)

The study made several assumptions in calculating the family budgets. It assumed, for example, that all the adults in the family were working 40 hours a week, 52 weeks a year. In one-child families, the child was a preschooler; in two-child families, one child was in preschool and the other in grade school. The families were very frugal. They shopped carefully for food, prepared all their meals at home, and never went out to eat, even to a fast-food restaurant. They rented modest apartments, and if they had two children, the children shared a room. They had telephones, but made no long-distance calls. Their cars were eight years old, and the families used them only for school and work. Because the parents were working, the children were in childcare, which was of at least average quality. Families spent money for clothing and personal items like diapers and school supplies, but nothing for recreation, sports, or entertainment, other than a television. They did not use credit cards and did not have life insurance. They didn't go to movies, and the children did not have money for special school activities. The families never took a vacation. They saved a little each month, but they used that for emergencies and not for long-term saving for education and retirement. The family budgets for Nevada as a whole are presented in Table 1 (figures updated to 2006).

Researchers then calculated the wage a full-time worker or workers would need to make in order to meet their family's basic expenses. This is a *living wage*, as presented in Table 2.

The report further concluded that the Nevada economy was not creating enough living wage jobs for all those who needed them, according to several indicators. These include the percent of current jobs that pay less than a living wage, the share of jobs that pay poverty-level wages (which grew from 20 to 25.8% in the three decades of boom), and the percentage of jobs in the 12 fastest growing occupations that pay less than a living wage. For example, according to estimates by the Research and Analysis Bureau of

TABLE 1 Monthly Family Budgets for Nevada

	1 Parent, 1 child	1 Parent, 2 children	2 Parents, 1 child*	2 Parents, 2 children*
Food	$371.70	$415.90	$460.60	$604.80
Rent/Utilities	$836.00	$836.00	$836.00	$836.00
Health care	$217.00	$248.00	$275.00	$304.00
Transportation	$269.00	$269.00	$367.33	$367.33
Child care	$367.33	$701.14	$367.33	$701.14
Miscellaneous/Household	$159.57	$176.89	$193.89	$211.21
Savings	$87.65	$92.29	$107.09	$116.17
Taxes	$221.67	$111.00	$234.33	$139.00
Total Costs:				
Monthly	$2,529.92	$2,850.22	$2,841.57	$3,279.65
Yearly	$30,359.04	$34,202.64	$34,098.84	$39,355.80

*Parents' *combined* incomes need to total this amount.

TABLE 2 Living Wage Levels

Family unit	Living wage level	
	Hourly rate	Annual income
1 Parent, 1 Child	$14.60	$30,359.04
1 Parent, 2 Children	$16.44	$34,202.64
2 Parents, 1 Child	$16.39*	$34,098.84*
2 Parents, 2 Children	$18.92*	$39,355.80*

*Parents' *combined* incomes need to total this amount. If both parents are paid at the same rate, they would each need to earn $7.52 per hour in the one-child family and $8.70 per hour in the two-child family.

the Nevada Department of Employment, Training, and Rehabilitation, 17.4% of the 1,062,020 jobs in Nevada in 2001 paid less than a livable hourly wage for one person ($8.53), while 57.3% paid less than a livable hourly wage for a single parent with two children ($14.57; Chandler, 2001).

Working Hard, Living Poor also examined short and long term trends in Nevada's economy from the perspective of workers and their families, and found that despite the fact that Nevada's economy had been performing at record-breaking levels for the past two decades (the Gross State Product had expanded seven times, close to a million jobs had been created, and unemployment, up until September 11, 2001, had remained low), most Nevada workers had not benefited from the economic boom. In the ten years from 1989 to 1998 the wages of middle-income workers in Nevada declined 7.3%—from $11.56 an hour to $10.72 an hour—the third sharpest decline in the nation. Income inequality increased significantly in Nevada during the last 20 years with high-income earners garnering nearly all the benefits of the economic boom. From 1978 to 1998, the average income of the poorest fifth of families decreased by $800, and the average income of the middle fifth of families decreased by $1,200. In contrast, the average income of the richest fifth of families increased by $26,010.

The report went on to draw a picture of inequality in Nevada using images with which readers would be familiar. It described Frank Fertitta, III, CEO of the Station Casinos in Las Vegas, whose annual salary in 1999 was $6,679,512.00. A janitor at the non-union Station Casinos, the report found, begins at $7.00 an hour. Working full-time, 52 weeks a year, it would take that janitor 459 years to earn what Mr. Fertitta makes in a year. Mr. Fertitta, on the other hand, could earn the janitor's annual salary, before he left for lunch—in just four and a half hours.

Working Hard, Living Poor was released in August of 2001, at PLAN-organized press conferences in both Reno and Las Vegas. Dignitaries, activists, people of faith, and the author presented the study and spoke about the situation of Nevada's working poor. Working people added their personal stories of multiple jobs, long hours away from their children, and meager annual raises to the report's analysis. The response was dramatic: television and radio stations throughout Nevada covered the report's release as did all the English and Spanish-language newspapers around the state—often on the front page. Following the flurry of press activity that accompanied its release, PLAN received many letters and requests to present the study. Over the next two years, the authors spoke at over 100 venues at both the state and national levels: churches, political groups, university classes, radio talk shows, a Ford Foundation conference for statewide progressive coalitions like PLAN, the Governor's Workforce Investment Board, the Economic Development Office, and so forth. The study was reprinted several times and translated into Spanish. Low-wage workers called to add their own stories to the report, which was especially gratifying.

IN THE CLASSROOM

Working Hard, Living Poor also became a valuable classroom resource. "Nickel & Dimed: On (not) Getting By in Northern Nevada" was a project designed for social welfare policy courses (and in 2003 won first place in the *Influencing State Policy* national curriculum contest). Based on Barbara Ehrenreich's popular book (2001), the unit was designed to engage students in a research effort that would bring to life issues of low-wage work, and then use students' newfound knowledge and enthusiasm as the basis for advocacy for living wages. The class first read *Nickel & Dimed* and *Working Hard, Living Poor,* and then created a working family (one class, for example, created a family composed of a mother—with a GED, some job experience, and a 1991 Ford—and two children, ages four and eight). The class was challenged to discover if the family could survive on low-wage work in Reno. The students, divided into six groups, were to imagine they were the mother and go out into the community and find (a) a job, (b) a place to live, (c) childcare, (d) food, (e) medical care, and (f) sources of help. Students went throughout the city looking at trailer parks, apartments, and motels; they shopped at Pak 'n Pay; they sat in health clinics; they found the mother a waitress job. Suddenly, a topic—low wages—that was on no one's mind at the beginning of the semester took on a whole new life. Students carefully calculated the budget figures and found that even with a job that inclued tips and 40 university students helping her, this mother could not make it.

Classes then discussed what social workers could do to impact wage structures. After studying collective responses to low wages, like living wage campaigns and union organizing, faculty and students focused their efforts on advocating for a minimum wage bill that had been recently introduced in the Nevada Legislature. The students' advocacy unfolded in multiple venues, each of which provided opportunities for them to hone macro-practice skills. Five students presented the "Nickel & Dimed" project at a widely-covered press conference calling for an increase in the minimum wage. A group traveled to the state capital where they were met by an assemblywoman who had introduced the bill and actually had some part in drafting it. Two students undertook a public opinion survey regarding raising the minimum wage in three Nevada communities. (The response indicated widespread—in fact, nearly unanimous—support for the measure.) Later, state NASW organizers asked students to present their work as part of testimony on a proposed welfare bill—testimony that resulted in their inclusion in a television special on grass-roots advocacy. When 200 people gathered at Grassroots Lobby Days, a three-day event at the State Legislature organized by the Nevada Women's Lobby, the students were among the featured speakers. Finally, when the bill was announced, students e-mailed every committee member, wrote letters to the editor, and joined casino maids, waitresses, and busboys in a march organized by the Culinary Union (the 60,000 member local of UNITE HERE that represents casino workers). Four students were chosen to testify at the legislature. On the day of the hearing, the room was packed with low-wage workers and students. The students, in an eight-minute presentation, gave a clear and passionate description of the "Nickel & Dimed" project and their own experience with minimum wage jobs. When it was over, faculty and students gathered outside the hearing room, the students grinning from ear to ear. The assemblywoman came out beaming. "Did you get an A?" she teased them.

The bill failed, but served to keep the issue alive. Two years later, a coalition of labor unions, people of faith, and progressive organizations like PLAN collected signatures to launch a ballot initiative to raise the minimum wage $1.00—and, critically, to tie the minimum wage to the cost of living. Minimum wage initiatives are extremely popular, and organizers hoped that the initiative would bring Nevadans out to vote; not only for a raise in the minimum wage, but also to participate in the 2004 presidential election. Volunteers sent out tens of thousands of campaign leaflets and called thousands of voters. In November, 2004, 68% of Nevada voters marked their ballots for a raise in the minimum wage, one of two successful minimum wage campaigns in the nation that election (the other was in Florida).

In Nevada, ballot initiatives must win a majority of the voters in two successive elections. In 2006, the initiative passed a second time, this time winning 73% of the vote. Nevada's victory was joined by ballot-initiative landslides in five other states—Arizona, Colorado, Missouri, Montana, and Ohio. It was, as analysts noted, a "sweet victory" (Vanden Heuvel & Graham-Felsen, 2007), and one that both reflected and foreshadowed the upsurge of political activity that has characterized the first decade of the 21st century.

The sweep was instrumental, too, in the passage of legislation increasing the minimum wage at the federal level. In 2007, convinced there was strong popular support for the bill that might have bearing on their chances for reelection, Congress voted to approve a measure raising the federal minimum wage from $5.15 to $7.25 in three stages over three years. It was the first increase in a decade, and included $4.84 billion in tax breaks for small business owners who might be negatively impacted. In the summer of 2008, the second of the three steps raised the federal minimum wage to $6.55 per hour. Twenty-three states—including Nevada—continue to have higher standards than the federal government's, and in Nevada, the wage is tied to the cost of living. Social workers can take some pride in having contributed to the movement that won that advance.

CONCLUSION

Who built Thebes of the Seven Gates?
In the books you will find the names of kings.
Did the kings haul up the lumps of rock? . . .

Bertolt Brecht, *Questions from a Worker who Reads, 1935*

This article has examined how social workers can contribute in multiple ways to the struggle for livable wages—and in so doing, reclaim the profession's historic relationship with the working poor. The walls that separate academia from the lives of workers are substantial; agency social work too often precludes action toward higher wages and better benefits for those at the low end of the economic ladder. If this is to change, social work students must be given opportunities to experience closely the lives of working people and to join with them in collective action for change. The Nevada experience illuminates one way in which "praxis for the poor"—a synthesis of theory and practice on behalf of working people— might unfold (Schramm, 2002). The *Working Hard/Living Poor* project provided social work faculty and students with an experience of collective political action that actually succeeded—rare in these times. It was also a chance for Nevadans, like the "factory girls" Jane Addams welcomed to Hull House, to know that social workers stand with them in the struggle for dignity and fair wages—not only philosophically, but in actual joint efforts on the front lines—at rallies, in the legislature, at the ballot box, in front of television cameras, and using their own particular practice and research skills. In so doing, it affirms the profession's commitment to "continued pursuit of social justice and social development" (International Association of Schools of Social Work, 2004) and demonstrates that social work can be part of making visible the labor of women like Alma Pacheco, who like the workers in Brecht's poem, daily create the world in which we live.

REFERENCES

Addams, J. (2002). The objective value of a social settlement. In J. B. Elshtain (Ed.), *Jane Addams reader* (pp. 29–45). New York: Basic Books. (Original work published 1892)

Appelbaum, E., Bernhardt, A., & Murname, R .J. (2003). *Low-wage America: How employers are reshaping opportunity in the workplace.* New York: Russell Sage.

Bonacich, E., & Appelbaum, R. (2000). *Behind the label: Inequality in the Los Angeles apparel industry.* Berkeley: University of California Press.

Brooks, F. (2007). The living wage movement: Potential implications for the working poor. *Families in Society, 88*(3), 437–442.

Cancian, M., Haveman, R., Kaplan, T., Meyer, D., & Wolfe, B. (1999). Work, earnings, and well-being after welfare: What do we know? In S. Danziger (Ed.), *Economic conditions and welfare reform* (pp. 161–186). Kalamazoo, MI: Upjohn Institute.

Cancian, M., & Meyer, D. (2000). Work after welfare: Women's work effort, occupation, and economic well-being. *Social Work Research, 24*(2), 69–86.

Cavanagh, J., & Collins, C. (2008, June 30). The new inequality: The rich and the rest of us. *The Nation, 286*(25), 11–12.

Chandler, S. (2001). *Working hard, living poor: A living wage study for Nevada.* Las Vegas, NV: Progressive Leadership Alliance of Nevada. Available from http://www.planevada.org/content/view/108/420

Chandler, S., & Jones, J. B. (2003). "Because a better world is possible": Women casino workers, union activism, and the creation of a just work place. *Journal of Sociology and Social Welfare, 30*(4), 57–78.

Chang, G. (2000). *Disposable domestics: Immigrant women workers in the global economy.* Cambridge, MA: South End Press.

Collins, C., & Wright, M. (2007). *The moral measure of the economy.* Maryknoll, NY: Orbis Books.

Donovan, R., Kurzman, P., & Rotman, C. (1993). Improving the lives of home care workers: A partnership of social work and labor. *Social Work, 38*(5), 579–585.

Dawson, S. (1993). Social work practice and technological disasters: The Navajo uranium experience. *Journal of Sociology and Social Welfare, 20*(2), 5–20.

Ehrenreich, B. (2001). *Nickel & dimed: On (not) getting by in America.* New York: Metropolitan Books.

Gray, K. (2005). Women who succeeded in leaving public assistance for a living-wage job. *Qualitative Social Work, 4*(3), 309–326.

Gringeri, C. (2001). The poverty of hard work: Multiple jobs and low wages in family economies of rural Utah households. *Journal of Sociology and Social Welfare, 28*(4), 3–22.

Heymann, J. (2000). *The widening gap: Why America's working families are in jeopardy—and what can be done about it.* New York: Basic Books.

Hondagneu-Sotelo, P. (2001). *Immigrant workers cleaning and caring in the shadows of affluence.* Berkeley: University of California Press.

International Association of Schools of Social Work. (2004). Statement of Principles. Retrieved January 23, 2009, from http://www.iassw-aiets.org

Karger, H. (Ed.). (1988). *Social workers and labor unions.* New York: Greenwood Press.

King, M. L. (1967). *Where do we go from here: Chaos or community?* New York: Harper & Row.

Klein, R. (2003). *Cruise ship blues: The underside of the cruise industry.* Gabriola Island, BC, Canada: New Society Publishers.

Kuttner, R. (1997, August 20). The "living wage" movement. *Washington Post,* p. A25.

Lambert, S. (2003). The work side of welfare-to-work: Lessons from recent policy research. *Work & Occupations, 30*(4), 474–78.

Louie, M. C. Y. (2001). *Sweatshop warriors: Immigrant women workers take on the global economy.* Cambridge, MA: South End Press.

Luce, S. (2004). *Fighting for a living wage.* Ithaca, NY: Cornell University Press.

Madonia, J. (1985). Handling emotional problems in business and industry. *Social Casework, 66,* 587–593.

Piven, F., Acker, J., Hallock, M., & Morgen, S. (2002). *Work, welfare, and politics: Confronting poverty in the wake of welfare reform.* Eugene: University of Oregon Press.

Pollin, R., & Luce, S. (1998). *The living wage: Building a fair economy.* New York: New Press.

Reisch, M., & Gorin, S. H. (2001). Nature of work and the future of the social work profession. *Social Work, 46*(1), 9–19.

Rocha, C. (2001). From plant closures to reemployment in the new economy: Risks to workers dislocated from the declining garment manufacturing industry. *Journal of Sociology and Social Welfare, 28*(2), 53–74.

Root, L. (1997). Social work and the workplace. In M. Reisch & E. Gambrill (Eds.), *Social work in the twenty-first century* (pp. 134–142). Thousand Oaks, CA: Pine Forge Press.

Rosen, E. (2002). *Making sweatshops: The globalization of the U.S. apparel industry.* Berkeley: University of California Press.

Rosenberg, J., & Rosenberg, S. (2006). Do unions matter? An examination of the historical and contemporary role of labor unions in the social work profession. *Social Work, 51*(4), 295–302.

Sassen, S. (1998). *Globalization and its discontents.* New York: New Press.

Scanlon, E. & Harding, S. (2005). Social work and labor unions: Historical and contemporary alliance. *Journal of Community Practice, 13*(1), 9–30.

Schram, S. F. (2002). *Praxis for the poor: Piven and Cloward and the future of social science in social welfare.* New York: New York University Press.

Sherraden, M. (1985). Chronic unemployment: A social work perspective. *Social Work, 25*(5), 403–408.

Shipler, D. (2004). *The working poor: Invisible in America.* New York: Alfred A. Knopf.

Simmons, L. (Ed.). (2004). *Welfare, the working poor, and labor.* New York: M.E. Sharpe.

Straussner, S., & Phillips, N. (1988). The relationship between social work and labor unions: A history of strife and cooperation. *Journal of Sociology and Social Welfare, 15*(1), 105–118.

Teixeira, R., & Rogers, J. (2000). *Why the white working class still matters: America's forgotten majority.* New York: Basic Books.

United Nations. (1948). *Universal declaration of human rights.* Retrieved November 10, 2005, from http://www.un.org/Overview/rights.html

Vanden Heuvel, K. & Graham-Felsen, S. (2007, January 1). Morality of the minimum. *The Nation*, p. 4.

Wagner, D. (1991). Reviving the action research model: Combining case and cause with dislocated workers. *Social Work, 36*(6), 477–482.

Wu, C. F., Cancian, M., & Meyer, D. (2008). Standing still or moving up? Evidence from Wisconsin on the long-term employment and earnings of TANF participants. *Social Work Research, 32*(2), 89–103.

Zippay, A. (2001). The role of social capital: A longitudinal study of occupational mobility among displaced steelworkers. *Journal of Sociology and Social Welfare, 28*(4), 99–119.

Zweig, M. (2000). *The working class majority: America's best kept secret.* Ithaca, NY: Cornell University.

Organizing for Immigrant Rights: Policy Barriers and Community Campaigns

JILL HANLEY

School of Social Work, McGill University, Montreal, Quebec, Canada

ERIC SHRAGGE

School of Community and Public Affairs, Concordia University, Montreal, Quebec, Canada

Immigration to Canada has changed in basic ways the composition of the labor force. Over the past 40 years, a large wave of immigrants has arrived from the countries of the "Global South". Many have arrived with high levels of education and qualifications; however, the jobs they receive are at the bottom of the labor market. The Immigrant Workers Center (IWC) in Montreal is an organization that provides individual services, education on rights, and organizes immigrant workers for workplace justice. This article describes three campaigns led by the center. They reflect the exclusion of immigrant workers from coverage in policy areas related to heath care, compensation for workplace injury, and benefits for collective lay-offs in the textile sector. The article concludes with some of the lessons learned in these campaigns.

INTRODUCTION

International migration has had a huge impact on the structure of labor markets throughout the world. The movement of people from poorer nations to richer ones in the search of greater economic opportunity has created a huge pool of workers, some with and others without formal immigration or legal status, who are willing and able to work under almost any conditions for both their own and family survival and in order to send money back home to their extended families. The mobility of labor can be understood as "labor reserve for global capital" (Sassen, 1988, p. 36, as cited in Bauder, 2003). There is a large literature on this movement of people, but less on the way that they have organized themselves to contest the resulting working conditions. Internationally, migrant workers and their allies have created new forms of organizations and strategies to respond to their conditions through innovative means as well as the traditional union model, which has not been able to effectively organize these workers given the fragmented and unstable marketplace.

This article will discuss one of these organizations, the Immigrant Workers' Centre (IWC) in Montreal, and the results of a research project undertaken to better understand the labor challenges facing its constituency. As members of the IWC Research Group, the authors helped conduct more than 50 semi-structured interviews between 2003 and 2007 with three distinct groups of immigrant workers: a group who had come for help to the IWC or were involved in the Centre; a group from Latin America who had been in Canada for at least ten years; and a group with precarious immigration status such as refugee claimants, temporary workers, or undocumented workers. The interview guide explored issues such as migration trajectory, their work experience, and their resistance in the workplace where appropriate.

The IWC is an example of a community-based strategy linked with labor issues. We begin with a discussion of the particular context of immigrant labor in Canada. Against this background, the article will focus on areas of public policy that exclude immigrant workers or make it difficult for them to access specific so-called universal programs. Three campaigns in which the IWC has recently been involved (Summer, 2008) will be discussed in order to examine these policy exclusions and an example of the IWC's grassroots response. The experiences of interview respondents will be used to illustrate the situations that led to these campaigns, revolving around: (a) the lack of benefits in case of workplace injury or illness for domestic workers; (b) a delay in free public health insurance for new arrivals; and (c) the difficulties in getting meaningful compensation in cases of large-scale layoffs. Each of these issues illustrates government's inadequate response to mass migration and labor market restructuring. The article's conclusion will discuss lessons for building opposition of immigrant workers in the contemporary context.

Both of the co-authors of this article participated the founding of the IWC in 2000, and have remained active in it. Shragge is president of the Board of Directors and is active in the campaigns related to both health and safety legislation for domestics and justice for laid-off textile workers described below. Hanley is also a member of the board and is involved in the access to healthcare campaign. Both participate in bi-weekly team/staff meetings and supervise social work students who do their field placements at the IWC. The information and perspectives of this article are derived from this ongoing involvement in the center over the past eight years.

IMMIGRANT WORKERS IN CANADA: AN OVERVIEW

In order to contextualize the emergence of the IWC and its practices, it is important to situate it within the transformations that have resulted from the immigration of the last 30 years. Historically, immigration has been used as a key component in the Canadian colonization project. Immigration policy contributes to maintaining a highly racialized construction of the Canadian nation with priority given to European immigrants up until the 1970s (Thobani, 2007). Non-Europeans were allowed in, often without full citizenship, to respond to specific demands for labor. Examples include the 19th-century importing of male Chinese labor to build railways while imposing extravagant landing fees (the "head tax") and prohibiting family reunification, versus the easy citizenship offered to early 20th-century female British nannies and maids (Iacovetta, Draper, & Ventresca, 1998).

In the past 40 years, the preponderance of European migrants has shifted, with a large increase in migrants from the south and a large influx of non-white immigrants. In 2007, for example, seven of the top ten source countries for permanent residents were "non-Western": China, India, Philippines, Pakistan, Iran, Korea, and Colombia. These top ten countries, with approximately 100,000 immigrants that year, represent nearly half the total permanent residents (Citizenship and Immigration Canada [CIC], 2008d). Forty years ago, the portrait was markedly different, with European, American, Australian, and New Zealand immigrants representing more than a third of all immigrants (Employment and Immigration Canada, 1978, p. 5–7). Many arrive with a high level of training and skills, usually including university education and advanced training (Picot, 2004). More than 60% of adult immigrants arrive with post-secondary diplomas, with an even higher proportion for those coming from developing countries (CIC, 2008b). Despite these qualifications, immigrant workers find themselves disproportionately in low-wage jobs, with new immigrants facing chronically high levels of unemployment and poverty (Picot, 2004; Picot, Hou & Coulombe 2007; Zietsma, 2007).

In his groundbreaking review of immigration outcomes over the last 30 years, Picot (2004) argues that the traditional pattern of earnings for immigrant workers—that is, relatively lower income in the early years after their arrival and catching up with Canadians afterward—has not happened over that time period. For the group of immigrants that entered Canada in the 1970s, the earning gap has not narrowed as quickly as it had for previous groups of European immigrants. For those arriving in the 1980s and 1990s, the gap has increased, and periods of economic growth and shrinking unemployment have not reduced this gap as would have been expected. Further, using the government's low-income cut-off (LICO) as a measure of poverty as a reference, immigrants have faced a deteriorating position. The proportion of recent immigrants with family incomes below the LICO rose from 24.6% in 1980 to 31.3% in 1990 and 35.8% in 2000. There has been a corresponding decrease for Canadians, from 17.2% in 1980 to14.3% in 2000. Poverty rates for recent immigrants were 1.4 times higher than other Canadians' in 1980, and this grew to 2.5 times higher by 2000. This increase in low-income rates is not restricted to new immigrants, but includes all immigrant groups (Picot, 2004, p. 11).

It is clear that despite high levels of education, immigrants tend to stay at the bottom of the labor market. This information challenges the myth that new immigrants are economically upwardly mobile. Lack of recognition of professional credentials has been identified as a major factor impeding the integration process (Aldridge & Waddington, 2001; Austin & Este, 2001; Krahn, Derwing, Mulder & Wilkinson, 2000; Li, 2001). Ahmadi (2006) adds that during 2005 to 2006, there was a rising trend of job discrimination for both immigrant men and women. Given the changes from European immigration to that from the developing world, one can ask about the labor market and income stratification across racial lines. Meanwhile, in keeping with neo-liberal policy trends, new immigrants are increasingly viewed as commodities (Abu-Laban & Gabriel, 2002; Arat-Koc, 1999). This "leads to an evaluation of people's potential contribution to and value to the country solely on the basis of their expected place in the labor market" (Abu-Laban & Gabriel, 2002, p. 65).

The period of arrival has a major impact on the material success of immigrant workers. Most of the users and members of the Immigrant Workers' Centre arrived in Canada in a period of labor market transition, a period of restructuring when the Fordist arrangement, with significant employment in unionized blue-collar jobs, was in decline and the new economy, characterized by services, new flexible working arrangements, and contingent work, was emerging. Such work includes "those forms of employment involving atypical employment contracts, limited social benefits and statutory entitlements, job insecurity, low job tenure, low wages and high risks of ill health" (Fudge & Vosko, 2003, p. 183). It is the fastest growing pattern of employment, and youth, women, and immigrants tend to be absorbed into the labor market through these jobs (Fudge & Vosko, 2003). This era of economic restructuring has been accompanied by cutbacks in social programs, such as language and job training, which have reduced the ability of new arrivals to gain skills that would help them in the Canadian job market (Abu-Laban & Gabriel, 2002).

Another important trend in Canadian migration is the shift away from permanent residency towards what critics term "guestworker" programs.[1] The current Conservative government has pushed ahead with a process started by the previous Liberal government to diminish the proportion of immigrants to Canada in favor of temporary foreign workers. This shift represents a major reduction in the state's obligation towards migrants and also is in close line with a "just-in-time", flexible management of the Canadian labor market; when we don't need them, we can just send them home. Migrants who arrive in Canada as permanent residents have a minimum level of security as a basis from which to refuse or resist substandard work conditions. Temporary workers, however, have their legal status in Canada tied to one specific employer and have very little leeway to object if they are not treated properly. They also have no guarantee of ever being able to remain in Canada on a permanent basis.

While this current trend toward guestworkers is striking, it is just a continuation of a differentiation among migrants that the state has imposed for quite some time and that shapes a lot of the work carried out at the IWC. We work with the concept of "precarious immigration status", the idea that when a person's immigration status does not confer the permanent right to remain in Canada and/or is dependent on a third party (usually a sponsoring employer or family member), that person is much more likely to experience exploitation and have a harder time defending themselves against it (Hanley & Shragge, 2008). Precarious immigration status is a continuum that ranges from the undocumented (with virtually no rights) to sponsored family members (who share almost all the same rights as citizens but whose status as "sponsored" has been shown to engender serious feelings of dependency and vulnerability). In between, the Canadian immigration regime distinguishes between refugees (claimants, accepted or refused), temporary residents (tourists, students, humanitarian) and temporary workers (professional, live-in caregivers, seasonal agricultural workers, low-skill).

Of particular concern to our work at the IWC are the undocumented and those under temporary work visas, although refugees and students may also have the right to work in Canada. The Live-In Caregiver Program (LCP) and the Seasonal Agricultural Worker Program (SAWP) are the two temporary worker programs now being used as a template for an expansion into other supposedly "Low-Skill" fields of work through the "Low-Skill Pilot Project" under the Temporary Foreign Worker Program. Both of these programs tie the worker to one specific employer and restrict the stay in Canada (up to 36 months for the LCP and 10 months for the SAWP). Both programs require that the worker live on their employer's property. And while the LCP holds out the carrot of possible permanent residency if the (usually female and usually Filipino) caregiver completes 24 months of live-in work before the end of her 36-month program, farm workers are denied the possibility of permanent status. In both cases, access to basic labor protections is severely limited due to policy exclusions, employer interference, extreme dependence on the job, socio-economic barriers or some combination thereof.

COMMUNITY LABOR ORGANIZING IN MONTREAL:
THE IMMIGRANT WORKERS' CENTRE

The IWC is part of a wider movement in immigrant communities to integrate community and labor organizing. It is estimated that there are approximately 130 centers of this type across the United States (Fine, 2005), mainly in immigrant communities. These centers work with those closest to the bottom of the labor market. They are an important innovation in the field of community organizing, focusing on issues of labor outside of the workplace. Gordon describes these centers as seeking ". . . to build the collective power of their largely immigrant members and to raise wages and improve working conditions in the bottom-of-the-ladder jobs where they labor" (2005, p. 280). Fine (2005), in her overview of these centers, states that they use a combination of the following approaches: service delivery including legal representation on issues such as wages and status; advocacy including research that exposes working conditions, and lobbying for policy or legislative change; and organizing including the development of leadership in immigrant communities in order to take action on their own behalf. As opposed to traditional labor organizing along craft or industry, these centers build on identification with race, ethnicity and place as key elements (Fine, 2005; Tait, 2005). In addition, they have tended to use direct action and lobbying as strategies rather than union and specific workplace organizing.

Fine (2005) argues that the success of these centers in improving working conditions for immigrant workers is derived from two sources. First, because of the limited power of immigrant workers, there are no other organizations that have succeeded in direct economic intervention on their behalf. Second, given the existing industrial structures and prevailing employment practices, only comprehensive changes in public policy can make a substantial difference. To understand the emergence of these centers, some elements related to their context will be examined, followed by an example of one center in Montreal, and conclude with lessons that emerge from practice.

The IWC was founded in 2000 by a small group composed of Filipino-Canadian union and former union organizers and their allies of activists and academics. The idea of the center grew out of the experience of two of the founders who had worked as union organizers. They observed that much of their recruitment and education to support a union drive had to take place outside of the workplace and there were few places where this could happen, particularly in a collective way. Thus, the idea of the center was to provide a safe place outside of the workplace where workers could discuss their situation. Further, they had a critique of the unions themselves, arguing that once they got a majority to "sign cards" and join the union, the processes of education and solidarity built into the organizing process were lost as union "bureaucrats" came in to manage the collective agreement. In its first year, the IWC was able to secure a grant from the social justice fund of the Canadian Automobile Workers to intervene on labor issues in the community. The IWC then got to work providing ongoing education and critical analysis that goes beyond the specific role of unions, as well as finding ways to address worker issues outside of the traditional union structures.

The activities of the IWC cover individual rights counseling, popular education and political campaigns that reflect the general issues facing immigrant workers, such as dismissal, problems with employers or, sometimes, inadequate representation by their unions. Labor education is a priority, targeting organizations in the community and increasing workers' skills and analysis. Workshops on themes such as the history of the labor movement, the Labour Standards Act and collective organizing processes have been presented in many organizations that work with immigrants as well as at the IWC itself. The "Skills for Change" program teaches basic computer literacy, while incorporating workplace analysis and information on rights. The goal is to integrate specific computer skills while supporting individuals in becoming more active in defending labor rights in their workplaces. There is also an ongoing link between the struggles of immigrant workers with other social and economic struggles; building alliances is a priority. In addition, the IWC supports union organizing in workplaces where there is a high concentration of immigrant workers. The IWC, as an organization crosses traditional boundaries and has characteristics of a social movement organization through its participation in the wider movements for migrant justice and its structure with a board of directors and service provision and education programs is more in the tradition of non-profits. (Hasenfeld, and Gidron, 2005). It can be understood as a social change organization. Drawing from Chetkovich and Kunreuther (2006), these types of organizations support collective action for change and encourage individuals to take actions to improve their lives. The IWC has a clear vision that it is an organization engaged in collective action that emerges from the experiences lived by immigrant workers themselves.

Campaigns are viewed not only as a way to make specific gains for immigrant workers but also a way to educate the wider community about the issues that they face. For example, the first campaign, in 2000, was to defend a domestic worker, here under the Live-in Caregiver Program, against deportation. She had been unable to complete her 24 months of live-in work because she was fired by her employer when she became pregnant and was unable to find a new employer willing to have her live in with her infant son. In addition to winning the campaign, the issue of importing labor as "indentured servants" was brought into the public sphere and many community organizations and unions became involved in this issue. Another example is how, along with many other groups in Quebec, the IWC became involved in a campaign to reform the Labor Standards Act in 2002. Because many immigrant workers do not work in unionized shops, the Labor Standards Act provides one of non-unionized workers' few recourses against their employers. The IWC brought to the campaign specific concerns including the exclusion of domestic workers from this Act and the difficulty in accessing information on workers' rights. In 2003, several victories were had, including the coverage of domestic workers by the reformed Labor Standards. However, despite the reforms won in this province-wide campaign, the Act still has many inadequacies in protecting workers in precarious and irregular jobs.

Another aspect of the IWC's work has been its contribution to the organizing of cultural events with political content. The first was an International Women's Day event organized in 2001. A coalition of immigrant women of diverse origins organized a cultural event, panels and a march to emphasize the concerns of immigrant women and international solidarity. This event has become an annual event and through its success has increased the profile and the issues faced by immigrant women within the wider women's movement in Quebec. The first MayWorks events, a community/union festival celebrating labor struggles through the arts, were launched on May Day of 2005. The festival was initiated by the IWC and found collaboration from trade unions and the wider activist community. The festival has been held annually since then, and includes a community event in a local park as its core.

Overall, the IWC is a place of intersection between the traditions of the labor and community movements. Work-related issues have been the concern of the labor movement, acting on the assumption that the best way for workers to have a strong voice is through the union movement. However, the IWC, along with other organizations, sees that this is limited because of the difficulties in organizing workers mentioned above. New forms of labor organizing are required in the current context that both include support for and from the trade union movement. The IWC works at both levels with the goals of serving, organizing and educating those who are not unionized. At the same time, it supports worker efforts to unionize and to help them get adequate representation from their unions. The union-community relationship is developed through many activities of the Centre, including building alliances with younger union activists, supporting immigrants in organizing and in helping them negotiate conflicts with their trade unions.

The work of the IWC has formed new alliances and has become a meeting place for a many groups of social activists. The core of the organization is a group made up of immigrant union and labor organizers and allies who have been active on both labor and community issues for many years. In addition, the IWC is connected to what may be described as student and anti-globalization activists. There are several reasons for this. The center has been fortunate to have student placements from law, social work and related fields from several Montreal universities and colleges. Many of these students have been involved in student organizing and this has helped to connect students to the issues raised by the IWC. At the same time, the

IWC's connection with these groups has pushed its own positions on broader social issues. The IWC is a place that brings together union-community and student activists, people of different ages, ethnic, cultural and class backgrounds to work together for social justice for immigrant workers.

EXCLUSION OF MIGRANT WORKERS FROM SOCIAL PROTECTIONS: GOVERNMENT POLICIES AND GRASSROOTS CAMPAIGNS

Canadian researchers have documented the policy and social barriers faced by immigrants in trying to access health and social services. They range from limited eligibility for programs, to systemic barriers within the health and social service networks, to socio-economic and cultural factors of discrimination or disconnect (Oxman-Martinez et al, 2005; Baines & Sharma, 2002; Zaman, 2004; Pierre, 2005). Issues of gender and immigration status have been shown to be of particular importance in understanding the barriers to health and social wellbeing (Preibisch, 2005; Guruge & Khanlou, 2004). Further, research in Canada indicates that immigrants do not benefit from equitable access to social rights. For instance, when accessing the health care system, research has shown a significant proportion of immigrants to Canada experience delays, complications or denial of medically necessary treatment (Caulford & Vali, 2006). This is particularly true of those with "precarious immigration status"—that is, those who are denied the permanent right to remain in Canada or whose status depends on a third party such as a spouse or employer (Hanley & Shragge, 2009).

For migrants to Canada, barriers to health services are likely a composite of legal, institutional, socio-economic, and cultural factors. Linguistic barriers often prevent or complicate communication and action (Gibson et al, 2005; Kopec et al, 2001; Zanchetta & Poureslami, 2006). Also, migrants to Canada report cultural barriers, such as a lack of understanding of ethnic-specific norms and cultural incompatibility as a barrier in accessing institutional settings (Lai & Chau, 2007; Stephenson, 1995). Such issues are likely exacerbated for those whose immigration status is precarious and for whom barriers to social rights are often systemic. Medicare policies, and the exclusion of temporary workers and recent immigrants from health services for the initial three months of their residency, act as a serious impediment to equitable health care (Oxman-Martinez et al, 2005). Also, health costs and loss of wages due to work related injury may not be compensable or compensated due to provincial workers' compensation restrictions that lead to the *de facto* exclusion of many migrants (Lippel, 2006; Preibisch, 2007). Such policies are compounded by bureaucratic barriers, such as misfiling or miscommunication, which increase the time for receiving social benefits (Gravel, Boucheron & Kane, 2003). We turn our discussion to the organizing around these policy barriers, offering examples of campaigns undertaken by the IWC in alliance with others.

Here we will discuss examples of policy exclusion and the campaigns organized to oppose them: (a) the exclusion of domestic workers from health and safety policies that provide financial compensation for workplace injury or relate illness; (b) a three-month exclusion from free public health insurance for new arrivals; and (c) the lack of meaningful compensation for workers being laid off from the textile sector. In the course of its day-to-day work, those seeking help have brought specific issues to the IWC. The experience of these individuals has led to campaigns; that is, going from case to cause. In each case, the policies and administrative structures of the provincial government are involved as all of the programs we will discuss below are legislated and administered through the provincial government.[2]

One of the key arguments that we will make is that these programs do not reflect an understanding of the recent wave of immigration to Quebec or the changes in the labor market such as increased flexibility, service sector development, irregular hours, and so on. Labor protection and other social programs assume full citizenship and the traditional structure of work. They do not take into account some of the situations facing immigrant workers, such as the type of jobs and the complex status questions described above. As we will see below, each campaign illustrates a wider issue facing immigrant workers and they are used to educate the general public and potential and actual allies about immigrant labor. We will describe the campaigns below and discuss lessons from them in the conclusion.

CSST for Domestic Workers

CSST is the French acronym for the Health and Safety Board or the Workers' Compensation Board of Quebec.[3] CSST legislation addresses health and safety prevention and protective measures in the workplace as well as the compensation to which workers' are entitled should they be injured or become ill due to their employment. From its inception, domestic work (including housework, as well as caring for children, elderly, or disabled people, whether the worker lives in the home or not) has been excluded from the compensation aspect of the CSST due to the argument that a private home cannot be considered a "place of business". While all other labor legislation applies equally to domestic workers (although some only as of 2003), the employers of domestic workers are exempt from paying into the collective insurance regime of the CSST that would compensate their employees in cases of accident or illness.

Domestic workers have limited options when it comes to protecting themselves, despite the fact that domestic work is not without workplace hazards. It is important to recognize that domestic workers face many risks in their daily tasks, such as illness, infection, exposure to chemicals, awkward and repetitive tasks, heavy lifting, fatigue, and stress. Apart from professional athletes, domestic workers are the only salaried workers who are not guaranteed CSST coverage by their employer. Domestic workers can register themselves or be registered through an association though in this situation, the cost of coverage is paid out of the worker's pocket, and not by their employer, as in the case of other employees. In case of accident or illness, they are told that they may pursue their employers through the civil courts but the unequal assets of the two parties make this a losing battle for the domestic worker.

Campaigns organized by the IWC often begin with an individual grievance. In this example, it was the case of a live-in domestic worker on the Live-In Caregiver Program, who became ill and unable to work due to unhealthy conditions in her employer's house, That was the beginning of the Centre's campaign around the CSST. Janet (not her real name), a live-in caregiver, came to Canada from the Philippines to work as a domestic. She had lived in a basement room and, because of certain chemicals in the room, developed a rash that was so severe that she could no longer work. She came to the IWC and asked for help. A representative of the IWC accompanied her to the CSST, expecting that she would receive a hearing about her workplace-generated illness. The CSST response was that if she had been working in any other workplace than a private home, she would have received compensation from CSST. Before the IWC decided whether to launch a campaign, a social work student did research on these policies in other provinces in Canada. She found that three provinces in Canada (Ontario, British Columbia, and Manitoba) offer compensation to domestic workers who suffer workplace injury or illness. This seemed like good leverage, given that the government of Quebec has a tradition of viewing itself as a leader in social policy, such as its universal $7 per day childcare system and network of community health agencies. After internal discussion, the IWC decided to launch a campaign to demand that domestic workers in Quebec be given full coverage in case of workplace accidents or illness.

A campaign committee was organized and led by three groups: the IWC, PINAY (a Filipina women's organization) and the Association des aides Familiales du Québec (AAFQ, which represents and serves domestic workers). The demands for the campaign were that current CSST legislation be extended to include the mandatory coverage of domestic workers, regardless of immigration status or validity of work permit; and that basic CSST information be available in languages other than French. In this context, the official language of Quebec is French; documents are available in English but many who work as domestics would be excluded by their inability to read these languages. The second demand was made to argue that the government has a responsibility to improve access to programs by informing people of their rights in a way that they can understand them and make appropriate claims. Representatives, volunteers and members from PINAY, the AAFQ, and the IWC met as the organizing committee for the campaign, discussed and agreed with the demands and took the first steps to mobilize support. The IWC took the responsibility to circulate demands with an explanation to unions and women's organizations and community groups across Quebec. Over 80 organizations, including the large union federations, gave their support.

The campaign was launched on International Women's Day, 2006. The strategy takes into account the fact that domestic work is not high on anyone's political agenda, including that of the groups and organizations supporting the campaign. The campaign therefore has a number of specific objectives: first, to keep the issue visible to both allies, and pressure the CSST bureaucracy and the Minister of Labor; second, to educate allies, potential allies, and the general public on the issues faced by domestic workers, including the fact that domestic workers are workers; and third, to mobilize domestic workers to participate in the campaign. To date there has been some success in all three. For the first two, visibility and pressure, it has been important to send material and updates to supporters of the campaign and remain in contact with labor representatives of the CSST board to inform them of the progress of the campaign and the response of both the minister and CSST officials. Education on the campaign, the LCP, and domestic work in general has continued. One tactic has been the preparation of a popular theatre production by domestic workers. This was put on in a number of different venues, such as during an educational event with women's organizations, and in demonstrations in solidarity with refugee claimants. These have acted to sensitize both allies and the general public to their situation and the demands for CSST reform and the general situation of domestic workers. The media did a story on the popular theatre presentation. Domestic work is often invisible work and the goals of the IWC, PINAY, and this campaign are to make it visible and point out that domestic work is work and domestic workers are workers, and entitled to the same rights as other workers.

The political target was both the CSST bureaucracy and the minister. A meeting with the minister was held in the summer of 2006, and he promised to involve representatives of the CSST campaign in an internal process within the CSST to examine the issue. This failed as the CSST bureaucrats did a superficial examination and did not appear to take the issue seriously. Subsequent pressure from the members of the campaign, union representatives on the CSST board, and a concern within the provincial government about the LCP resulted in a renewal of pressure on the CSST, and a new proposal for investigating how the government of Ontario has implemented this plan. The results of this are to be shared with the campaign committee in the fall of 2008.

Despite all the activity in this campaign, the direct mobilization of domestic workers has been difficult. PINAY is the group that works directly with those women arriving in Canada on the LCP. It has used a variety of means to reach people as part of its overall organizing and specifically on the campaign, including a survey to discuss workplace health and safety questions. They have successfully built an organization base among Filipina domestic workers. Other mobilizing has been less successful. The general orientation of community organizations in Quebec is to represent what they see as the "interests" of their clients/constituency and not to mobilize them. This has resulted in a process of broad-based collation building as a way to promote a particular issue rather than direct organizing and mobilizing. Further, it is difficult to mobilize domestic workers as they are isolated, are vulnerable in their workplaces and only have Sundays off, not the best day for rallies or meetings targeting politicians and bureaucrats. PINAY has been successful in doing this because there is a basis of identity as migrant domestic workers arrive under a common program from the same country. The AAFQ, although in touch with many domestic workers, has not mobilized as they define themselves as a service and advocacy group and have received official recognition from the provincial government as "the" representative of domestic workers. Thus the basic challenge is to find ways to reach domestic workers to engage them and help them organize themselves. On the whole, it has been hard going for the campaign with periods of some success such as getting a meeting with the minister of labor and periods of without progress, but the commitment is there, many domestic workers are involved organized by PINAY, and the struggle continues.

Health Care for All

Another important campaign for the IWC has been the Health Care for All Campaign, demanding the abolishment of the 3-month waiting period (the *délai de carence*, or the DDC) for Medicare imposed on migrants to Quebec (in the short term) and the extension of free healthcare to all (including the undocumented, in the long term). In the area of health care, Canada and the provinces have the legislated principles of universal, free and accessible care; however, in the case we discuss below, this is deliberately violated by the province of Quebec and several others. In theory, at least, the DDC was implemented to discourage people moving from one province to another, seeking better services. For people moving within Canada, the issue is not so serious since they will still be covered by their province of origin's Medicare for the first three months. The problem is most serious among new immigrants and temporary workers who usually do not have alternate coverage and are therefore left uninsured.

Since 2001, all new residents in Quebec, especially immigrants and temporary workers, have had to wait three months from their declared arrival before being covered by public health insurance (DDC). More than 67,000 landed immigrants and temporary workers a year face this exclusion in Quebec. Under the DDC, new immigrants and temporary workers get stuck in the bottom tier of health care. The DDC is part of a larger trend toward the privatization of Quebec and Canada's health care systems. The costs of this policy are being borne by new immigrants, to the profit of private insurance companies.

In the analysis of the IWC, the DDC ignores provincial, federal, and international human rights by preventing immigrants and temporary workers their right to physical and mental health. In theory, those rights should be exercised without discrimination of any kind. In reality, 84% of people that are not receiving Medicare for 3 months are new immigrants! For live-in caregivers and other temporary workers, they may even go through more than one 3-month delay, facing major obstacles to protecting their health.

When the DDC was implemented, the IWC started to see cases of people avoiding seeking health care when they needed it or, nearly as bad, people being saddled with debt into the tens of thousands of dollars. The first case that really illustrated this problem for the IWC was a man saddled with $37,000 of debt when he fell on the ice outside his apartment building and broke his femur. He was absolutely unable to pay down this debt while supporting his family, and he was terrified that this debt to the government would have a negative impact on his eventual goal of becoming a citizen. Another early case was a woman who came to work as a nanny in Canada on a temporary work permit under the Live-In Caregiver immigration program. Six weeks into her new job, she became very ill. Soon afterwards, she was diagnosed with cancer and was no longer able to work. Although she had been told that she would be covered by provincial health insurance, she discovered that there was a 3-month waiting period before she would become fully insured. Unfortunately, she had become ill before the three months were up and was facing hospital bills in the tens of thousands of dollars. Although she recovered from her cancer, the debt she accumulated has become a significant barrier to her dream of sponsoring her family to join her here in Canada.

Cases involving children have been particularly salient with the public and the media. Two recent cases involved very serious conditions. For example, within weeks of finishing their 3-month waiting period, a young girl suffered from repeated convulsions. Terrified, her family took her to the hospital where the doctor ordered a battery of tests. Her mother describes the horrible ordeal of having to discuss with the doctor which tests could wait so that Medicare would cover them once their 3 months were finished. Nevertheless, the family incurred a huge debt for their child's treatment. In another case, a young boy fell from the play structure at a park after only a few days in Canada. He was rushed to the hospital and treated for a ruptured liver. The enormous bill was impossible for the family to pay, since they had just spent all their savings to travel and settle in Canada.

Convinced that this was discriminatory and bad for Quebec society overall, the IWC teamed up with a number of other organizations to work on a campaign to abolish the DDC. Project Genesis, a neighborhood social rights organization, and PINAY, the Filipina Women's Association of Quebec (representing many live-in caregivers) are the two other groups in the coordinating committee. With support from more than 20 other organizations, including the biggest immigrant-serving coalitions of Quebec, the strategy has been to target the Health Minister and the provincial health insurance board in order to pressure them to remove the regulation from the books. Tactics have ranged from press conferences, to camping out in front of the Health minister's office, to public education on the issue, to supporting individual families facing DDC debt.

In the case of the DDC campaign, it was Project Genesis (an ally of the IWC located just up the street) that took the first steps in initiating a campaign. They operate a drop-in storefront rights information clinic and had seen numerous cases of immigrant families saddled with massive debt due to unforeseeable medical problems (childhood appendicitis, car accidents, slipping on ice) shortly after their arrival in Canada. Given Canada's supposedly universal Medicare system, this situation seemed to go against the spirit of the law, and Project Genesis organized a press conference with major immigration coalitions to call on the Quebec government to reverse its exclusion of new arrivals. When IWC organizers and activists saw this, it echoed a problem that we had been seeing among temporary foreign workers, especially LCP workers and in our collaborations with PINAY. We contacted Project Genesis in the summer of 2006 and, along with PINAY, the Health Care for All organizing committee was born. Since that time, dozens of Quebec organizations have signed on to our campaign and participate in specific events and actions.

Similar to the CSST campaign, the DDC campaign has had limited direct mobilization of those most affected by the issue. New arrivals to Quebec who don't encounter health problems (and most don't, having been pre-screened for health problems before being selected as immigrants or workers) don't often notice the lack of health coverage. And for those who do encounter problems, their relatively short time in Canada does not help them feel comfortable contesting publicly. Nevertheless, the campaign has documented a disturbing number of cases and research is beginning to show the negative effects of avoiding the use of health care services by those under the DDC. There is a core of about 10 families that are willing to speak publicly about the debt and stress they incurred as a result of the DDC, and they participate in demonstrations, lobbying, and media interventions.

There has been some movement on the issue. Several of the families who have gone public with their situation have had the debt collectors mysteriously back off and have been approached by opposition parties willing to support the campaign demands. Not so surprisingly, political insiders are encouraging the campaign to lessen its demands to ask only that children be covered immediately upon arrival. To date, campaign members have refused, finding this to be more of the same logic seen elsewhere in our social system (i.e. children deserve our sympathy, but their parents are just trying to abuse the system). Interestingly, it seems to be the connection to the LCP that is really moving the issue forward at the level of the Health Insurance Board.[4] Years of organizing around the trampled rights of LCP workers have moved the current Quebec Minister of Immigration to put pressure on the CSST and the Health Insurance Board to reexamine their treatment of LCP workers, and the DDC falls under this category. The Quebec Human Rights Commission is also investigating the DDC and CSST exclusion to determine whether these rules contravene Quebec's Charter of Human Rights. Activists are hopeful for change in the coming year.

Justice for L'Amour Workers

With globalization and the shifting of jobs to developing countries, the textile sector in Montreal has been in serious decline. Once a prosperous and key sector of employment for immigrants back in the early 20th century, the sector has recently lost many of its jobs to "offshore" production in poorer countries. Since its beginning, the IWC has dealt with cases of workers in this sector. Often, these cases have concerned unjust dismissal and lack of representation either because there were no unions or the unions were weak and did not adequately represent their members. Since 2007, there was an increase in the number of workers reporting job loss to the IWC. One company in particular came to the attention of organizers: L'Amour, a knitting factory that manufactured socks. There had already been cases brought through the IWC against L'Amour for its working conditions, such as the front door being kept locked and chained during the night shift. Under these conditions, workers were always in danger of being trapped because escape routes were limited in the case of an industrial fire. Often those doing piecework were not paid when machines broke down and they could not produce quotas. Workers were often forced to have meals at their stations while they continued to work, which meant that they virtually had no breaks. All of this was made worse by a union set up in 2004 and believed by many workers to be a "pro-management" union, preventing workers from organizing themselves and pressuring for changes in working conditions. This time, however, it became clear that company was shutting down production in Montreal with no compensation to the workers. A group of 25 workers, who have on average been working for this company for more than 10 years and some more than 20, was organized and began meeting. Another 50 at the beginning of August 2008 joined this group. The question is, how does one respond to lay-offs?

Interviews with the workers reveal the depth of their anger and frustration with L'Amour[5]. One former employee recounted how he had worked for 40 hours a week for 13 years, but was then laid off by L'Amour with no compensation beyond what he had earned. In our conversation, he empha-sized how skilled he was, consistently pressing as many as 11,000 socks a day: "I was one of the special guys on the tube machine. Nobody like me." Another worker, who had worked as a knitter's helper for 5 years and then as a knitter for 10 years until he was laid off by L'Amour, also emphasized his skill and dedication to his work, and his sense of outrage that he had been so little val-ued: "I gave thirteen years of my life to them, and what I got, I got nothing."

Both workers also pointed to problems with their working conditions. They noted that workers on the night shift were locked in, often having to wait for half an hour after their shift for the security guard to unlock the main door and let them out. The knitter said that workers had to work con-tinuously for 8-hour shifts: "During that time we had no break, the machine running. We have no choice to go to eating place, to cafeteria, get fresh air." He was especially vexed by the fact that the L'Amour management played favorites among workers:

> If they like employees, they say, "OK, OK, OK! We want to keep that person." Let's say I have no back up. Some person backs up the person. I hadn't back up. If I had back up, I would still be working at L'Amour. That's the policy at L'Amour. Let's say you are manager, you are so close to me, you save me, you say, "Don't touch this person, I recommend this person." But we are all good. We are all able to work. We are all skilled . . . so why do I need that person to back me up? I know how to work. I know how to work 25 machines. I was working a long time. Ten years, I was knitter. Five years, I was a knitter's helper. Why do I need someone to help me?

In discussion with the committee of workers from L'Amour, it became clear that returning to their old jobs was impossible, and there were workers from other factories in the sector who reported similar layoffs. As well, L'Amour has become a very profitable company for its owners, boasting that it is a leading company in the apparel industry and has operations in places like China, Pakistan, Bangladesh, and India with over 2,500 workers worldwide. A long-time partner of the retail giant Wal-Mart, it recently broke into the U.S. manufacturing market in July, 2007, by taking over Terramar Sports, a company based in Tarrytown, New York.

Through discussion, the workers decided on one significant demand, fair compensation for the years of loyalty they've shown this company. The situation is complex. If the company had shut down entirely or laid off large numbers, the workers would be eligible for "collective lay-off benefits". The company has chosen to lay off workers in small numbers, but systemati-cally, avoiding collective lay-offs and the related benefits.

The strategy chosen is to pressure both the Labor Relations Tribunal for inadequate labor representation and the Labor Standards Board. The call is for these bodies to intervene and treat lay-offs as collective so that the workers will be eligible for much higher benefits. At the same time, a wider committee of workers from L'Amour and a couple of other factories facing similar conditions, along with allies, are working toward the development of a policy covering the workers in the declining textile sector. This campaign is one that involved workers who are either not unionized or are represented by weak or pro-boss unions. In contrast, another company closed in Montreal with a strong union and the workers received a decent compensation package.

The situation of L'Amour workers is typical of that of other workers who come to the IWC who have experienced the failure of government institutions that regulate the labor market to protect them. These state policies were established in a period in which most jobs were stable and regular. Those jobs currently in textiles are increasingly irregular, with a drive to reduce labor costs. This type of labor is difficult to regulate through existing policies and programs. Without the collective action of the L'Amour workers, there would have been no recourse and the individuals would have received little compensation with their lay-offs. News of this campaign has even traveled through word-of-mouth and ethnic media, so that workers from other factories and even other cities have begun contacting the IWC with similar situations. Although it is difficult, the way forward is through political campaigns that not only challenge employers, but also state bodies that are supposed to protect workers' rights.

CONCLUDING COMMENTS

The immigration tendencies in Canada over the past 30 years have been well documented. This wave of immigration is mainly non-white, from the South. Immigrant workers tend to be concentrated in sectors of the economy that are at the bottom despite their relatively high levels of education, and they remain there over long periods. The impacts of globalization and neo-liberalism are seen in massive human displacement, restructured labor processes, and cutbacks in public services. The consequences include a rising demand for cheap labor, particularly in the service sector such as its privatization, and in just-in-time production. Immigrant workers face precarious, low-paid, non-unionized jobs and exclusion from many health, safety, and workplace policies. Beyond this are migrant workers without official status, who are forced to work below the minimal standards that theoretically protect other workers.

The campaigns being undertaken by the IWC reflect both the situations of immigrant workers and some of the emerging forms of organizing. Both the CSST and the DDC show how new immigrants are disproportionately excluded from public policies-health and safety. The L'Amour campaign demonstrates the precarious nature of the production in Canada and the arbitrary, unregulated working conditions. There are important lessons that the IWC has learned from these campaigns. First, it is difficult to organize immigrant workers around their workplaces, particularly those with precarious immigration status. There are many reasons for this, but it is important to be present and consistent and support people who come forward to challenge their employers. Working with individuals can be a precursor to building broader collective work. It is important to emphasize the mobilization of the workers themselves and to help support their leadership on the issues they face. Second, coalition building is necessary but not always easy. It takes a lot of time and work to educate allies about the conditions faced by immigrant workers, and the fact that they bring their own organizing and political traditions that do not always fit well with a more bureaucratic style in Quebec. As these issues are put in the public sphere, immigrant workers can begin to take their place as political and social actors in the struggle for social and economic justice. Third, campaigns have to be addressed at both the employers and the state, in order to work toward justice for immigrant workers. It is difficult to win demands from employers who function within a liberalized market without changes in government policies and programs that would benefit workers in precarious jobs in unstable sectors of the economy.

Organizing labor in the community is a new form that gives voice and some power to groups of immigrant workers, who are the most marginalized group in the labor market. The related organizing processes and advocacy cross traditional boundaries of community and work. With some exceptions, labor has been the domain of the union movement. However, with the changes described above, worker centers have been founded to counter the difficulties faced by unions in the restructured labor market. However, it is not only linking community and labor that is an important crossover. Organizations like the IWC have been able to bring together younger activists, who began their engagement with the anti-globalization movement, with older activists and immigrant workers. This is a way that those involved in broader social and political questions can bring their energy and analysis into local activities. On the other side, these exchanges have brought the IWC closer to wider "movement" activities such as Solidarity Across Borders. This exchange broadens both and brings the global and local together in a concrete way and creates an exchange between activists from different generations and different countries and traditions. Learning is a significant consequence for all involved, and the resulting alliances have grown out of these exchanges. One result is that the IWC, as with the revival of new forms of labor organizing in the United States, takes on elements of a wider social movement and is not limited to local work (Clawson, 2003). The IWC through its many activities has become a place for building alliances and bring social actors, who are promoting social and economic justice, together.

There has often been a distinction drawn between direct service and organizing. Many community organizations are pushed to provide direct service by their funders and, as a result, their organizing activities become secondary. The IWC and similar community centers see individual service as a key way to attract people to their organizations. For an individual to step forward to challenge their boss on an issue of working conditions is an act of courage and is inherently political. And because individual problems are based in a workplace and in a policy context, they are often shared by others and form the basis for collective action. So, for organizations like the IWC, the issues brought in by community members contribute to building collective action and campaigns (Delgado, 1996; Gordon, 2005).

For community and labor organizing in general, the concept of working with individuals as a beginning point to initiate collective action is an important one to grasp and one that allows for more creative targets for change. It is often impossible to organize directly in the workplace because of the precarious nature of many of the jobs of immigrant workers. Therefore, the target of their campaigns has been the state, demanding improvements in conditions for everyone at the bottom end of the labor market. Policy-oriented campaigns, such as demanding improvements in labor standards or extending coverage of health and safety, are the result. In the current climate in which immigrant labor is used as a cheap pool that can be brought into workplaces or excluded as needed, new strategies that challenge exploitation are needed. The traditional union model has not been able to respond and organize most of the workers in these conditions. The emergence of worker centers with an immigrant membership is a start on the road to building a class movement for workplace justice alongside the union movement.

NOTES

1. Canada's immigration system has traditionally been conceived to respond to demand for labor through the admission of "Permanent Residents" (immigrants) based on a point system that takes into account such factors as age, education, language ability, and employment prospects. They share all the same rights as Canadian citizens, apart from the right to vote. Three years after arrival, they are eligible for full citizenship. Temporary Foreign Workers (TFW), however, are restricted to work for the employer on their visa and are granted a 6- to 24-month work permit, after which time they have no guaranteed right to remain in Canada. For the first time in 2007, TFWers outnumbered the employment-oriented permanent residents admitted to Canada, with 115,000 TFWers (CIC, 2008a) versus only 94,000 permanent residents admitted for employment purposes as opposed to family or humanitarian motivations (CIC, 2008c).

2. In Canada, the provinces have the major responsibility for health, social services, and labor. Even though there is federal transfer of funds, the provinces retain full control.

3. CSST=*Commission de la sécurité et la santé au travail.*

4. Health Insurance Board=RAMQ=Régie de l'assurance médicale du Québec

5. These interviews were carried out by Yumna Siddiqi and were part of Siddiqi and Shragge (2008).

REFERENCES

Abu-Laban, Y., & Gabriel, C. (2002). *Selling diversity: Immigration, multiculturalism, employment equity and globalization.* Peterborough, ON: Broadview Press.

Ahmadi, E. (2006, June). *Current employment conditions and learning practices of Canadian immigrant workers.* Paper presented at the annual conference of the Work and Lifelong Learning Research Network (WALL), Ontario Institute for Studies in Education, University of Toronto.

Aldridge, F., & Waddington, S. (2001). *Asylum seekers' skills and qualifications audit pilot project.* Leicester, UK: National Institute for Adult and Continuing Education.

Arat-Koc, S. (1999). Neo-liberalism, state restructuring and immigration: Changes in Canadian Policies in the 1990s. *Journal of Canadian Studies, 34*(2), 31–56.

Austin, C., & Este, D. (2001). The working experiences of underemployed immigrant and refugee men. *Canadian Social Work Review/Revue canadienne de service social, 18*(2), 213–229.

Baines, D., & Sharma, N. (2002). Migrant workers as non-citizens: The case against citizenship as a social policy concept. *Studies in Political Economy, 69,* 75–28.

Bauder, H. (2003). "Brain abuse", or the devaluation of immigrant labor in Canada. *Antipode, 35*(4), 699–717.

Caulford, P., & Vali, Y. (2006). Providing health care to medically uninsured immigrants and refugees. *Canadian Medical Association Journal, 194,* 1253–1254.

Chetkovich, C., & Kunreuther, F. (2006). *From the ground up: Grassroots associations making social change.* Ithaca, NY: Cornell University.

Citizenship and Immigration Canada (CIC). (2008a). *Facts and figures 2007: Immigration overview: Initial entry of foreign workers by top source countries.* Ottawa, ON: Author.

Citizenship and Immigration Canada (CIC). (2008b). *Facts and figures 2007: Immigration overview: Permanent residents 15 years of age or older by source area and level of education.* Ottawa, ON: Author.

Citizenship and Immigration Canada (CIC). (2008c). *Facts and figures 2007: Immigration overview: Permanent residents by category (principal applicants).* Ottawa, ON: Author.

Citizenship and Immigration Canada (CIC). (2008d). *Facts and figures 2007: Immigration overview: Permanent residents by top source countries.* Ottawa, ON: Author.

Clawson, D. (2003). *The next upsurge: Labor and new social movements.* Ithaca, NY: ILR Press, Cornell University Press

Employment and Immigration Canada. (1978). *Immigration statistics 1977.* Ottawa, ON: CIC.

Fine, J. (2005, March). Community unions and the revival of the American labor movement, *Politics and Society, 33*(11), 54–199.

Gibson, N., Cave, A., Doering, D., Ortiz, L., & Harms, P. (2005). Socio-cultural factors influencing prevention and treatment of tuberculosis in immigrant and aboriginal communities in Canada. *Social Science & Medicine, 61,* 931–942.

Gordon, J. (2005). *Suburban sweatshops: The fight for immigrant rights,* Cambridge MA: Belknap Press.

Gravel, S., Boucheron, L., & Kane, M. (2003). Workplace health and safety for immigrant workers in Montreal: Results of an exploratory study [Electronic version]. *Perspectives interdisciplinaires sur le travail et la santé, 5*(1). Retrieved May 5, 2009, from http://www.pistes.uqam.ca/v5n1/articles/v5n1a3.htm

Guruge, S., & Khanlou, N. (2004). Intersectionalities of influence: Researching the health of immigrant and refugee women. *Canadian Journal of Nursing Research, 36,* 32–47.

Hanley, J., & Shragge, E. (2009). Economic security for women with precarious immigration status: Enforcing labour rights for all. In J. Pulkingham & G.M. Cohen (Eds.), *Imagining public policy to meet women's economic security needs* (pp. 353–373). Toronto, ON: University of Toronto.

Hasenfeld, Y., & Gidron, B. (2005). Understanding multi-purpose hybrid voluntary organizations: The contributions of theories on civil society, social movements and non-profit organizations. *Journal of Civil Society, 1,* 97–112.

Iacovetta, F. (with Draper, P., & Ventresca, R.). (Eds.). (1998). *A nation of immigrants: Women, workers, and communities in Canadian history, 1840s –1960s.* Toronto, ON: University of Toronto.

Kopec, J. A., Williams, J. I., To, T., & Austin, P. C. (2001). Cross-cultural comparisons of health status in Canada using the health utilities index. *Ethnicity & Health, 6,* 41–50.

Krahn, H., Derwing, T., Mulder, M., & Wilkinson, L. (2000). Educated and underemployed: Refugee integration into the Canadian labor market. *International Journal of Migration and Integration, 1*(1), 59–84.

Lai, D. W. L., & Chau, S. B. Y. (2007). Predictors of health service barriers for older Chinese immigrants in Canada. *Health & Social Work, 3,* 57–66.

Lippel, K. (2006). Precarious employment and occupational health and safety regulation in Quebec. In L. Vosko (Ed.), *Precarious employment: Understanding labour market insecurity in Canada* (pp. 241–255). Montreal-Kingston: McGill Queen's University Press.

Oxman-Martinez, J., Hanley J., Lach, L., Khanlou, N., Weerasinghe, S., & Agnew V. (2005). Intersection of Canadian policy parameters affecting women with precarious immigration status: A baseline for understanding barriers to health. *Journal of Immigrant Health, 7,* 247–258.

Picot, G. (2004). *Deteriorating economic welfare of immigrants and possible causes.* Ottawa, ON: Statistics Canada. (Catalogue No. 11F0019MIE, No.222)

Picot, G., Hou, F., & Coulombe, S. (2007, January). *Chronic low income and low-income dynamics among recent immigrants.* Statistics Canada, (Catalogue No. 11F0019MIE, No. 294)

Pierre, M. (2005). Factors of exclusion blocking the socioeconomic integration of certain groups of immigrant women in Quebec. The current state. *Nouvelles Pratiques Sociales, 17,* 75–94.

Preibisch, K. L. (2007). *Patterns of social exclusion and inclusion of migrant workers in rural Canada.* Ottawa, ON: The North-South Institute.

Preibisch, K. L. (2004). Migrant agricultural workers and processes of social inclusion in rural Canada. *Canadian Journal of Latin American & Caribbean Studies, 29*(57/8), 203–239.

Shields, J. (2003). *No safe haven: Markets, welfare, and migrants* (CERIS Working Paper No. 22). Toronto, ON: CERIS.

Siddiqi, Y., & Shragge, E. (2008, September-October). The Empire's new clothes: Where does boutique capitalism leave Montreal's garment workers? IBON *Education for Development, 7*(5), 20–24.

Stephenson, P. H. (1995). Vietnamese refugees in Victoria B.C.: An overview of immigrant and refugee health care in a medium-sized Canadian urban centre. *Social Science & Medicine, 40,* 1631–1642.

Tait, V. (2005). *Poor workers' unions: Rebuilding labor from below.* Cambridge, MA: South End Press.

Thobani, S. (2007). *Exalted subjects: Studies in the making of race and nation in Canada.* Toronto, ON: University of Toronto.

Zanchetta, M. S., & Poureslami, I. M. (2006). Health literacy within the reality of immigrants' culture and language. *Canadian Journal of Public Health, 97,* S26–S30.

Zietsma, D. (2007, September). *The Canadian immigrant labour market in 2006: First results from Canada's labour force survey.* Ottawa, ON: Statistics Canada. (Catalogue No. 71-606-XIE)

Outcomes of Two Construction Trades Pre-Apprenticeship Programs: A Comparison

HELENA WORTHEN

Labor Education Program, School of Labor and Employment Relations, University of Illinois, Champaign, Illinois

REV. ANTHONY HAYNES

Building Bridges Project, Arise Chicago, Chicago, Illinois

Jobs in unionized construction trades are among the few forms of employment that provide significant, rapid, upward mobility to people who fall into the category of "hard to employ." However, such jobs have also historically been racially exclusive. In many cities, community-based organizations have acted as workforce intermediaries to address this issue of access. Judging the success of these programs is difficult. This paper compares and offers explanations for the different outcomes of two construction trade pre-apprenticeship programs that targeted a hard-to-employ demographic. Both were run by the Building Bridges Project of Arise Chicago. Both were intended to increase minority access to unionized building trade apprenticeship programs, and ultimately to union work in construction. The self-selection process, the high level of support provided to participants in one class but not the other, and a close organizational relationship to the United Brotherhood of Carpenters (UBC) at a time when that union explicitly linked training with organizing made the critical difference in outcomes. These factors should be considered when planning future jobs programs. A jobs program designed to open up access to good jobs for the hard-to-employ should proceed by self-selection, substantial support, and viable links to the

The authors would like to acknowledge their debt and gratitude to Emanuel Blackwell, Dwight McDowell, Reverend CJ Hawking and Jonnita Condra, and to the anonymous reviewers who helped improve this article.

entities that control access to the work such as, in this case, union apprenticeship programs.

OUTCOMES OF TWO CONSTRUCTION TRADES PRE-APPRENTICESHIP PROGRAMS: A COMPARISON

To address locally the complex problems of unemployment and poverty, community-based organizations (CBOs) have emerged that serve as work-force intermediaries (Giloth, 2003) often bridging a particular population and a particular industry. These CBOs may be private-public partnerships involving churches, school systems, community colleges, private entities such as banks, and, in an industry where training is done via an apprenticeship program, as in construction, unions, contractors, and community develop-ment corporations. They may operate with grant funding, state or federal funding, or donations and volunteer labor. As organizations, they tend to be vulnerable to changes in the political context because the enactment of their mission places the organization directly into the heart of the politics of the industry. If, in the upcoming period, a major new infusion of funding for jobs creation occurs, organizations like these will have an important role to play. If they function as a mirror of the general labor market, by applying traditional criteria and selecting by sorting and eliminating, they will only repeat and reinforce legacies of discrimination.

Anecdotal reports suggest that CBO-based workforce intermediary programs are successful. However, systematic evaluations of outcomes of these programs are hard to obtain for many reasons, among them the limited budgets, low overheads, and dependency on soft money that makes doing training and case management a much higher priority than evaluating out-comes. In the case of programs where the goal is to gain access to the unionized construction trades, gathering outcome data is made more diffi-cult because the process of applying to an apprenticeship program may take up to two years, several times longer than the training itself. Therefore, any information that can help answer the question, Does a program like this work? is valuable.

A unique opportunity enabled the Building Bridges Project (BBP) of Arise Chicago to research and compare the outcomes of two of its training programs, both pre-apprenticeships that prepare participants to apply to unionized construction trades apprenticeships. The three core lessons that emerged from this research were the positive results of the selection strategy, which relied on self-selection rather than elimination; the importance of financial support which included stipends for participants and wages for journeymen instructors; and the importance of having a close relationship with a union apprenticeship program, in this case, the United Brotherhood of Carpenters (UBC).

DEFINITION OF OUTCOMES, GOALS AND LESSONS

For this study, a successful outcome is defined as acceptance of a graduate of a class into a unionized construction trades apprenticeship program. The outcomes of two different classes are compared. From the first of the two classes, called the Night Class, about one third (32%) of those who graduated and applied to an apprenticeship program appear to have been accepted, although tracking these graduates was problematic, for the reasons mentioned above and others to be explained. From the second of the two classes, called the Carpenters Class, 29 out of 29 (100%) of those who graduated and applied were accepted. What follows includes explanations of the reasons for this difference as well as cautions about its implications.

The goal of both these classes was to increase minority employment in unionized construction. The two classes recruited from the same population. They were both projects of the BBP, one of the over 60 affiliates within the national network of the non-profit Interfaith Worker Justice. The authors are a member of the BBP Advisory Board and the Director of the BBP, respectively. The classes differed in funding, recruiting, selection strategy, instructional design, relationships with building trades unions, curriculum, types and quality of case management, and other support for participants, and outcomes.

EXTERNAL FACTORS THAT SHAPE OUTCOMES

Circumstances specific, if not unique, to the building trades influence outcomes. These include the historic exclusion of minorities from construction unions, the number and type of minority hire requirements embodied in project labor agreements for publicly funded construction projects, the relationships between local elected officials, their constituents, and the processes by which building projects get approved, the opportunities for non-union work, and the contractions and expansions of the construction labor market. These not only shape opportunities for advancement through the apprenticeship period to journeyman status by accumulating on-the-job training hours, but also the commitment of participants to the program.

Minority Exclusion

The problem of access of minorities into the unionized trades in the United States has long seemed intractable (Fletcher & Gapasin, 2008; Goldfield,

1997; Paap 2008). After Bacon's Rebellion in 1676, Blacks were explicitly prohibited from being allowed to learn mechanical trades (Allen, 1994). Philip S. Foner wrote:

> But from the time the first trade unions were formed by white workers in the 1790's to the Civil War—in which period the free black population grew from 59,000 to 488,000—no free Negro wage-earner was a member. To be sure, the trade unions of the 1850's were exclusively craft unions composed of skilled mechanics. Unskilled workers found it impossible to join most of these unions, and several such as the printers, hotel waiters, shoemakers, and tailors, excluded women as well. But not one of the unions allowed a black worker, skilled or unskilled, male or female, to join its ranks. (Foner, 1974 p. 5)

In *Black Reconstruction,* W.E.B. DuBois (1935/1998) told how White workers in organized trades opposed the abolitionist movement for fear that free Black workers would underbid and compete for jobs held by White workers. After the Civil War and up through the Civil Rights movement, Jim Crow trade unions abounded (Frymer, 2003). After the passage of the Civil Rights Act of 1964, changes in the procedures for litigating made possible a wave of lawsuits that charged discrimination. Initially, the focus of litigation was on voting rights and integration of schools, but then it turned to employment, and the building trades were in the crosshairs. Between 1965 and 1985, the civil rights litigation against building trades unions was so relentless that some went bankrupt (Frymer, 2003). In Chicago, in the mid 1980s, some of the major building trades apprenticeship programs were placed under consent decrees as a result of civil rights lawsuits. Among these were the electricians, plumbers, pipefitters, ironworkers and insulators. The consent decrees stipulated and oversaw minority access.

In those same decades, the 1980s and 1990s, studies of the construction labor force predicted a shortage of skilled workers (Allen, 1997) partly because of an oncoming wave of retirements. When there is a skills shortage, organizing becomes easier. Not coincidentally, construction in the 1990s was the only private sector industry that experienced significant union growth (Belman & Smith, in press). In 1999 there was so much construction going on in the Chicago area that according to the President of the Chicago Federation of Labor, the hiring halls were "empty from Chicago to Arkansas" (D. Turner, personal communication, October 1999). In Chicago, when the consent decrees were lifted in the early 2000s and oversight ceased, community-based organizations attempted to fill this shortage with training programs directed toward minorities. In 2007, construction was still identified as a sector that was steadily increasing its share of the total employment picture. But that same year, according to the Center for Tax and Budget Accountability, African American workers constituted only 4% of the construction workforce in Illinois, as compared to over 8% for Latinos (a high percentage of whom are in non-union work), less than 1% for Asians, but 78% for Whites (http://www.stateofworkingillinois.niu.edu).

Political Advocacy for Increasing Minority Access

In 2004, community organizers approached leaders of the Illinois legislature, in particular the Illinois Black Caucus, for help. The goal was framed aggressively, as in "break open the unions," or "force the unions to open up." This strategy included intensive committee work in which the BBP and another Chicago non-profit, Chicago Women in the Trades (CWIT), partici-pated as well as reports, proposals, and newspaper publicity. This effort underwent transformation as several years passed, but it consistently got support from the Black leadership of the Illinois legislature.

Finally, in January, 2007, $6.25 million was set aside by the legislature in a straight party line vote to fund a program that would create a pipeline to bring minorities into the building trades. The funding would be disbursed as grants to community-based organizations (CBOs) and closely overseen by the Department of Commerce and Economic Opportunity (DCEO). The fact that general funds money (as compared to federal job training money such as funds distributed to states under the Workforce Investment Act) could be set aside for this program at a time when the budget of the state of Illinois was troubled and state workers were being laid off is an indication of the political effectiveness of its advocates. Characteristics of the DCEO program are described below.

The organizations that received grant money to carry out recruiting and training included the BBP, CWIT, New SkillBuilders (which made common cause with CWIT and set up its own training space in a warehouse on the South Side), two programs run out of the Chicago Public Schools, two pro-grams that worked in the desperately poor far South suburbs, a program from Peoria (one hundred and fifty miles south of Chicago), and United Services. These organizations formed a consortium of partners to exert continuing pressure to advocate for their programs. The pressure was directed both at the political establishment and at contractors who might consider hiring their graduates.

The Challenge Facing the DCEO Grant Recipients

The partners faced two challenges. They were not only to train and prepare applicants but to recruit them from a demographic of the most hard-to-employ: ex-offenders, people who had been on public aid, people who had been homeless, youth aging out of foster care, ex-drug addicts and alcohol abusers. Then they were to track these recruits not only into apprenticeship programs, but also through completion and into regular work as journeymen.

Only survival of a significant cohort through the whole process would count as "breaking open the unions." How the CBOs would continue their tracking and case management after the 18-month funding ran out was not addressed. This has always been one of the weaknesses of funding training programs run by small community-based advocacy organizations; budgets based on soft money mean that sustaining overhead past the accomplishment of the immediate goal of a grant rarely if ever gets accomplished.

THE BBP NIGHT CLASS AND THE CARPENTERS CLASS OUTCOMES

The $500,000 awarded to the BBP as one of the partner grant recipients came at a time when the BBP had already been running another class, called the Night Class, for six years. This was the program that had built the credibility of the BBP as a training provider. The request by the DCEO that grant recipients track recruits all the way from initial contact to journeyman status, if achieved, caused the BBP to try to track all participants in their Night Class, since a database of 587 enrollees (as of 2008) going back to 2003 existed. Short-term tracking had been done each year but long-term tracking would shed light on the effectiveness of the program and the experience of their graduates over time. It would also identify problems anticipated in the tracking challenge set by the DCEO. Therefore, at the same time that the DCEO grant was awarded, the BBP, working with the University of Illinois, started doing phone interviews with its entire list of Night Class Graduates. The phone interview process was completed within a few months (November 2008) of the graduation (September 2008) of the last group from the DCEO-supported program, which was called the Carpenters Class because of its close linkages to the UBC.

A summary of the tracking results of the Night Class is shown in Table 1. This table can be read as follows: of the 587 individuals who originally attended at least one BBP Night Class meeting, 184 (90 + 94) were reached by phone. One hundred and twenty-nine phone numbers reached either an

TABLE 1 Tracking Results of the BBP Night Class

In database	No telephone number originally given or number given is wrong number	Phone number correct and possible to reach	Called, not reached	Called, reached, but did not graduate from program; no interview	Called and interviewed	Applied to apprenticeship program	Accepted into apprenticeship program
587	274	313	129	90	94	63	20

TABLE 2 Tracking Results of the BBP Carpenters Class

In database	Accepted into carpenters class	Attended carpenters class	Graduated from carpenters class	Applied to apprenticeship program	Accepted into apprenticeship program
100	41	38	29	29	29

answering machine belonging to the person sought, or a person who knew the person sought, but the person was never reached. Of the 184 who were reached, 90 had not graduated. Of that same 184 who were reached, 94 had graduated from the BBP Night Class and were interviewed. Of those interviewed, 63 or about two thirds, had proceeded with the apprenticeship program application process, and 20 had been accepted, for an acceptance rate of about 32% of those who graduated and who applied. An explanation for the extremely high dropout rate, from 587 to 94, follows below.

These results are to be compared with the results of the class funded by the DCEO, called the Carpenters Class, in Table 2. This table can be read as follows: of the 100 individuals who originally were potential candidates (see below for explanation of first level of selection), 41 were accepted into the Carpenters Class, 38 attended, 9 dropped out or were expelled during the class, and 29 graduated. All those who graduated applied to the UBC apprenticeship program and all were accepted, following an additional test.

These very different success rates should be evaluated in the light of the different selection strategies and levels of support provided to both the BBP and to individual participants in the program.

THE NIGHT CLASS AND THE CARPENTERS CLASS: DESCRIPTIONS

The Night Class

The Night Class is a 14-week once-a-week evening class that takes place in church, community, and fellowship rooms in various low-income Chicago neighborhoods (Worthen & Haynes, 2003). It is ongoing as of this date. About 10 Night Classes are in operation every year. It is a walk-in program: there is no selection process. Anyone, no matter what age, ability, gender, or race, is welcome. This means that among the 587 individuals in the database there are people who would never physically be able to do the work of the building trades, or who do not have the high school diploma, birth certificate, immigration documents, or driver's license that would be required. Some attend simply to learn the basic math skills that are being taught. But the principle of the class is to exclude no one.

In the early years of the program the Night Class was, outside of one paid staff member, a virtually all-volunteer, all-donation program, relying heavily on the good will of the UBC to cover photocopying and sometimes provide journeymen or organizers as teachers, and to allow participants to tour their training facility. The UBC at that time had explicitly strategized training, including this type of training, to be part of organizing and increasing minority presence in their membership (D. McMahon, personal communication, December 2005). Journeymen from other unions (e.g., plumbers, bricklayers, laborers, electricians) also came to classes as guest speakers and hosted tours. As the program built relationships with unions, minority contractors, and minority developers in order to place graduates in on-the-job training opportunities, and the program grew, ten classes per year were graduated, teachers became paid, a textbook was written and printed for use in the class, and a small fee was paid to churches for the use of their premises. By 2007, the point at which the DCEO grant was awarded, the budget for each Night Class, including in-kind donations, was estimated to be between $20,000 and $25,000, covering teachers, staff, and office administration, which came to about $1,000 to $4,000 per participant given a class of 20–25 participants and depending on requirements set by funders for a specific class, such as drug testing. Funding came from a combination of donations and grants.

The Night Class involves no hands-on construction training. Instead, classroom sessions are devoted to basic math, some reading comprehension, and financial literacy. Time is also spent providing the kind of information that a person already familiar with the world of unionized construction might have internalized informally: what the different trades do, how to interview, and above all, the complex multi-deadline application process itself which varies from one trade to another.

The Night Class has a modest degree of case management. The director and one case manager are available by phone. Participation is the criterion for graduation; there are no tests. Upon graduation, participants are expected to take advantage of contacts at various union apprenticeship programs and keep informed of dates of different stages in the apprenticeship program. A jobs club for graduates who have not obtained work meets bi-monthly and hosts visits from prospective employers. But the initiative for making the application to the apprenticeship program and following through on the process is in the hands of the applicant.

The Carpenters Class

The terms of the $500,000 DCEO grant awarded to the BBP both enabled and required a program with a much higher level of support. State Representative Marlow Colvin, a member of the Illinois Black Caucus, saw the grants as addressing the various obstacles that face minority applicants to the building trades apprenticeship programs directly. He said, "We've removed all the obstacles to success. We'll get a group of people, remove the obstacles, and see what they're capable of doing" (M. Colvin, personal communication, January 17, 2008). The grant would provide support for child care, a bus pass, text books, tools, and a much higher level of case management. Specific requests for items such as car repair could be made by grant recipients. Participants would receive stipends of $300 per week, or Illinois minimum wage, so that they would not have to survive the 11 weeks without income.

Given these stipulations, it was determined that for $500,000 the BBP could run three classes of 12 students each. It would be an 11-week full-day program that included hands-on carpentry training. The class would take place in the Carpenters Training Facility and would be taught by journeymen carpenters who were paid union scale including benefits. Most of the costs, which included building materials, stipends, a physical exam, workman's compensation insurance and textbooks, were not flexible. Compared to the Night Class, the Carpenters Class was an expensive program, at $14,000 per participant. Therefore the BBP strategized carefully about its selection process, as each failed participant would in effect waste a $14,000 slot.

The Selection Process

The selection process began like the Night Class with open meetings in low-income neighborhood churches. Over the course of four meetings, 100 applicants filled out an application form and showed that they had a birth certificate, high school diploma or GED, and a driver's license. Many who attended these meetings could not produce these documents. When the BBP staff reviewed the application forms, it became apparent that no individual could be accepted or eliminated on the basis of the information they provided: even the best-written applications were scanty and uninformative. Therefore a decision was made to rely on self-selection and sequence of hurdles was created to measure commitment through action. The first hurdle was to appear at a distant, unfamiliar address (the UBC apprenticeship program site) at a specific time three weeks later. Half the applicants did not pass that hurdle. The second hurdle was to take an hour-long math test that included addition, subtraction, fractions, decimals, measurements, geometry, and some mechanical reasoning, followed by an hour-long reading comprehension test. A third test put applicants together in groups of three and asked them to use magic markers to draw maps of Chicago. This tested social skills as well as awareness of the major highways they would need to take to get to construction sites.

The math and reading tests were scored immediately, onsite. Although about half the applicants could get no further than the first fraction problems on the math test, they were not eliminated by a cut-off score. Instead, they were referred to math tutoring, held at yet another location on a set of other dates. The hurdle, in this case, was attendance. The tutoring was intensive and often one-on-one. All students who attended tutoring improved their scores enough to enter the program. Thus, the screening process was essentially self-selection by the most motivated and able applicants.

The last phase of the selection process involved an interview, a physical agility test, and a drug test. At this point there were 52 remaining applicants out of the original 100. The physical agility test, which involved carrying 4' × 8' sheets of plywood and climbing a two-story scaffold carrying a large wrench, eliminated several who were afraid of heights. Another four or five either declined to take or failed the drug test, which eliminated them. The remaining 41 were ranked and assigned to classes. As it happened, because of the sagging housing market, several others who had employment withdrew, preferring to keep a current job rather than risk an increasingly tight job market. This meant that everyone who survived the hurdles and still wanted to enter the program was accepted. Of those last 41, 38 showed up for classes. Nine were expelled for attendance, failure to do home work, or unsafe use of tools during class. Thus, 29 graduated. Because of their training under UBC journeymen, the tutoring, and intensive case management to resolve academic, family, health, and transportation problems, all 29 of these passed a final test and were indentured into the UBC.

WHO CAME TO THE TABLE?

A Snapshot of a Population

One of the intentions of the DCEO grant, expressed at an early meeting of all stakeholders, was to see who came to the table and "take a snapshot of a population." The population in question was the target demographic of hard-to-employ minorities, including previously incarcerated, unemployed, working part-time, history of drug of alcohol abuse, single parent or parenting youth, homeless, past or present public housing or public aid recipient, or youth aging out of foster care. The BBP had not kept such data on applicants to the Night Class, but it did have data for the Carpenters Class. All these characteristics were represented in the first group of 100 for the Carpenters Class. This group included 95 African Americans, 5 Latinos, and 13 women. Among the 52 who were invited to be interviewed, there were 22 previously incarcerated, 28 who had been in public housing or on public aid, 11 with a history of drug and alcohol abuse, 4 who had been homeless, and 4 who had been in foster care. Among the 29 graduates, there were 24 African Americans, 5 Latinos, 1 woman; 11 who had been previously incarcerated, 14 who had lived in public housing or had been on public aid, 5 who had had drug or alcohol abuse problems, and 1 each who had been either homeless or in foster care. In other words, the original target demographic survived into the graduating cohort; neither the selection process nor the actual class creamed out the hard-to-employ whom the grants were intended to reach. This information has relevance for design of future jobs programs intended to avoid historic patterns of discrimination.

The applicants' original written applications also revealed information about their economic condition. Out of 100, there were 55 who were living on less than $5,000 per year income, and only four who were living on $30,000 to $35,000. The majority, in other words, were living outside the formal economy. Ten out of 100 applicants reported working full-time and seven of those were making $15,000 to $25,000 per year. Full-time jobs were in recycling, food service, and warehousing.

Because the recruiting for the Carpenters Class took place in the same neighborhoods through the same network that the recruiting for the Night Class takes place, the participants in both classes can be assumed to be similar. This information about income levels and social situation can help explain why out of the 587 names in the Night Class database, so many had moved, left no forwarding address, had never had a telephone number, or were no longer available at the number they gave at the time.

An important question was whether the high level of support provided by the DCEO grant was necessary, adequate, or effective. The stipend was clearly the most valued type of support. Instructors and case managers for the Carpenters Class reported that among the obstacles identified by the grant, child care posed the most problems, especially for women (only one woman graduated). The child care support guidelines had not anticipated the extent to which extended family, sibling and elder care, in addition to child care responsibilities, were an obstacle. Physical fitness was also a problem, especially for women. Among other critical problems, homelessness seemed to be a strong predictor of inability to complete the program.

This is the snapshot that the Carpenters Class provided: a population of very disadvantaged hard-to-employ people among whom there were neverthe-less some who, with significant support, could survive an intensive training program.

The Perspective of the Stakeholders

The political forces activated to move this grant through the legislature were not natural allies, but their interaction created a moment in time in which different stakeholders could be brought to the table. Viewed as a whole, the design of the DCEO program suggested that the stakeholders were at the table as much to place a bet as to see the program succeed. The bet could be expressed this way. Some stakeholders would say that apprenticeship recruitment strategies were already color blind and that outreach programs were good enough as is. Others would say that recruitment strategies were not color blind and that outreach programs and the application process itself had to be modified to remove obstacles identified as systemic features of the legacy of racism. This would mean that if outreach was modified to reach the target demographic most likely to be deterred by such obstacles, and if key support to overcome obstacles was provided, then the partners would find good candidates who could make it through the pre-apprenticeship programs and get accepted into union apprenticeship programs. Some stakeholders were betting yes; some were betting no.

For example, the Chicago Building Trades Council (CBTC), representing the unions, declared its willingness to work with any and all minority organizations, but argued that training a candidate for unionized work took four to five years from apprenticeship to journeyman, and that especially among the target population, finding candidates who could survive even the application process, much less the rigorous apprenticeship training, would be extremely difficult. Also, the CBTC made it clear that the Council would only support a pipeline into union work. If funds were spent on training for non-union work, the CBTC warned that it would withdraw support and block the program. Chicago commercial construction ranges, depending on the trade, from 75% union on up; most work in Chicago is union. Withdrawal of union support from this program would have been fatal to the program because participants would lose their link to eventual good jobs.

The Builders Association, made up of major contractors and developers, also expressed concern about the quality of the candidates that would come through any selection process that drew from the target population. Once the grant was awarded, they distributed a list of topics such as "work ethic" that they wanted the CBO grant recipients to teach." They warned the grant recipients that the Builders Association had not made a commitment to hire any of the graduates of the trainings. The minority hire requirement applies only to public and federally-funded construction projects; privately funded construction has no minority hire requirements.

Another stakeholder was the DCEO itself, through which the grant came. The DCEO proposed the database to track every applicant from the first moment of contact during recruiting to final status, if achieved, of journeyman, five or six years later. This database was what was described as "a snapshot of a population." This raised the question of what kind of claim would be validated or nullified by such a snapshot. Was it the claim that there existed many good candidates for building trades apprenticeships in the "hard-to-employ" demographic, but that they were being excluded on the basis of race and could be successful if certain obstacles were removed? Or was it the claim that qualified candidates could not be found at all in that demographic?

The CBO partners were also stakeholders. They were the vehicles through which the funding would get disbursed and which would actually have to design and implement the programs. They existed because of their advocacy role. They were, of course, betting that they would be able to find good candidates and produce good outcomes. Banding together as a consortium of partners, meeting regularly, sharing strategies and practicing collective advocacy both toward the funders and toward the contractors in the Builders Association helped the project avoid the pitfall of competition among the partners.

The various unions that have worked with the BBP are also stakeholders. In particular, the UBC first by explicitly using training as a strategy for organizing, and second by opening its resources to a program that was designed to bring in members from a hard-to-employ demographic, was betting on the success of the program.

However, a major factor that would affect the progress of program graduates in their positions as apprentices was the labor market itself. Work in construction is essentially temporary work; when the project is over, the job is over. A few workers may be carried over onto the next job, but if there is no next project, there is no next job. Making progress toward journeyman status requires accumulating the required 4,000 to 10,000 hours of on-the-job apprenticeship work (Construction Industry Service Organization, 2006). If an apprentice can't get hired, he or she can't advance. In 2008, the labor market for construction was shrinking rapidly. The jobs that depended on federal and state funding, which are the jobs that have minority hire requirements, were stalled. Therefore despite success in the BBP pre-apprenticeship program, progress beyond indenture of both the Night Class and the Carpenters Class graduates was slowed. This, however, was not within the power of any of the stakeholders to control or influence.

IMPLICATIONS AND CAUTIONS

This article is about outcomes of two community-based organization training programs. This particular set of outcomes was developed because, in the case of the Night Class, some funding became available that enabled a systematic round of telephone interviews (actually two rounds, with a third ongoing) with an entire database, and, in the case of the Carpenters Class, the cohort was recent enough and small enough so that the numbers were easy to see. In general, outcomes are costly and difficult to collect, easily misunderstood or misinterpreted, and rarely shared. Nevertheless, they are important because they help answer the question, Does this program work?

Immediate implications from this comparison can be summarized as follows. Long-term tracking of participants in this target demographic is hampered by the high frequency of changing residences and telephone numbers among low-income populations and by the limited resources of CBOs that have to prioritize training above evaluating training. But a systematic effort, even if imperfect, generates information which can be interpreted and built upon. Two different programs offered to the same population produced different results, but both demonstrated that good candidates can be found even among the most hard-to-employ. The high level of support provided by the DCEO grant made the critical difference. Self-selection rather than testing and use of cut-off scores to eliminate participants allowed the most committed participants to survive. Intensive tutoring accelerated recapture of basic math knowledge. As expected, targeted solutions to previously identified obstacles (Worthen & Haynes, 2003) in the form of various kinds of case management and support lowered or removed those obstacles. However, a program of this sort (the Carpenters Class) is expensive, and not all obstacles can be anticipated or addressed on a short-term, individual basis.

Challenges of Tracking

The outcomes presented for the Night Class should be taken with a grain of salt. As of this writing, a third round of phone calls is being made to the 129 phone numbers on the Night Class list where the participant was known but not available. Ultimately, time and budget will determine when these attempts cease. Therefore the result of 32% of graduates who applied to apprenticeship programs, or 20 individuals, is based on only 94 interviews. When and if the remaining 129 contacts are made, will this percentage go up? Short-term data collection (yearly) by the BBP had also indicated that about two thirds of Night Class graduates applied to apprenticeship programs. Since the application process can be a multi-year effort, those who applied one year might not show up as accepted until the next year. However, assuming the same rate of acceptance (one third of two thirds), based on 100 graduates per year for six years (600), about 120 graduates of BBP should have been expected to have been accepted as apprentices. In fact, the BBP's anecdotal records (not systematic) showed 59 graduates accepted, still in apprenticeships or working as journeymen in the building trades. This difference between the short-term, informal and the long-term systematic results may be partly a measure of the difficulty of tracking members of a transient workforce in a population that changes residences and contact information frequently.

The Value of Links to Unions

The high rate of successful outcomes with the Carpenters Program can be attributed in part to the close cooperation and support of the UBC, into which all of the graduates who applied (all of them applied) were accepted. Another Chicago pre-apprenticeship program that works closely with the electricians has had a similar rate of acceptance, if not quite 100% (M. King, personal communication, July 2008). By working closely, or being actually sponsored by, a union with an apprenticeship program, the pre-apprenticeship program not only focuses on the same curriculum and channels expectations but also becomes linked to a chain of interlocking commitments that culminate in the contracts for employment that are negotiated at the level of master contracts. A participant, once accepted into the initial training phase, becomes connected, if only distantly, to this contract. This link does not exist in non-union construction. Generalizing from these programs to training programs that prepare people for work in fields other than construction, however, is risky. In construction, at least in states with high rates of unionization, the apprenticeship programs essentially control access to the work. This is not the case in other fields of work. For example, nursing and teaching, both heavily unionized, are not fields where the unions dominate preparation for work. In other fields there are programs where training is linked to the union that represents workers in that field (culinary workers, machinists, and healthcare workers, for example) but these are illustrations of what is possible, not the norm.

Public Funding and Union Training Programs: Thinking Ahead

Finally, this raises the overall question of strategic planning of job training programs. Job training programs may be designed to address a shortage of skilled labor or designed to find workers who can be prepared for good middle-class jobs who might otherwise face impossible obstacles to getting those jobs. Federal job training funds under the 1998 Workforce Investment Act (WIA), which supplanted the Jobs Training Partnership Act (JTPA) and served as an employment response to welfare reform, were intended to fill a labor shortage, not strengthen unions. This was made clear in the language of the act and in the design of the committees, state and local, that would disburse WIA funds, on which representation of the labor movement was usually kept the minimum of two. The opposite was the case for the Illinois funding for the Carpenters Class and the other partner classes, which was not WIA funding, and which was explicitly intended to be spent in cooperation with construction trades unions and to recruit and prepare hard-to-employ participants for union work. The contrast between a selection process that relies on sorting and elimination, and a selection process that relies on self-selection, as has been described here, should be kept in mind when designing jobs programs that are intended to avoid repeating past histories of exclusion.

REFERENCES

Allen, S. G. (1997). Developments in Collective Bargaining in Construction in the 1980s and 1990s. In P. B. Voos, (Ed.), *Contemporary collective bargaining in the private sector* (pp. 411–445). Madison, WI: Industrial Relations Research Association.

Allen, T. W. (1994). *The invention of the White race: The origins of racial oppression in White America.* London, UK: Verso.

Belman, D., & Smith, A. (in press). Reconstructing construction unionism: Beyond top-down and bottom-up. In G. Gall (Ed.), *Union organizing—Current practice, future prospects*. New York: Palgrave, Basingstoke.

Construction Industry Service Corporation. (2006). *Build your future with a career in construction: A guide to apprenticeship programs in Northeastern Illinois*. Oak Brook, IL: Author.

DuBois, W. E .B. (1998). *Black reconstruction in America: 1860–1880*. New York, NY: Simon & Schuster. (Original work published 1935)

Fletcher, B., & Gapasin, F. (2008). *Solidarity divided: The crisis in organized labor and a new path toward social justice*. Berkeley: University of California Press.

Foner, P. S. (1974). *Organized labor and the Black worker*. New York: Praeger.

Frymer, P. (2003). Acting when elected officials won't: Federal courts and civil rights enforcement in U.S. labor unions, 1935–85. *American Political Science Review, 97*(3), 1–17.

Goldfield, M. (1997). *The color of politics: Race and the mainstream of American politics*. New York: New Press.

Giloth, R. P. (Ed.). (2003). *Workforce intermediaries for the twenty-first century*. Philadelphia, PA: Temple University Press.

Paap, K. (2008). How good men of the union justify inequality: Dilemmas of race and labor in the building trades. *Labor Studies Journal, 33*(4), 371–392.

Worthen, H., & Haynes, A. (2003). Getting in: The experience of minority graduates of the Building Bridges Project pre-apprenticeship class. *Labor Studies Journal, 28*(1), 31–52.

One Small Revolution: Unionization, Community Practice, and Workload in Child Welfare

TARA LA ROSE

School of Social Work, Ryerson University, Toronto, Ontario, Canada

This article presents the finding from a community based research project reflecting workers' retrospective analysis of the enduring effects of a strike over issues of workload. The 273 bargaining unit members of CUPE Local 2190 took a stand against fundamental changes to their work processes resulting in standardization of practice and the introduction of neo-conservative/neo-liberal values to child welfare services in the province of Ontario, Canada. Workers utilized the rights afforded them through their collective agreement, collaboration with the labor movement as well as the skills and techniques of community practice to engage in resistance and challenge workload from inside and outside the system.

INTRODUCTION

Social workers concerned with community practice rarely look to child welfare intervention as a place to explore excellence in this approach. The profession's tradition of dichotomizing clinical and community based interventions has resulted in assumptions that child welfare work is limited to case management

The author wishes to thank: Maureen La Rose, Yvonne LaRose, Melissa Redmond, Henry Parada, George Bielmeire, Ben Carniol, Donna Baines, Angela Miles, and CUPE Local 2190, with a special and gracious thanks to Nancy Jackson for her support and assistance with the editing process.

activities, individual intervention and clinical work. This article seeks to present a different view of child welfare workers and their practice by presenting research findings that demonstrate the significance of community practice and resistance in the context of child welfare work.

Throughout the 1990s the culture of child welfare in Ontario shifted dramatically with the tide of political change. At the start of the decade, government-funded child welfare services in Ontario included community development, prevention services, investigation and protection functions, as well as supportive treatment services. By 2000, the system was stripped of most prevention services; in place of prevention, the new system's remedial focus highlighted client assessments using tight eligibility criteria within standardized service durations, investigation of abuse complaints and enforcement of minimum parenting standards.

The changes to the Ontario child welfare system brought significant increases in workload and a reorientation of the objectives and processes of work. Social workers experienced a total work redesign with greater focus on administrative work and what Mullaly (2007), has described as documentation of "defensible decisions" in casework. Standardization reduced workers' professional autonomy and led to an assembly line style of case work. These types of work system changes have been described in the social work literature as hallmarks of neo-liberalism as embodied by the social service sector (Baines, 2007; Caragata, 1997; Carniol, 2005; Mullaly, 2007).

Many social workers practicing in the sector at this time were deeply disturbed by these changes, and I was among them. At that time, I was working as a Family Service Worker in the second largest child welfare agency in Toronto, the capital city of Ontario with a population of about 3 million people. Like many social workers in Ontario, we were unionized with the Canadian Union of Public Employees and our workplace was represented by Local 2190. Our affiliation with the labor movement proved to be an important resource in not only resisting the reforms but also in working toward our own goals for systemic change. Rather than resign ourselves to the new political reality and assume nothing could be done to resist, many of us opted to engage in what Smith (2007) has described as "underground practice," resisting systemic restrictions from invisible locations within the sector. We also challenged from outside of the system by seeking alliance with organizations and associations positioned for critique (Baines, 2007; Caragata, 1997; Carniol, 2005; Mullaly, 2007*)*.

After months of unsuccessful bargaining, members of CUPE Local 2190 went on strike in the spring of 2000, and stayed out for six weeks. In the end, this collective action paid off, winning precedent setting new clauses in the union contract that increased protection on many issues of workload and working conditions, successfully challenging the implementation of a whole package of neo-liberal social policy and legislative changes introduced by the Conservative government of the Province of Ontario. These actions demonstrated that child welfare workers can be both politically oriented and active, and that community practice techniques are important tools for resistance.

This article highlights the complex process that led to the strike, as well as the depth of response by the participants involved. This material may be useful to other labor organizers and to community organizers seeking to organize social workers. It may also be useful for agency managers and government officials as a guidepost for strike avoidance. Ideally, it might even help to challenge the clinical/community divide in social work. The actions of these workers and the community based research project which followed were both informed by a number of theoretical traditions that underpin a community practice approach to social work. The next section of the article will highlight several key concepts from relevant literature, and the following section will give details of the research process.

THEORY: COMMUNITY AND SOCIAL ACTION

Community Practice Social Work

The concept of community practice in social work stems from transformative traditions of social change engagement. It draws on skills, knowledge, and activities associated with the broad traditions of community development (Absolon & Herbert, 1997; Heron, 2008; Wharf & Claque,1997), and community organizing (Alinsky, 1989a, 1989b) that go well beyond the scope of this article. It also draws from related concepts like social movements and social action, discussed briefly below. All of these perspectives are rooted in progressive theoretical positions including structural social work theory, anti-oppressive perspectives, theories of feminism and Black feminist thought, as well as queer theory (Barnoff & Moffatt, 2007; Carniol, 2005; Mullaly, 2007).

In social work, the ways and means of community practice are tied to political understandings of social roles, responsibilities and the benefits of "community." George (2006), Armitage (2003), and Hardina (2002) suggest that the most ethical and effective community processes begin as collaborative undertakings, moving to more conflict based activities only after other options are exhausted. All of these concerns, commitments, and tensions are visible in the case study discussed in this article.

A community practice approach to social work often has commonalities with various social movements that seek to address specific issues. This perspective holds that by changing individuals' values and beliefs, community values, priorities and beliefs are also changed (Wharf & Claque, 1997). Social movements produce oppositional culture and call into question what may have been long held social norms (Carroll & Ratner, 2001). Social movements may take up issues of marginalized identities (e.g., gay liberation) or acts of exploitation (e.g. environmental degradation). Solidarity, or "standing in alliance with" those affected by an issue, is the crux of the social movement philosophy. Work for the elimination of negative social phenomena is seen to benefit all because, as Freire (2007) has suggested, the liberation of all people is tied together.

A social action perspective shares many of these same goals and is often focused on social policy advocacy and changing the minds of the people who make those policies in the hope of eliminating exploitation (Weil, 1996). Social action embraces Freire's (2007) work for critical consciousness building which sees developing skills and "knowledge" with oppressed people as the basis of the empowerment process. Within the social action education framework concepts of "expert" knowledge are deconstructed. Knowledge and skills develop through engagement in the practices we seek to learn and so from this perspective, the best way to learn to do social action is to do social action (Newman, 1995). Social action education demands that those who have learned lessons at the grass roots level engage in knowledge transfer (Newman, 1995). Community-based research projects are by their very nature a form of knowledge transfer.

Unions and Social Action

Social work and the labor movement share many similar values around social action, making for a natural alliance. In defining social work, the International Federation of Social Workers (IFSW) asserts that "[t]he social work profession supports social change" and that ". . . social justice serves as the motivation and justification for social work action" (International Federation of Social Workers, 2000, Definition section, para. 1). Authors like Mullaly (2007) and Carniol (2005) define social work as meeting the immediate needs of people while at the same time working for systemic change aimed at eradicating exploitation and oppression.

Unionization in the social service sector provides social workers with resources to improve their working conditions as well as providing opportunities for engagement in social justice activities (Barth, 2003; Carniol, 2005; Mullaly, 2007; Scanlon, 1999). Mullaly (2007, p. 338) argues that unions provide concrete opportunities for social change engagement including: "empowerment in the work place . . . better understanding of class issues, . . . development of economic and social alternatives and . . . participat[ion] in coalitions with other workers, consumer groups and progressive social movements.

Burawoy (2008, p. 373) suggests "labor movement" unionism has grown out of greater focus on organizing unorganized workers by unions in North America. Hassan (2000, pp. 1, 6) reflects that unions nationally and internationally have moved away from exclusionary representation of "workers in niche sectors" to more inclusionary unionism, where "organizing all who can be organized" is the central focus of the union. Amassing large bodies of unionized employees is beneficial because it increases the power of the working class, therefore increasing the potential for social change to occur (Burawoy, 2008; Hassan, 2000; Weil, 1996). Rosenberg and Rosenberg (2006) have suggested:

> . . . for social workers, traditional work-place concerns such as wages, benefits, job security, and working conditions, which typically dominate the collective bargaining agenda, may be less important than an ideological affinity between the goals of social work and organized labor. (p. 299)

The shared values of inclusionary unions and social work have been understood throughout social work's history. In the era of the U.S. Settlement House Movement, close ties developed between labor and social work. Jane Addams, one of the foremothers of the movement, worked directly with workers to form unions and strengthen union solidarity (Benjamin, 2007; Montegomery, 1992). Addams saw the potential of the collective power of the labor movement to support social work's ongoing work for social and economic justice.

Unionization in both Canada and the United States is said to be in decline. The rate of unionization reported by the U.S. Bureau of Labor Statistics sat at 12.4% in 2008. The 1983 rate of unionization was recorded as 20.1%, demonstrating a significant decline in unionization in the last 24 years (U.S. Bureau of Labor Statistics, 2009). Unionization among social workers is significantly higher than the general trend. Barth's (2003, p. 6) analysis of the U.S. Current Population Survey (CPS), identifies that "twenty-four percent of social workers report membership in a union." The U.S. public sector has the greatest level of unionized social workers with, ". . . almost 9 out of 10 social workers who belong to unions . . . [employed] in the public sector" (Barth 2003, p. 6). In Canada, the trend is similar, with social workers demonstrating greater unionization than the general population. Statistical data suggests that:

> Between 2002 and 2006, union density in the community services sector grew from 35.6% to 38.7%, compared to a density of only 29% for the total workforce. (D. Baines, personal communication, July 16, 2007)

Preliminary data from the first half of 2007 shows "unionization in community service occupations far outpaced that in others" (D. Baines, personal communication, July 16, 2007).

Scanlon (1999) has called for social work and the labor movement to develop direct partnerships, stating, "Social work, acting boldly in an alliance with labor, might restore itself by becoming the discipline that helps to bring families, communities, and labor together in a new progressive era" (p. 3). The social work profession in both Canada and the United States gleans overall benefit from unionization, because unionized workers in both countries are more active in work-life and professional issues than non-unionized social workers (Antle et al., 2006; Rosenberg & Rosenberg, 2006). Weil (1996) has argued that together social work and labor can produce greater social change than either movement alone. Scanlon (1999) sees the labor movement as an untapped resource system with financial reserves and people power that could be mobilized for socially just objectives and outcomes. To bring this potential to light, Hick (2007), Carniol (2005) and Barth (2003) have demonstrated that union pressure has led to the implementation of social service programs in Canada and in the United States.

As demonstrated in this article, unionization provided a forum for social workers to work for tangible change. By utilizing the rights guaranteed under their collective agreement workers were able to take the politics of child welfare to the street. When attempts to work with management failed, the collective agreement gave workers the power to hold the employer accountable for its lack of attention to workers' issues. In the end, the strike process led to precedent-setting contract language that established caseload caps while allowing for binding arbitration in workload disputes. From a practical position, for the first time a limit had been placed on the amount of work employees within the Ontario child welfare sector could be expected to complete at any one time.

THE RESEARCH: BACKGROUND AND METHODOLOGY

Six years after the Ontario strike, social workers were preparing for more changes as part of a package of measures called the Child Welfare Transformation. Some of us who had been involved in the "strike of 2000" decided to revisit our experiences in that struggle, to see how they could help us in the present. We did this through a community-based research project, which is the subject matter of this article. Throughout the period of the strike, I served as a member of the negotiation team and union executive. As a member of the executive and bargaining team, I was heavily involved in the administration of the strike and negotiation process, but much of my time was spent in negotiation sessions away from the day-to-day reality of picketing and working for change through the "on the ground" strike management process. I had no exposure to the return-to-work process because at the very end of the strike, just one day before the return to work, I began an educational leave.

When I returned to Ontario several years later and reconnected with my colleagues, I was shocked to learn that no academic, labor, or community-based literature had captured the events of the strike. Without a written account of CUPE 2190's strike activities, it was as though strike never existed. I was concerned about what this loss meant to my union, to my profession, and to my community.

After discussing the issue with the Local president, the idea of the research project came to light. The local was about to enter bargaining and with more changes to the Child Welfare system via Ontario's "Transformation" agenda, CUPE 2190 was looking for ways to stimulate worker involvement. Empowering workers through a reconnection with their previous success seemed like a logical way of meeting many needs with one activity. In the spring of 2006, I developed a research proposal that was approved by the Union Executive and the bargaining unit members.

Without easy access to an ethics review process, ethical consideration of the research was sought through allies in the academic community. A member of the faculty at the Ryerson University School of Social Work reviewed the proposal, and a second review was completed by a researcher employed by one of the local hospitals. All of their recommendations were implemented. Initially, it was hoped that the project would be more participatory in nature, but as things unfolded other workers increasingly indicated a desire to have the project completed by me, as "the researcher". Bargaining unit members saw some political advantages to me completing the research because I was no longer employed by the agency, meaning there was less possibility for reprisal by the employer.

Several workers volunteered to assist with recruitment of other bargaining unit members through E-mail and telephone outreach. The recruitment process involved telephone calls and e-mail contacts to current members of the Local, as well as notices posted on the union bulletin boards. "Eligible participants" were defined as individuals who had been union members working at the agency on the last day of the strike, and who did not currently hold a management position within the agency. This restriction addressed concerns that individuals who occupied a management position at the time of the research might be seen as authority figures in the groups. Such a power imbalance could negatively affect the study by silencing workers or causing difficulty for bargaining unit members back at work. Another concern about recruitment included the fact of fairly high turnover in child welfare work; therefore, many people involved in the strike may not have learned about the research project. There was the potential that workers who remained employed over those years had some different values and attitudes than those who left the agency. These are limitations of the recruitment process, but given the resources available they were accepted by our reviewers as reasonable compromises.

The Local president coordinated the focus groups, booking locations and scheduling participants. As the researcher, I was an unpaid volunteer and did not receive payment of any kind for the data collection, analysis, and written reports. Local 2190 provided refreshments and supplies, as well as providing parking and care-giving honorariums to participants. The union has allowed me to use the data for various academic activities including conference presentations and this article.

Our primary data collection was completed in five focus groups with a total of 24 participants in attendance. The size of focus group ranged from three people to eight people. Each group lasted approximately two hours. Three focus groups were held in the union office, a familiar location where workers regularly attend meetings and activities. One focus group was held in the home of a bargaining unit member which facilitated the child care needs of some participants, and one group was held in the private room of a local restaurant where union events are regularly held.

The participants completed consent forms that adhered to standard university style consent requirements. Participants received written and oral consent information. The consent information was read aloud at the beginning of each focus group and the process audio taped. A standardized set of questions was used in each focus group with supplemental clarification questions asked in specific focus groups. Audio cassette recordings of the focus groups were made and the tapes were transcribed verbatim with the exception of names and identifying information. Thematic coding was completed manually; no coding software was used.

The majority of research participants were seasoned child welfare workers, with the average length of service in the field being 17.4 years and the median being 16.75 years. Participants in the five focus groups represented a broad cross-section of job classifications within the organization. All but one of the different bargaining unit job categories that existed during the strike were represented among the focus group participants. Most workers no longer held the same positions they held during the strike, but moved on to other jobs within the same agency. One participant no longer worked for the agency but returned to participate in the focus group process.

The findings of this research are descriptive and exploratory, and cannot be statistically generalized to any other situation. However, readers may see evidence of "soft generalizability" in this study wherever the conditions described are similar and thus findings may have relevance to other settings. Such inferences could only be confirmed by subsequent research.

A demographic survey was completed to highlight participant identities and roles within the agency. The focus groups were supplemented by a review of other strike related materials including CUPE 2190's strike "scrapbook", photos, and strike memorabilia maintained by the local or donated by bargaining unit members, the strike song book, the strike song compact disk recording, picket signs and boards, government documents and manuals, and newspaper and journal articles accessed through Internet and library database searches. These materials were used to expand on themes and issues, to clarify information provided by participants, and to analyze themes presented in the focus groups.

THE "STRIKE OF 2000:" WORKING INSIDE AND OUTSIDE

Setting the Scene

Child welfare services in the province of Ontario are provided by not-for-profit agencies mandated and sanctioned by the Provincial Government. The agencies are managed by professional managers and governed by a volunteer board of directors but operate within the confines of the Child and Family Services Act, a piece of provincial legislation. Jurisdictional boundaries designate service areas and in many cases, jurisdictions are further subdivided by ethnic, cultural, or religious traditions. While operated at "arms length" of the government, child welfare agencies experience significant power and control by government through policies, procedures, and practice standards. The legislation also leaves space for implementation of various administrative processes that reflect the values, beliefs, and ideological leanings of any government in power (Herd, Mitchell, & Lightman, 2005).

Those of us working in the field recalled the 1990s as a period of great change in child welfare services. Focus group participants described these changes as broad and deep. Accepted clinical understandings of abuse, neglect, and trauma were expanded; greater awareness of issues of family violence and its aftermath existed within the field; and the relationship between attachment and caregiver permanence were seen as important practice issues (Caragata, 1997; Trocme, et al., 1999). Changes in the clinical philosophy of child protection work led to greater demands for services, while at the same time neo-liberal social and political values promoted deficits reduction (Carniol, 2005; Mullaly, 2007). Changes in funding policies that reduced available services were justified as governments reframed social services as "a burden rather than a collective responsibility and a moral right" (Ledwith, 2001, p. 172).

High Stress and Low Morale

Amidst this picture of massive change, research participants described a climate where high levels of stress and low worker morale were the norm; physical and emotional exhaustion resulted from increased case volume and case acuity (CUPE, 1999). Workers stated that the pace of change was so rapid they felt overwhelmed. With more work to do and an unfamiliar work system, participants reflected it was almost impossible to analyze what was happening to their work in time and place. Workers were told the changes were "service improvements" and "good for clients," yet workers were not witnessing these outcomes. One participant summarized her experiences of the change process:

> . . . we have a revolving door in child welfare . . . you just keep going around and around, and depending on when you stepped into the door,

you will get a new theory, a new coach, a new way of thinking . . . but by the time you step [out of the system], it may be completely different. You are required to think and do things in so many different ways. At that time it was crazy there were so many different [approaches]! You couldn't even learn one approach before you [were] asked to take on two or three other approaches. (La Rose, 2006, T1, line 73)

Bargaining unit members identified cuts to in-house support services as directly affecting their work and clients' experiences of service. Workers recalled that throughout the 1980s and early 1990s many child welfare agencies provided family support interventions including counseling, community work, and group work services. These support services assisted families in practical ways and bolstered the agencies' core protection functions by providing clinical and prevention services to voluntary and involuntary clients at high risk for abuse.

Social group work was offered to prevent and remediate abuse while allowing for peer support. Akin to Community Policing initiatives present in many communities today, child welfare community work challenged stereotypes on both sides of the intervention system. Community work established links between personal troubles and systemic issues. By building rapport and relationship with community leaders and specialized community services, child welfare workers had allies they could call on when necessary. In the context of Toronto as one of the most multi-cultural cities in the world, these alliances were significant in facilitating culturally appropriate services both inside and outside the agency (Kopun & Nicholas, 2007).

Significant changes occurred in Canada's economic policy during this time that led to service cuts, including child welfare support services. As Federal Government priorities changed, funding transfers to the provinces demonstrated these new priorities (Hick, 2007; Mullaly, 2007). In Ontario, the social democratic New Democratic Party (NDP), a long-time ally of both working people and labor, was forced by powerful players in the finance sector to cut spending, which translated into amalgamation of services, with larger mainstream agencies swallowing smaller community based alternative services.

Service amalgamation posed a risk for unionized workers, sometimes resulting in lost jobs. Members of CUPE Local 2190 watched their own ranks shrink as the group work, community development, and other prevention services were cancelled by the agency. Between 1991 and 1995, the Ontario child welfare workforce was reduced by more than 300 workers ("How Cuts Hit," 1999).

The loss of internal support services necessitated external referrals. But without the support of community workers, protection workers had to research and assess community supports in addition to their regular tasks and activities; the tacit knowledge of the community workers had been lost to the agency (Baines, 2004). External referrals required more monitoring and more administrative work (Caragata, 1997; Carniol, 2005; Mullaly, 2007). Workers found themselves completing hours of paperwork work instead of engaging in face to face work with clients.

In 1995, the NDP government was replaced by the Conservative Government led by Mike Harris. Harris promised sweeping change to the social service sector and extensive "welfare reform" (CBC.CA, 1995). As a part of these reforms, the Ontario Risk Assessment Model (ORAM) was introduced into the child welfare system. The foundation of ORAM was a series of standardized practice tools and service eligibility criteria. Safety and risk assessment check lists replaced workers' professional assessment skills as the final word in determining risk in families (Goodman & McFadden, 1996). Understandings of child wellbeing became finite and quantitative, and the new system claimed that standardization meant more effectiveness and more efficiency.

The introduction of the Eligibility Spectrum, a type of risk assessment tool, saw an alpha-numeric coding system used to describe types of child abuse. Mullaly (2007) suggests that risk assessment tools serve a variety of functions oriented towards neo-conservative industrialization in social work. Risk assessments tools are seen to downplay structural issues affecting clients, while highlighting individuation of problems by categorizing issues in terms of "pathological or dysfunctional characteristics" (Mullaly, 2007, p. 23). The author further asserts that standardized tools are not about client care, but rather are focused on creating a paper trail of the case-based decision making process, establishing adherence to rules and regulations. Workers were told that the spectrum would assist in the process of protecting children, yet at the time the spectrum was introduced, there was little research data to support the benefit of the Spectrum (Goodman & MacFadden, 1996).

Workers did not experience these changes as positive outcomes and were left feeling devalued, deskilled and disrespected. One worker summed up her experience:

> . . . we moved from being seen as professional with the ability to assess and determine things and to work collaboratively with managers about decision making to being forced into a particular way of functioning that was restrictive. We were told, before we even saw the family what was expected of us. So, [it] wasn't about me having skill . . . or you having skill, it was about "did you tick off all the things on the safety [assessment tool]?". "Did you tick of all the things on the risk assessment?" (La Rose, 2006, T2, line 1413)

Participants in the focus groups described what they understood as a "culture of disrespect" present in the sector at the time. Many workers reflected that the Harris government called into question the value and validity of social service interventions and vilified the workers providing the services. One worker described the wide spread nature of the culture of disrespect:

> . . . we felt that [disrespect] from some of those involved . . . Ministry
> policies, social climate, hostility from clients and from police . . . Upper
> management did not fully respect the work we did. We were treated as
> you know, just disposable. You leave and someone else [comes] . . . the
> worker would just become the cog. Your relationship, your skills, your
> ability, were just secondary to being able to deal with the type of system
> they were implementing. (La Rose, 2006, T2, line 77)

Standardization under ORAM included a new funding formula commonly
described as a "zero-based" funding model. The funding model established
an audit culture by embedding funding metrics in mandatory documentation
processes and time/activity/payment ratios created an "invisible" work
quota system. Workers had to produce certain case outcomes in certain
time frames in order for the agency to receive adequate funding to justify
the employments costs of each social worker (Lindgreen, 1998; Ministry of
Community and Social Services, 1999). Paperwork took on a new importance within the ORAM system because completion of paperwork activated
the government payment systems (Lindgreen, 1998; Ministry of Community
and Social Services, 1999).

At this time, the government also undertook a series of inquests known
as the Child Mortality Task Force (Blackwell, 1997). This investigation into
the deaths of children who died while in the care of Children's Aid Societies
in Ontario led to a series of recommendations for changes to the system.
Among the final recommendations was a call for public education about
personal and professional "duty to report" suspected child abuse. As awareness spread, referral volume increased and agencies struggled to keep up
with service demands (Szklarski, 1997).

The inflexibility of the zero-based funding model further complicated
this issue: agencies could not hire workers in immediate response to the
increased demand but rather had to wait until the audit trail provided
"evidence" of increase ("How Cuts Hit," 1999). Direct service workers had
to take on extra work to compensate for the lack of flexibility in the system.
Increased work led to increased overtime. Overtime within the system
became normalized and expected. One worker described the experience of
her work team:

> . . . you would walk in the office at 7AM and everyone was in the office
> [and] at 7PM or 8PM . . . You were putting in a lot of time, you were
> accumulating a lot of hours. You were just exhausted, you would crawl
> home and sleep and just get up the next morning and go to work, you
> would just manage to try and manage. (La Rose, 2006, T5, line 1449)

In the early summer of 1997, the death of an infant who came to be
known in the press as "Baby Jordan" became a turning point for the members of CUPE 2190. Placed in his mother's care under the supervision of

child welfare authorities, the infant died just weeks after his premature birth, in spite of the involvement of numerous social and health care services (Grange, 1997; Hess, 1997). In August, 1997, criminal charges were laid against the child's mother and the investigating social worker (Grange, 1997; Hess, 1997). The charges against the social worker had a ripple effect throughout the social work community.

The members of CUPE Local 2190 were directly affected by the situation as the worker charged in the case was a member of the bargaining unit. The bargaining unit members were outraged and saw the worker as receiving punishment for doing her job in system that was overwhelmed. One worker reflected on this moment: "It woke us up. We deal with a high risk population. Children die in this high risk population . . . we cannot guarantee this won't happen."

In Canada, criminal charges against social workers in child welfare practice are extremely rare, but workers were forced to now consider their own liability and to acknowledge a change in the landscape of practice (Kanani, Regher, & Bernstein, 2002). One worker recalled her feelings about the potential of liability:

> . . . people thought "Oh, I am overworked and now I can be charged. Not just disciplined but changed criminally." People felt really scared and people knew the only way to protect themselves was to reduce their workload. (La Rose, 2006, T3, line 18)

Solidarity became an important response for the members of CUPE 2190. Discussion of the criminal charges at the union level gave workers a place to reflect and develop their own understanding of the situation. With no previous precedent of criminal liability, Local 2190's collective agreement lacked procedures and resources to assist workers in these circumstances. Collectively, members wanted to ensure that the worker received support and tangible resources as well as demonstrating personal, emotional, and profession support to the union sister.

Many in the union called for a "wildcat" (illegal) strike as a protest against the criminalization of practice, but this did not occur. Instead, the union executive members negotiated with the employer to develop a shared response. The executive wished to ensure the worker's needs would be met and guarantees of certain behaviors by the bargaining unit members was one way of mobilizing these supports, a tool only available in a unionized workplace. In the end, the chief negotiator in this process guaranteed the bargaining unit would remain on the job and silent in the immediate future in exchange for agency support of the charged worker.

During the preliminary inquiry into Baby Jordan's death, workers continued to support their employer and their coworker. In the end, the charges against the mother and the worker were both overturned. Baby Jordan's death was declared the resulted of systemic problems rather than individual negligence (Black, 1999; Kanani et al., 2002).

With a follow-up inquest scheduled, workers could not just put the issue behind them. In the post-trial pre-inquest period there was little improvement in working conditions and the collective agreement expired during this same time period. The solidarity that had allowed for the support of one worker became a tool for workers to use in collective bargaining and to challenge the issues that affected us collectively.

Strike Aversion: Working from the Inside Out

Even before the contract expired in 2000, pressure for change had been building for some time. Management feared that the criminal charges meant the agency was under scrutiny by the government and by the public. Worker cooperation was treated as an entitlement and the threat of criminal charges was at some points used to silence and manipulate workers. The workers were angered but had little recourse to address the issue. With the issue of criminality settled, workers were able to turn their attention to their workplace challenges. At the direction of the union, workers regularly raised the issue of over work and informed management of their dissatisfaction and desire for change. In meetings and supervision sessions workers questioned case assignments and asked about increasing the workforce. Workers monitored vacancies and leave applications, asking when these positions would be filled and reporting the information back to the union executive.

Managers frequently closed down these conversations claiming the governing Ministry of Community and Social Services was not open to any feedback on ORAM. Workers interpreted the managers' refusal to resist or advocate as abandonment of the agency's value system and of their professional value systems. Workers felt these reactions were an embodiment of the values embedded in the "new" child welfare system. One worker recalled: "People didn't feel that we were being taken serious[ly] . . . and there is nothing more frustrating than saying to a supervisor 'I just can't do it' and being told '. . . oh well, you have to'" (La Rose, 2006, T1, line 12).

While some branch level managers acknowledged connection between systemic change and workload issues, many others did not. Some managers deflected criticism by stating it was "not a worker's role" to interpret what reasonable workload should be. Other managers appeared too stressed to integrate and process workers' concerns or to consider alternative work arrangements. Still other managers interpreted negative workload outcomes as individual problems assessing these as "time management" or "training" issues. Managers who supported workers did so "off the record" stating that while they agreed with the workers, there was nothing they could do to stop the flow of work.

The focus group participants demonstrated empathy for the supervisors by suggesting they too were over worked and undervalued by the employer. Some participants felt managers were culpable for contributing to the "culture of denial" by refusing to speak out against excessive work demands even though everyone knew the workload was impossible. One worker assessed the situation:

> We [were] facing two conflicting needs . . . The agency [was] making a choice for the demands of the Ministry and what they [were] asking for . . . to come before what the workers [were] saying [was] the absolute need. That [was] at the expense of the kids. (La Rose, 2006, T5, line 133)

Union meetings and pre-negotiation consultations afforded workers the opportunity to share their experiences of workload and work processes and to discover that heavy caseloads and high case acuity were experiences shared across the agency. For many who thought these issues were limited to their work team this was both welcoming and frightening news. In light of this new realization, union meetings became strategy sessions where collective plans for resistance were made and the individualization of systemic issues was challenged. As the workers gained greater critical consciousness of their shared experiences they became more confident in expressing their concerns with managers. One worker remembered the development of her own critical awareness of the issues:

> Do you remember . . . a branch meeting [where a] very senior worker who had been with the agency for probably 20 years, who had been through the 'ebb and flow', getting up in a meeting and screaming . . . "I can't take this stress, you are not listening to me, you are not hearing me . . ." and left the room crying. I remember looking around at all of my co-workers and thinking, because we had been told . . . "Young people, you don't under-stand, you're inexperienced workers, you're not efficient, you need to team with older more experienced workers so that you can understand how to do this properly. . . ." I remember thinking "Okay, if she can't do it then no wonder I feel like this. . . ." (La Rose, 2006, T2, line 719)

In a previous round of bargaining members won the right to establish a Labor Management Workload Committee. The committee was mandated to develop collaborative solutions to workload issues. Optimistically, the bargaining unit members developed suggestions and brought them to the committee but management regularly rejected the suggestions. Rejection of the workers' efforts left the many bargaining unit members feeling it was impossible to work collaboratively with management on the issue of workload.

Preparation for collective bargaining began with a bargaining survey that illustrated quantitatively that workers' priority was reduced workload. A dynamic negotiation team was elected by the members and mandated to seek nothing less than the inclusion of workload language that placed clear limits on caseloads in the collective agreement.

As negotiations unfolded, the employer remained resistant to negotiating workload issues directly. Workers pushed their agenda by engaging in a series of "work to rule campaigns". Within these campaigns, workers worked to the letter of their contract, executing many of the rights and privileges not normally exercised by workers. In a concrete and tangible way this demonstrated that worker flexibility and selflessness was an important and routine aspect of making the system work. But flexibility was also a resource the workers could ethically withdraw. The campaigns resulted in a slowing down of work simply because the workers began to take breaks and refuse overtime. Another campaign saw workers wear black t-shirts with the slogan, "It's About Fairness and Respect" in hot pink lettering. Yet another saw workers utilize their "union leave clause", a clause that allowed workers to complete union work during work hours. Through union leave, workers held information pickets at various public locations and outside of the hotel where negotiations were underway. Finally, the workers talked about negations and plans for a strike in their offices and informed managers directly that strike plans were being put in place.

In spite of ongoing negotiations and work to rule activities, the employer and the members of Local 2190 were unable to develop a negotiated settlement before their legal strike deadline. As contract negotiations broke down, the employer declared that workers had their "final offer" and it did not include workload language. Unwilling to continue to work in conditions of extreme stress and constant overtime, the workers of Local 2190 voted overwhelmingly in favor of a strike. As workers hit the pavement the struggle moved from a collaborative strategy to a conflict based approach.

Strike Strategy: "Working from the Outside In"

Drawing on Robert Mullaly's (2007, p. 331) theory of structural social work, workers described their strike strategy as "working from the outside in". Mullaly suggests that working from the outside in occurs when social workers seek social change engagement through larger social movements as a means of avoiding the "restrictions placed on formal social work practice" (p. 331). During negotiations and the work to rule campaigns, workers had to be mindful that the employer held greater power than the workers. Once outside the agency, bargaining unit members reflected that they gained a greater sense of empowerment.

On the picket lines, workers began to draw strongly on their community practice skills. The social action education perspective of "learning by doing" was a regular part of the strike process (Newman, 1995). Some of the more veteran workers had previous strike experience, but most workers were inexperienced. The Canadian Union of Public Employees provided guidance and advice to the striking workers, as well as linking more experienced trade unionists with the Local Executive. While these resources were helpful, for the most part, workers were blazing their own trail and loving it!

From a practical standpoint, meeting the needs of the picketers was extremely important. Distributing information, water, sunscreen and food to picket lines across the city became part of day to day strike management. Strike outreach activities included liaising with local businesses and residents to ensure peaceful interactions between the local community and the striking workers. Communication teams worked with national union representatives to deal with media and advertising issues, as well as mobilizing letter writing campaigns and solidarity work with other union locals.

Leadership opportunities abounded during the strike. Picket captains were trained and assigned branch locations where they monitored and coordinated picketing processes. Picket captains were asked to respond to needs and issues as they presented themselves. They administered the lines, dealt with crises, and promoted morale boosting activities. Workers were encouraged to express themselves and to find creative ways of reducing boredom on their lines.

Each of the five picket lines developed their own personality and picketing style. At one picketing location "irreverence" became the style of engagement. The members developed a series of theme days which included, "bring your pet to the line day," "pajama day," and a "make-over day" that saw a number of estheticians, recruited by bargaining unit members, provide workers with manicures, pedicures, and hair styling while on picket duty. At one point, a picket captain voluntarily shaved her head in an effort to encourage workers' continued commitment to picketing.

Management described this line as a "circus" and a "disgrace," but the community embraced and supported the workers. Local restaurants regularly sent lunch. Groups of other unionized workers located in the same building regularly visited the site and conducted "solidarity picketing" joining the line with their own flags and banners. Drivers honked when they passed by. Neighbors in the area visited to see what the striking social workers might do next.

At another picketing location, music proved to be the avenue for self expression and strike song writing became a daily activity. Using popular tunes, children's songs and traditional industrial ballads workers rewrote song lyrics reflecting their lived experience of child welfare work and the strike process. Over the six and half weeks of the strike, a strike song book was developed and distributed to workers on all picket lines. A Local 2190 choir was established and charged with the task of teaching songs and leading singing at mass rallies. With so much great music present on the picket lines, CUPE Ontario recorded a CD album of strike songs with the help of Canadian folk singer Faith Nolan. The album was sold nationwide as a union fundraiser. One worker recalled:

I think the fact that we did become united, cohesive, [and] creative and . . .
I thought "oh my god, there are the people who do social work, but
look at their other talents . . ." I think [management] were totally blown
away by that. (La Rose, 2006, T1, line 184)

The strike organizing committee coordinated weekly rallies at the central
branch of the agency. Labor and political leaders from the NDP regularly
attended the rallies as did a number of other union locals. Members of the
Foster Parent's Society of Ontario gave a speech in support of the workers.
One worker remembered:

Picketing was a positive thing. We really got to know each other, especially
when we went to [central branch] all together. We would get a chance to
stand next to people and say ". . . where are you from . . ." Really get a
sense of very, very important information . . . their experiences. I think
there was more of a shared experience which you don't normally get. People are normally isolated, in their own bubble. (La Rose, 2006, T1, line 496)

The solidarity of the union movement showed itself in unexpected
ways. Workers on the picket lines built alliances with external workers, asking
them to support the strike by refusing to cross the line. One worker
reflected the success of these strategies:

. . . we were so peaceful, so good and yet we got our point across.
I remember the courier driving out in front of [the branch] and us stopping
him and saying, ". . . we would really appreciate it if you wouldn't deliver
that package . . ." And he said, "well what are you going to do . . ." and I
said, "Well, we are a bunch of women and we are social workers. We are
not about to attack you or anything. We would just really appreciate it if
you wouldn't bring the package in" and he said "Okay . . ." and drove off.
That was a different way of doing business. (La Rose, 2006, T1, line 402)

Picketing was a magical process that greatly reduced workers sense of
alienation. On the line, new relationships formed, old relationships deepened
and a healing occurred. One worker recalled:

There was so much fraternizing during the strike . . . To some extent,
my boss might now say, "Too much enmeshment!" But I got to know
people, people who had been labeled and branded as uncooperative, as
a pain in the butt. You got to see another side of the person. That was
kind of fun and refreshing. . . . (La Rose, 2006, T5, line 577)

On some of the lines, managers were important allies and resource
providers. At one location the workers reflected that the management
team made great efforts to support the picketing process. The support of

the managers reduced the potential for conflict on the line. One worker commented:

> One supervisor ran a tab for us at the local [coffee shop]. [Another supervisor] told us "if it rains don't stand and get wet. You make sure you go and stand under that over-hang" right up by the building. They were always bringing us treats . . . bringing us food. Telling us they missed us. Waiting while we sang. . . . (La Rose, 2006, T1, line 303)

Though there were many picket line victories, it wasn't all bread and roses on the sidewalk, and a number of challenging issues developed. In some cases, work accommodations needed to be put in place for workers with special needs, and members sometimes had to wait while processes were put in place. Alternative work arrangements, such as administrative duties and driving duties, were reassigned to individuals with mobility challenges or other health, wellness, and safety needs.

Some workers of color felt their voices were overshadowed by White workers and that the needs, issues, and experiences of people of color were not reflected in the strike process. The majority of people in positions of power in the union were White women, and the majority of picket captains were also White women. Some workers questioned this structural reality. On one line, disagreements flared and issues of homophobia and racism intersected. Rumors circulated and tensions bubbled, but never quite boiled over on these issues. The biggest challenge for the union executives was that the issues were never brought directly to them and questioning brought silence, a clear symptom of mistrust.

As Carniol (2005) has suggested, racism is an issue that has haunted the labor movement. The issue of racism was at best unresolved and at worst avoided during the strike. In looking back it seems clear that more resources and time should have been committed to equity issues. Greater anti-oppression training was needed and should have been accessed by the local. Anti-racism and anti-oppression training continues to be an ongoing area of focus for the Canadian Union of Public Employees and more training resources have been developed and made available since the time of this strike.

SETTLEMENT AND LEGACY: CONCLUSIONS AND IMPLICATIONS

After six and a half weeks of running the agency without direct-service staff, under widespread pressure from the public as well as the union, the employer conceded to the workers demands. Caseload caps and workload language became a part of the collective agreement. Where workload disputes could not be settled through internal grievance procedures, the Ministry of Labor would make a ruling on the issue through binding arbitration. While one other child welfare agency had succeeded in having their employer acknowledge workload in the contract language, never before had a quantitative limit been set in a child welfare sector contract (CUPE.ca, 2000). Negotiation of workload became a standard practice in future contract talks across the province. One worker reflected on the language victory: "There is workload language spread right across the province and that started out with us . . . Every time someone goes to negotiations they take the language, the most recent language and they push it [further]" (La Rose, 2006, T4, line 827).

The focus group participants recalled that the return to work processes went smoothly. At several work locations managers and the non-unionized administrative workers demonstrated their support by celebrating the workers' return by hailing the language victory as an important win for the entire field of child welfare. Some workers suggested that managers were more aligned with workers at the conclusion of the strike. The focus group participants assessed the managers' exposure to direct service work as a process that demonstrated concretely the challenges and complexities that the front line workers faced on a day to day basis. This experiential knowledge softened some of the managers' attitude towards the employees they supervised.

Many workers commented that taking part in the strike gave them a greater sense of personal empowerment. The focus group participants stated they gained greater confidence in their own abilities, regained self esteem and renewed their sense of personal efficacy as a result of the strike. This reclaimed confidence helped workers evaluate how deeply they had been affected by overwork and stress. Even six years after the strike, the critical consciousness developed during the strike process appears to have protective qualities for these workers. The participants provided numerous stories where workers refused to internalize negative feelings and beliefs about their capabilities. One participant commented:

> Truthfully, for me I thought the strike was important in that I thought the way we were treated, the way the clients were treated, the way the system [worked] was so incredibly unjust . . . What I couldn't understand was why all the social workers let it happen when we were supposed to be the people who are empowered and empower others . . . We can't empower anybody if we let them walk all over us. . . . (La Rose, 2006, T2, line 1382)

Empowerment for many workers expressed itself as a greater sense of confidence to engage in self-advocacy. Workers reported that they were more likely to question decisions made by management and directives given in supervision, and a greater willingness to exercise the rights won in collective bargaining. The workers felt that exercising these rights did not undermine their relationship with the employer. One worker stated:

I feel more empowered than I did before the strike. When things happen now, within the workplace, when I feel that our rights as employees are being infringed upon by management, I think ". . . Hey, let me just check my collective agreement." "Are you sure?" I say to my supervisor, "Are you sure that's allowed? Because, these things are in the collective agreement . . ." I ask, "Have you checked with HR?" You feel a little stronger. (La Rose, 2006, T1, line 418)

Six years after the strike, the collective empowerment of the workers remained strong. The participants stated they felt their concerns were taken more seriously by the employer after the strike and that this continued to the present. Workers felt the employer was mindful of the workers' capacity to build solidarity around specific issues and to express this solidarity through legal job action. Through the strike process the workers achieved their goals in the moment and left a legacy that they continued to benefit from after the strike. One worker summed up her appreciation for these outcomes:

We gained respect. We empowered ourselves too. We realized . . . that sometimes radical does work, it does get you what you want and it doesn't have to be a bad thing . . . We empowered ourselves from a professional stand. We had a revolution. (La Rose, 2006, T5, line 1374)

Overall, the workers' resistance and strike process explored here represents a concrete example of the use of community practice in the pursuit of social justice and social change. The direct service workers who participated in the strike action demonstrated how workers can engage in processes that raise critical consciousness and community awareness. Use of the labor movement to challenge the negative effects of systemic change also highlights the legal and ethical means available to professional social workers to engage in protest on their own behalf and on behalf of service users.

The contract language won by the striking workers was precedent-setting within the Ontario child welfare sector, and allowed workers across the sector to seek greater control over their work-life. For the field of social work, the example set by these workers demonstrates that by engaging in social action and using resistance to produce changes in the system, we reaffirm that we learn about social change best through active participation.

REFERENCES

Absolon, K., & Herbert, E. (1997). Community action as a practice of freedom: A First Nations perspective. In B. Wharf and M. Claque (Eds.), *Community organizing: Canadian experiences* (pp. 205–227). Don Mills, ON, Canada: Oxford University Press.

Alinsky, S. (1989a). *Rules for radicals*. New York: Random House.

Alinsky, S. (1989b). *Reveille for radicals*. New York: Random House.

Antle, B. J., MacKenzie D. J., Baines, D., Angell, B., Dawson Haber, M., Paulekat, P., et al. (2006). *OASW quality of work life survey: Final report*. Toronto, ON, Canada: Ontario Association of Social Workers.

Armitage, A. (2003). *Social welfare in Canada* (4th ed.). Don Mills, ON, Canada: Oxford University Press.

Baines, D. (2004). Losing the "eyes in the back of our heads": Social service skills, lean caring, and violence. *Journal of Sociology & Social Welfare, 31*(3), 31–50.

Baines, D. (2007). "If you could change one thing": Restructuring, social workers and social justice. In D. Baines (Ed.), *Doing Anti-oppressive Practice: Building transformative politicized social work* (pp. 83–94). Halifax, Nova Scotia, Canada: Fernwood.

Barnoff, L., & Moffatt, K. (2007). Contradictory tensions in anti-oppression practice in feminist social services. *Affilia, 22*(1), 56–70.

Barth, M. (2003). Social work labor market: A first look. *Social Work, 48*(1), 9–19.

Benjamin, A. (2007). Afterword–Doing anti-oppressive social work: The importance of resistance, history and strategy. In D. Baines (Ed.), *Doing anti-oppressive practice: Building transformative politicized social work* (pp. 191–204). Halifax, Nova Scotia, Canada: Fernwood.

Black, S. (1999, December 4). Mother will not face trial over baby's death: Judge blames system. *National Post,* p. A11.

Blackwell, T. (1997, August 22). Province plans to study child neglect and abuse: Cash to hire front-line workers would do more good, critics say. *The Spectator,* p. D3.

Burawoy, M. (2008). The public turn: From labor process to labor movement. *Work and Occupations, 35*(4), 371–387.

Canadian Union of Public Employees (CUPE). (1999). *Overloaded and under fire.* Paper presented at the annual meeting of the Ontario Division Social Service Sector, Toronto, ON, Canada.

Caragata. L. (1997). How should social work respond? Deconstructing practice in mean times. *Canadian Social Work Review, 14*(2), 139–154.

Carniol, B. (2005). *Case Critical* (5th ed.). New York: Between the Lines.

Carroll, W., & Ratner, R. (2001). Sustaining oppositional cultures in 'post-socialist' times: A comparative study of three social movement organizations. *Sociology, 35*(3), 605–629.

CBC.ca. (1995, June 8). *Who is Mike Harris?* [Internet streaming of video recording]. Retrieved January 17, 2009, from http://archives.cbc.ca/politics/provincial_territorial_politics/clips/5197

CUPE.ca. (2000, April 27). *Durham CAS workers strike*. Retrieved December 27, 2007, from http://cupe.ca/s44f3302f7c125/288

Freire, P. (2007). *Pedagogy of the oppressed*. New York: Continuum.

George, P. (2006). Social action with pavement dwellers in India. In B. Lee & S. Todd (Eds.), *A casebook of community practice: Problems & strategies* (pp. 192–210). Mississauga, ON, Canada: Common Act Press.

Goodman, D., & MacFadden, R. (1996). A comprehensive tool for determining eligibility for child welfare intake: The intervention spectrum—a framework for social services [Electronic version]. *OACAS Journal, 40*(1). Retrieved February 16, 2009, from http://www.robertmacfadden.com/writings/SPECT.html

Grange, M. (1997, August 12). Charged colleague weighs on case worker: Pressure mounts on children's aid societies as legal ramifications become part of the job. *The Globe and Mail*, p. A10.

Hardina, D. (2002). *Analytical skills for community organization practice.* New York: Columbia University Press.

Hassan, K. (2000). The future of the labor left. *Monthly Review, 52*(3), 60.

Herd, D., Mitchell, A., & Lightman, E. (2005). Rituals of degradation: Administration as policy in the Ontario Works Programme. *Social Policy and Administration, 39*(1), 65–79.

Heron, B. (2008). *Desire for development: Whiteness, gender and the helping imperative.* Waterloo, ON, Canada: Wilfred Laurier Press.

Hess, H. (1997, August 9). Charge against colleague shocks children's aid workers: Resources are not adequate to do the job, spokeswoman says. *The Globe and Mail,* p. A3.

Hick, S. (2007). *Social welfare in Canada: Understanding income security* (2nd ed.). Toronto, ON, Canada: Thomson.

How cuts hit child protection services. (1999, April 16). *Hamilton Spectator: Final Edition,* p. A11.

International Federation of Social Workers. *Definition of social work.* Retrieved January 20, 2009, from http://www.ifsw.org/en/p38000208.html

Kanani, K., Regehr, C., & Bernstein, M. (2002). Liability considerations in child welfare: Lessons from Canada. *Child Abuse and Neglect, 26*(10), 1029–1043.

Kopun, F., & Nicholas, K. (2007, December 5). Revealing statistics: A city of unmatched diversity. *Toronto Star.* Retrieved January 17, 2009, from http://www.thestar.com/News/GTA/article/282694

La Rose, T. (2006). [CUPE 2190 focus group transcripts 1–5]. Unpublished raw data.

Ledwith, M. (2001). Community work as critical pedagogy: Re-envisioning Freire and Gramsci, *Community Development Journal, 36*(3), 171–182.

Lindgreen, A. (1998, December 5). Critics attack CAS rules: New funding formula rewards agency for seizing children, family lawyers say. *The Ottawa Citizen; Final Edition,* p. G8.

Ministry of Community and Social Services. (1999). *Guide to child welfare funding framework.* Toronto, ON, Canada: Queens Printer for the Province of Ontario.

Montegomery, E. (Producer), & Johnson, M. A. (Director). (1992). *The women of Hull House: A documentary production* [Videorecording]. Chicago: University of Illinois at Chicago/ Jane Addams Hull House Museum.

Mullaly, R. (2007). *The new structural social work* (3rd ed.). Toronto, ON, Canada: Oxford University Press.

Newman, M. (1995). Adult education and social action. In G. Foley (Ed.), *Understanding adult education and training* (pp. 267–281). Sydney, Australia: Allan & Unwin.

Rosenberg, J., & Rosenberg, S. (2006). Do unions matter? An examination of the historical and contemporary role of labor unions in the social work profession. *Social Work, 51*(4), 295–302.

Scanlon, E. (1999). Labor and the intellectuals: Where is social work? *Social Work, 44*(6), 590–593.

Smith, K. (2007). Social work, restructuring and everyday resistance: "Best practices" gone underground. In D. Baines (Ed.), *Doing anti-oppressive practice: Building transformative politicized social work* (pp. 145–159). Halifax, Nova Scotia, Canada: Fernwood Press.

Szklarski, C. (1997, July 3). Children's aid needs more workers, say observers [Report on Child Mortality Task Force]. *Canadian Press NewsWire: Toronto.* Retrieved December 4, 2006, from the ProQuest Database (ID No. 404741311).

Trocme, N., Fallon, B., Nutter, B., MacLauren, B., & Thompson, J. (1999). *Outcomes for child welfare services in Ontario.* Toronto, ON, Canada: Queens Printer for the Province of Ontario.

U.S. Bureau of Labor Statistics. (2009). *Economic news release. Union members summary, union members in 2008* [USDL 09–0095]. Retrieved May 5, 2009, from http://www.bls.gov/news.release/pdf/union2.nr0.htm

Weil, M. (1996). Model development in community practice: An historical perspective. *Journal of Community Practice, 3*(3/4), 5–67.

Wharf, B., & Claque, M. (1997). Lessons and legacies. *Community organizing: Canadian experiences.* Toronto, ON, Canada: Oxford University Press.

Index

Page numbers in *Italics* represent tables.